Lecture Notes

ORDINARY DIFFERENTIAL EQUATIONS

Fourth Edition

P. K. Subramanian

Melisa Hendrata

Department of Mathematics
California State University
Los Angeles, CA

Copyright © 2017, 2013, 2012, 2011.

All rights reserved. Reproduction or translation of any part of this work beyond that permitted by 1976 United States Copyright Act without the written permission of the authors is unlawful. Requests for permission should be addressed to the authors.

Contents

Preface   **7**

1 Preliminaries   **11**
   1.1 Introduction 11
   1.2 First order differential equations and initial value problems 12
   1.3 The differential 13
   1.4 Direction Fields 15
   1.5 Exercises 18

2 First Order Equations   **21**
   2.1 Separable equations 21
   2.2 Linear equations - Integrating Factors 23
   2.3 Exact equations 26
   2.4 Homogeneous equations 30
   2.5 Applications 34
       2.5.1 Introduction 34
       2.5.2 Motion of an object under gravity 35
       2.5.3 Newton's law of cooling 40
       2.5.4 Malthus' law of population dynamics 43
       2.5.5 Mixture problems 46
       2.5.6 Applications to Geometry 49
   2.6 Exercises 65

3 Higher Order Homogeneous Linear Equations   **71**
   3.1 Introduction 71
   3.2 Solution of the homogeneous linear equations 76
       3.2.1 Special case: Auxiliary equation has equal roots 77
       3.2.2 Special case: Auxiliary equation has complex roots 78

	3.3	Applications	80
		3.3.1 Catenary	81
		3.3.2 Curve of pursuit	83
		3.3.3 Simple harmonic motion	87
	3.4	Exercises	97

4 Nonhomogeneous Linear Equations — 101

4.1	Introduction	101
4.2	Method of Undetermined Coefficients	105
	4.2.1 How the UC method works	106
	4.2.2 Determining coefficients	111
4.3	Differential Operator Method	114
	4.3.1 Meaning of the operator $\frac{1}{p(D)}$	115
	4.3.2 Exponential rule $Q(x) = e^{kx}$	116
	4.3.3 Exponential shift $Q(x) = e^{kx}V(x)$	117
	4.3.4 $Q(x)$ is a polynomial	121
	4.3.5 $Q(x)$ is a circular function: $Q(x) = \sin x, \cos x$	124
	4.3.6 Substitution for D^2	125
4.4	Exercises	127

5 Linear Equations with Variable Coefficients — 131

5.1	Introduction	131
5.2	Method of Reduction of Order	132
5.3	Method of Variation of Parameters	135
5.4	Cauchy–Euler equations	138
5.5	Exercises	142

6 Power Series Solutions — 145

6.1	Introduction	145
6.2	Analytic functions and ordinary points	148
6.3	Relationship between $\{a_n\}$ and $\{f^{(n)}(0)\}$	153
6.4	Successive differentiation and Leibniz's Theorem	156
6.5	Leibniz's Theorem and differential equations	157
6.6	Exercises	160

7 Systems of Linear Equations — 163

7.1	Introduction	163
7.2	A mathematical model	163

7.3	How do we solve such a system?	165
7.4	Pathologies	167
7.5	Exercises	171

8 The Laplace Transform — 175
- 8.1 Introduction 175
- 8.2 Properties of Laplace transform 177
- 8.3 The inverse transform 181
- 8.4 Solving initial value problems 182
- 8.5 Exercises 187

9 Numerical Methods — 191
- 9.1 Euler's Method 191
- 9.2 Truncation error of Euler's Method 195
- 9.3 Modified Euler's Method 197
- 9.4 Higher order Taylor Methods 200
- 9.5 Runge-Kutta Methods 204
- 9.6 Applications 207
  - 9.6.1 Systems of first order equations 207
  - 9.6.2 Predator-prey model 212
  - 9.6.3 Higher order equations 219
- 9.7 Exercises 222

A Review of Basic Linear Algebra — 227
- A.1 Introduction 227
- A.2 Linear independence 228
- A.3 Bases 229

B Operator Methods with Complex Coefficients — 231
- B.1 Introduction 231
- B.2 Exercises 234

Answers and Hints to Selected Exercises — 235

Preface

The *Lecture Notes on Differential Equations* ("Notes") presented here are simply a collection of all the handouts I have given to my students in our elementary differential equations course (Math 215) over the past several years.

In the presence of a good text, I don't normally bother giving handouts. Occasionally I give handouts on topics that seem somewhat muddled or deal only with sheer drudgery, or solution methods that are just laborious. What started out as one handout slowly expanded into many!

1. The first time I taught the course, I found that none of the books talked about operator methods for finding particular solutions. In most cases, it is far simpler to use operator methods instead of the method of coefficients which can be extremely laborious. Ever since student days in India, I have always been captivated by the sheer beauty, elegance and power of the operator methods. So as I taught this topic it became necessary to give fairly detailed handouts on this topic. Thus the first handout was born. Somewhat to my surprise, they were really well received.

2. Most books treat the method of undetermined coefficients as if it is simply a piece of intelligent guess work. My students asked for a handout that would clarify the actual process of writing the correct form of a particular solution and the process of finding the coefficients. This was the second handout.

3. The usual process for solving second order equations using power series methods is to substitute an assumed power series, manipulate indices, collect coefficients, etc., to find the recurrence relations satisfied by the coefficients. Like the method of coefficients, however, this is also a laborious method where it is easy to make mistakes. But one can dispense with this drudgery and instead find the recurrence relations more elegantly by simply using Leibniz's theorem on derivatives of products. This gave rise to my third handout.

Thus, over the years I wrote more handouts on other topics that can be treated more simply or directly such as systems of equations, Cauchy-Euler equations, etc., where the underlying method is the operator method. Often I was impelled by my students to write on just about every other topic that was in the syllabus. By now the Notes had grown to a good size and I started using them as the basis for my lectures supplemented by reading material from other texts. Another important reason has been the sharp rise in the cost of textbooks with prices beyond the reach of many of our students.

Our department surveys have shown that the students surely read the notes more than they read their text books (my experience is that except for some very bright students, most avoid whatever book is prescribed!). To make the Notes somewhat self contained, I included handouts on practically all the topics in our syllabus including several applications. These notes have been class tested by other instructors as well. They could be used by themselves or as a supplement to a text book.

The Notes however do not form a text book. Our students (math majors, engineering and science majors) who take this course have completed the usual calculus sequence but not a linear algebra course, so there is little discussion of eigenvalues, etc. In discussing power series methods, we restrict our discussion to solutions around ordinary points. Numerical solution of differential equations is a very important topic, but it does not find a place in Notes. Nor do partial differential equations. Even so, there is possibly too much material here to be covered in a quarter or even a semester, and instructors may want to skip some material. We would urge that they certainly include some of the applications.

I am much indebted to Melisa Hendrata, my former student and protégé. Now a colleague in the department, she joins me as a coauthor. Some of the applications and the chapter on Laplace transforms are due to her. She has transformed what was once an unattractive TeXdocument into a beautiful monograph. Her keen eye has caught many errors.

It is now my pleasant duty to acknowledge my indebtedness to the many authors from whose books I learned the material or used in my teaching. The classical texts by Forsyth, Piaggio, Murray, Coddington were suggested texts for me at the University of Delhi, India. I have taught from the books by Simmons (an all time favorite), Ross, Tennenbaum & Pollard, Boyce & DiPrima and many others.

Carlos Arcos and David Beydler of the department used the notes as text when they taught the course. I am grateful to them for pointing out the typos and other minor errors.

Above all, I am grateful to the several generations of students who took my course, made teaching them all a joyful experience, and were primarily responsible for the Notes to come into existence!

Los Angeles *P. K. Subramanian*
August 2011

Changes in the Second Edition

We received many comments from several of our colleagues who used these Notes in their courses. Based on their suggestions, we have rewritten portions of Chapters 2, 3, 4 and 6 to make the Notes more readable. We thank them all, especially Professor Stewart Venit for his constructive criticisms. We have additional applications in Chapter 2 (motion under gravity) and added more exercises.

Los Angeles *P. K. Subramanian*
August 2012 *Melisa Hendrata*

Changes in the Third Edition

Several of the instructors teaching out of these Notes had requested we add more exercises, especially simple ones. We have added new exercises, with hints to solutions in many cases, in practically every chapter. We have also taken the opportunity to rewrite some sections. We wish to thank Professor Gary Brookfield for letting us use many problems from his exercise collection.

Los Angeles *P. K. Subramanian*
July 2013 *Melisa Hendrata*

Changes in the Fourth Edition

We have received many suggestions from our colleagues in our department to include additional material to our book, especially on numerical methods and also additional applications of the first derivative. Accordingly a new chapter, Chapter 9, is now devoted to a discussion of numerical methods including the well known

Euler and Runge-Kutta methods. There is also a discussion of predator-prey and interspecies competing models.

In Chapter 2, several new applications of the first derivative have been added including simple mixture problems. In geometry, we have included a discussion of orthogonal trajectories and envelopes. We include a discussion of using polar coordinates to find orthogonal trajectories when using cartesian coordinates may not be advantageous.

We have used this opportunity to remove additional typos that were pointed out to us. Many new exercises with answers have been added with hints for solution on the more difficult ones.

It is a pleasant duty to thank our colleagues who have taught out of our book and made important comments. We would like to especially thank Professor Gerald Beer for his very thoughtful suggestions to improve the book.

Los Angeles *P. K. Subramanian*
August 2017 *Melisa Hendrata*

Chapter 1

Preliminaries

1.1 Introduction

A ***differential equation*** is an equation that involves a function $y = f(x)$ and one or more of its derivatives. For example,

$$\frac{d^2y}{dx^2} + 2x\frac{dy}{dx} + y = \sin x \qquad (1.1)$$

is a differential equation. Sometimes one uses shortened notations to write the same equation as

$$y'' + 2xy' + y = \sin x$$

or using the differential operator $D \equiv \frac{d}{dx}$,

$$D^2 y + 2x D y + y = \sin x.$$

The ***order*** of a differential equation is the order of the highest derivative in the equation. For example, equation (1.1) is a second-order equation, while $y' - \sin(x + y) = 0$ is of the first order.

A solution of a differential equation is a relationship that involves only y and other functions of x either *explicitly* like

$$y = 2c_1 e^x + c_2 \sin x$$

or *implicitly* as

$$\frac{y}{x-y} = \tan y$$

but not any of its derivatives. Notice that often implicit solutions cannot be expressed as direct explicit solutions.

It is much *easier* to verify that a function (given either implicitly or explicitly) is a solution of a given differential equation.

Example 1.1. *Verify that $y = c_1 \sin 2x + c_2 \cos 2x$ is a solution of $y'' + 4y = 0$.*

Solution: Since the second derivative is involved, we differentiate y twice to get

$$y' = 2c_1 \cos 2x - 2c_2 \sin 2x, \quad y'' = -4c_1 \sin 2x - 4c_2 \cos 2x$$

and substituting these in the given equation,

$$\{-4c_1 \sin 2x - 4c_2 \cos 2x\} + 4\{c_1 \sin 2x + c_2 \cos 2x\} = 0.$$

Example 1.2. *Verify that $x^2 = 2y^2 \ln y$ is a solution of $y' = xy/(x^2 + y^2)$.*

Solution: We differentiate both sides of the given solution to get

$$2x = 4yy' \ln y + 2y^2(1/y)y',$$
$$= 2yy'(2\ln y + 1)$$

from which we get

$$y' = \frac{x}{y(1 + 2\ln y)}$$
$$= \frac{xy}{y^2(1 + 2\ln y)}$$
$$= \frac{xy}{x^2 + y^2}.$$

1.2 First order differential equations and initial value problems

For our purposes, we shall define the general differential equation of the first order as an equation of the form

$$\frac{dy}{dx} = f(x, y).$$

Here x is the independent variable and y the dependent variable. If y is the independent variable and x the dependent variable, a first order equation would be of the

form
$$\frac{dx}{dy} = f(x,y).$$

Consider the simple first order equation

$$y' = \cos x.$$

It is easily verified that $y = \sin x + c$ defines an *infinite family* of solutions all dependent on the values of c chosen. In most differential equations, this is usually the case. Suppose that we want a specific solution such that when $x = \pi/2$, we have $y = 2$, often written as $y(\pi/2) = 2$. By substituting these values in the solution $y = \sin x + c$ we see that $c = 1$, and the required solution is $y = \sin x + 1$. The extra condition $y(\pi/2) = 2$ is called *an initial condition*. The given equation together with the initial condition, in this case $y' = \cos x$, $y(\pi/2) = 2$ is called an *initial value problem (IVP)*.

How do we know that a given IVP has a solution? The answer is given by the following theorem whose proof is beyond the scope of this book.

Theorem 1.1. *(Picard) Suppose that $f(x,y)$ and $\partial f/\partial y$ are both continuous on a closed rectangle R in the xy-plane and let (x_0, y_0) be a point in R. Then the IVP*

$$\frac{dy}{dx} = f(x,y), y(x_0) = y_0$$

has a unique solution.

1.3 The differential

If $y = f(x)$ is a differentiable function of x, the **differential** dy of $f(x)$ is defined to be

$$df = f'(x)\,dx$$

and sometimes written simply as $dy = f'(x)\,dx$. Notice that this leads to the familiar derivative or *differential coefficient* $y' = dy/dx = f'(x)$. Although there are other interpretations for the differential, for our purposes in this book, this should suffice. It is important, however, to observe that dy is a function of both x and dx and for this reason some authors write the differential as $dy(x, dx) = f'(x)dx$.

One immediate use of the differential is that it helps us solve differential equations! If we know the differential of f, $df = f'(x)\,dx$, it is immediate that $f(x) = \int f'(x)\,dx + c$, where c is a constant of integration. Another observation is that the

solution is not a single function but *a family* of similar curves ("parallel") in some sense. For example, if
$$dy = 2x\,dx,$$
then $y = x^2 + c$, which is a family of parabolas all opening upwards and with y-axis as their axis. There is one such parabola through every point on the y-axis. If $c = 0$, it goes through the origin. If $c = 1$, we get the parabola $y = x^2 + 1$ which goes through (0,1).

Given a differential equation such as
$$y' = \frac{xy}{x^2+y^2},$$
we can easily convert it into the differential form. Rewrite y' as $\dfrac{dy}{dx}$ to get
$$\frac{dy}{dx} = \frac{xy}{x^2+y^2}$$
from which we easily get
$$xy\,dx = (x^2+y^2)dy \tag{1.2}$$
which is the corresponding differential equation. The general form of a first order differential equation can usually be written as
$$M(x,y)dx + N(x,y)dy = 0.$$

As an example, the equation
$$(x^2+y)\,y' = (y-x)$$
can also be written as
$$(y-x)\,dx - (x^2+y)\,dy = 0.$$

The differential form is particularly useful in solving a differential equation. For instance, given
$$y' = 2\sin x \cos x$$
we rewrite it using differentials as
$$dy = 2\sin x \cos x\,dx$$

and solve it as
$$y = \int 2\sin x \cos x\, dx + c.$$

One way of evaluating the integral is to use the substitution $t = \sin x$ to get $dt = \cos x\, dx$. Substituting we get
$$y = 2\int t\, dt + c = t^2 + c = \sin^2 x + c.$$

If on the other hand, we make the substitution $t = \cos x$, we would get
$$y = -\cos^2 x + c = \sin^2 x + (c-1) = \sin^2 x + c_1,$$

where c_1 is a different constant. Finally, we can also use the trigonometric identity $\sin 2x = 2\sin x \cos x$ to get $dy = \sin 2x\, dx$ from which
$$y = -\frac{\cos 2x}{2} + c = -\frac{1 - 2\sin^2 x}{2} + c = \sin^2 x + (c - 1/2) = \sin^2 x + c_2$$

and we see that although there are apparently three different solutions, they are all equivalent!

1.4 Direction Fields

Often times it is not easy to solve a differential equation, even for a first-order equation. Yet we may need to know at least the *behavior* of the solution.

First note that the first-order equation
$$\frac{dy}{dx} = f(x,y)$$

gives us the slope of the tangent to the solution curve y at each point (x,y). If we draw the slope at various points on the xy-plane as short line segments, we will get what is called the **direction field** (often also called **slope field**). The direction field will give us an idea of how the solution might look like. Consider, for example, the equation
$$\frac{dy}{dx} = y. \tag{1.3}$$

The solution curve to (1.3) has the x-axis as the asymptote and has the slopes of 3 and -4 at the points (2,3) and (-1,-4), respectively. The direction field of (1.3) is shown in Figure 1.1(a).

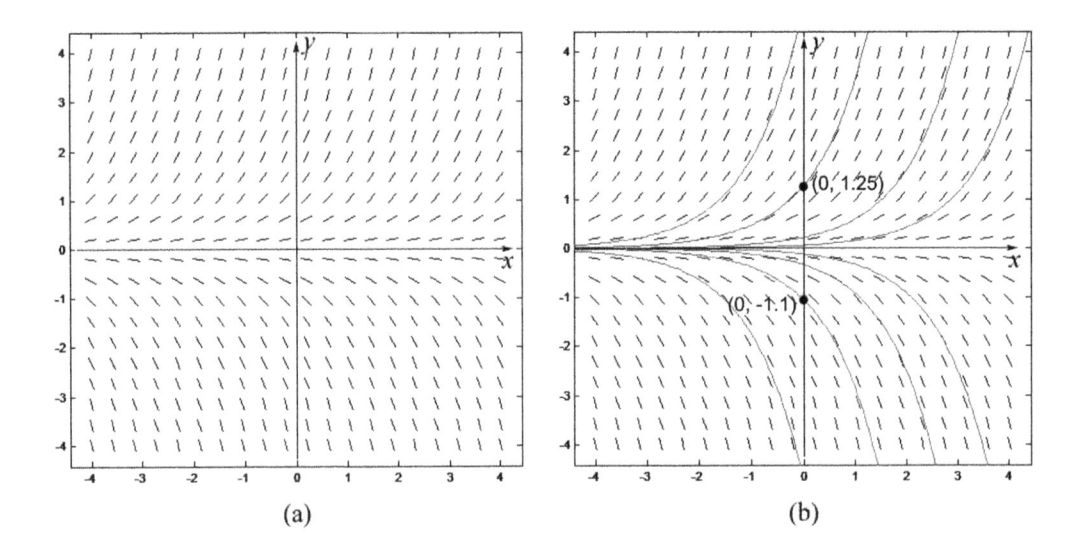

Figure 1.1: (a) Direction field of $dy/dx = y$. (b) Family of solutions of $dy/dx = y$. The solution curves satisfying the initial conditions $y(0) = 1.25$ and $y(0) = -1.1$ are also shown.

One can get much information by looking at this direction field. First, its "flow" pattern shows that as $x \to \infty$, all solutions diverge to either $+\infty$ or $-\infty$. In fact, equation (1.3) can be easily solved using the method of separation of variables (will be discussed in the next chapter) and the solution is given by $|y| = ce^x$, where c is the constant of integration. Note that the solutions are a family of exponential functions whose behavior matches the flow pattern shown by the direction field.

Secondly, given an initial condition $y(x_0) = y_0$, we can look at the point (x_0, y_0) and trace the slopes to get the solution curve that passes through (x_0, y_0). In this particular example, we see that a small change in the initial condition can cause a very different behavior of the solutions. With the initial condition $y(0) = 1.25$, the solution $y \to \infty$ as $x \to \infty$, while the initial condition $y(0) = -1.1$ causes $y \to -\infty$ as x gets larger. See Figure 1.1(b).

Example 1.3. *The elk population in a small mountain area is given by a first-order equation*
$$\frac{dP}{dt} = 0.1\, P(t)\left(1 - \frac{P(t)}{300}\right),$$
where $P(t)$ is the number of elks at any time t. This equation is called the logistic equation. More details on this type of equation will be discussed in Section 2.5.4. By sketching the direction field,

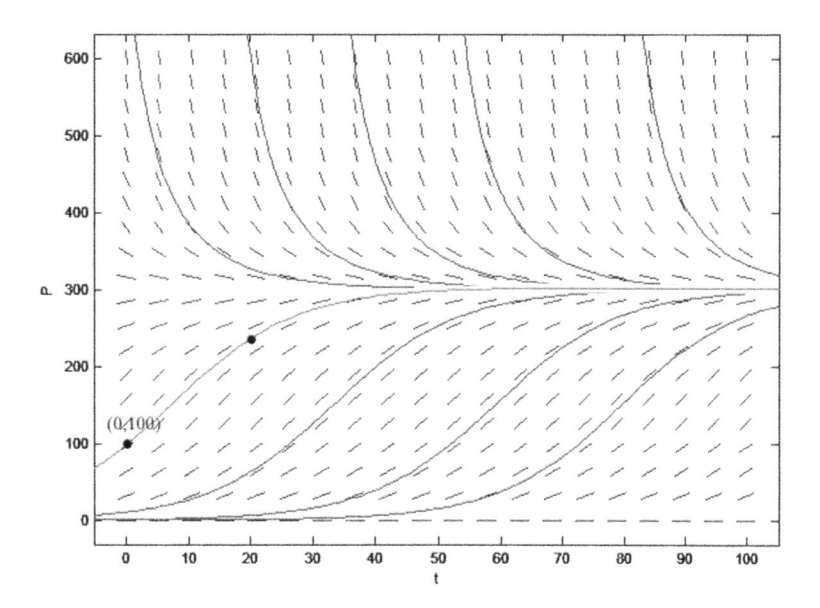

Figure 1.2: Direction field and family of solutions of $\frac{dP}{dt} = 0.1\,P(t)(1 - (P(t)/300))$. The solution curve satisfying the initial condition $P(0) = 100$ is also shown.

> (a) Estimate the limiting size of the population as $t \to \infty$.
>
> (b) If the initial elk population is 100, estimate the size of the population in 20 years. Can the population ever reach 500?
>
> (c) If the initial population is 600, can it decrease to 200?

Solution:

(a) Since the variables t and P represent the time and the number of elks, respectively, they cannot be negative. Thus, we only need to sketch the direction field for $t, P \geq 0$ and it is given in Figure 1.2. From the flow pattern, we can see that all solutions tend to P-value of 300 as $t \to \infty$. In Section 2.5.4 we will see that this is indeed the case.

(b) The initial condition here is when $t = 0$, $P = 100$. We trace the solution curve that passes through the point $(0, 100)$ and see that when $t = 20$, $P \approx 233$. It is clear that the population will increase to 300, but never reaches 500.

(c) The population will steadily decrease to 300, but it can never decline to 200.

Sketching direction field is straightforward, but it can be very tedious without the aid of computer software packages. If one really needs to hand sketch a direction field, the ***method of isoclines*** can help ease the job. For a first-order equation $dy/dx = f(x,y)$, an *isocline* is any member of the family of curves $f(x,y) = c$, where c is an arbitrary constant (Yes, it is very much the level curve for $f(x,y)$). At each point on an isocline, the solution curve has slope that is equal to c.

We illustrate the technique in the following example.

Example 1.4. *Sketch the direction field for $y' = x+3y$ using the method of isoclines.*

Solution: The isoclines for the given equation is $x + 3y = c$, which is a family of parallel lines. Pick several values for c and draw short line segments with slope c along the isocline $x + 3y = c$. Figure 1.3 shows isoclines for $c = 0, \pm 3, \pm 6, \pm 9$ and the resulting direction field. Some solution curves are given in Figure 1.4

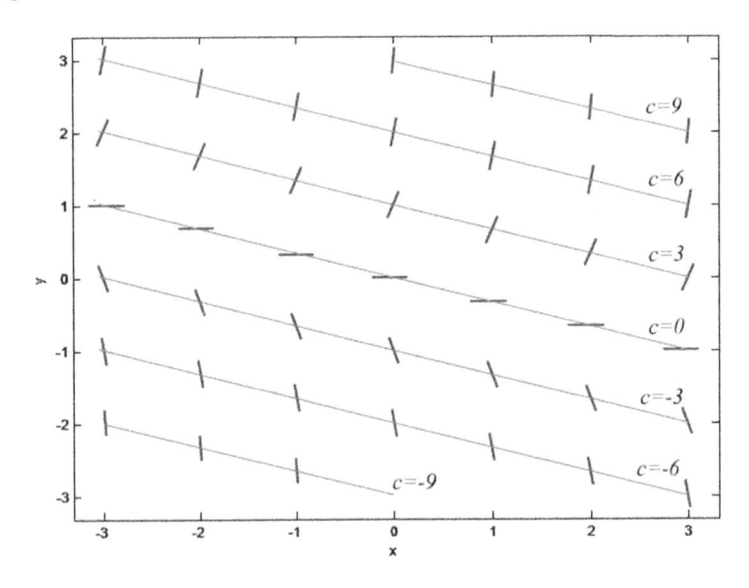

Figure 1.3: Isoclines for $y' = x + 3y$

1.5 Exercises

1. Determine the order of the following differential equations:

    (a) $2xy' = x^3 + y^2$

    (b) $2y''' - y'' = x^5 + 3xy$

    (c) $xy' - y = y''\sqrt{1 - xy}$

    (d) $x^3 D^2 y + Dy + xy = x^4$

    (e) $2\left(\dfrac{d^2y}{dt^2}\right)^4 + \left(\dfrac{dy}{dt}\right)^{10} - t^2 = 0$

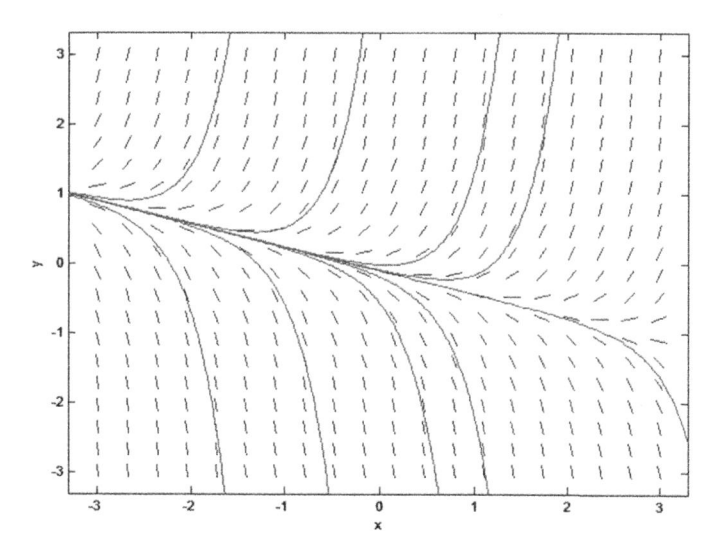

Figure 1.4: Family of solutions to $y' = x + 3y$

2. Verify that the following functions are solutions to the corresponding differential equations. In each case, give the order of the differential equation. Also state whether the solution is *explicit* or *implicit*.

    (a) $y = 2\sqrt{x} + c$, $\quad y' = 1/\sqrt{x}$
    (b) $y^2 = e^{2x} + c$, $\quad yy' = e^{2x}$
    (c) $y = \arcsin xy$, $\quad xy' + y = y'\sqrt{1 - x^2 y^2}$
    (d) $x + y = \arctan y$, $\quad 1 + y^2 + y^2 y' = 0$
    (e) $y = a \sin x + b \cos x$, $\quad y'' + y = 0$

3. Find the differential df of the following functions:

    (a) $f(x) = \sin x \cos x$
    (b) $f(x) = c_1 e^x + c_2 e^{-x}$
    (c) $y = \sin^{-1}(2x)$
    (d) $y = cx\sqrt{1 - x^2}$
    (e) $f(t) = c_1 e^{-t} \cos t + c_2 e^{-t} \sin t$

4. Rewrite the following differential equations in the form $M(x,y)dx + N(x,y)dy = 0$.

    (a) $2xy' = x^3 + y^2$

(b) $xy' - y = y'\sqrt{1-xy}$

(c) $y' + y\cot x = 0$

(d) $yy' = e^{2x}$

(e) $y' = \dfrac{x^2 + y}{x^3}$

5. Write the following equations in derivative form:

   (a) $(2xy^2 + y)\,dx - x\,dy = 0$.

   (b) $(y - xy^2)\,dx + (x - x^2y^2)\,dy = 0$.

   (c) $dy - y\,dx = (1 + x^2)\,dy$.

   (d) $y = e^{y'+x}$

   (e) $e^x y' = y' + 2x$

6. Draw the direction field for the following first-order equations using the method of isoclines, including the curve satisfying the given conditions. From the sketch of the direction field, what can you say about the behavior of the solution?

   (a) $\dfrac{dy}{dx} = 2y, \quad y(0) = 1$

   (b) $\dfrac{dy}{dx} = 2x - y, \quad y(0) = 0$

   (c) $\dfrac{dy}{dx} = x^2 - y, \quad y(1) = 0$

   (d) $\dfrac{dy}{dx} = 2y(3 - y), \quad y(0) = 1$

Chapter 2

First Order Equations

2.1 Separable equations

A differential equation is said to be **separable** if it can be rewritten so that terms involving the differential of y are on one side of the equation, and those of x on the other side. One then integrates to get rid off the differentials leading to an equation that implicity or explicitly gives y.

Example 2.1. *Solve* $y^2 y' + 2x = 0$.

Solution: We rewrite this as $y^2 \{dy/dx\} = -2x$ and in differential form as

$$y^2 \, dy = -2x \, dx.$$

Integrating both sides we get

$$\int y^2 \, dy = -\int 2x \, dx + c,$$

that is,

$$\frac{1}{3} y^3 = -x^2 + c,$$

or as is commonly written

$$\frac{1}{3} y^3 + x^2 = c.$$

This equation can be solved for y explicitly but that is not necessary.

Example 2.2. *Solve the Initial Value Problem:*

$$y' = \frac{y \ln y}{x}, \quad y(1) = 2.$$

Solution: We rewrite the equation in differential form as

$$\frac{dx}{x} - \frac{dy}{y \ln y} = 0$$

from which by integrating

$$\int \frac{dx}{x} - \int \frac{dy}{y \ln y} = c.$$

The first integral is easy. To evaluate the second, put $t = \ln y$, $dt = dy/y$ to get

$$\int \frac{dx}{x} - \int \frac{dt}{t} = c$$

$$\ln |x| - \ln |t| = c,$$

that is,

$$c = \ln |x| - \ln |t| = \ln |x/t| = \ln |x/\ln y|.$$

This is equivalent to

$$\left|\frac{x}{\ln y}\right| = e^c = c_1,$$

where c_1 is another constant. Finally we get $|x| = c_1 \ln |y|$ or $|y| = e^{|c_2 x|}$ where $c_2 = 1/c_1$. To find the particular solution required, we have $2 = e^{c_2}$ from which $c_2 = \ln 2$ and the required solution is $|y| = e^{|x \ln 2|} = e^{|x| \ln 2} = 2^{|x|}$. We can rewrite this as $y = 2^x$, $x \geq 0$.

Notes:

1. Simply because an equation is separable, it does not follow that it is solvable! The resulting integrals may not be expressible in terms of known functions, e.g. $dy = e^{x^2} dx$.

2. An equation may not be *apparently* separable but a little effort can make it so. As an example, $y' = x^2 y + x^2 e^y - y - e^y$ does not seem separable but if you look carefully, the right side is factorable: $y' = (x^2 - 1)(y + e^y)$ which is now readily separable.

2.2 Linear equations - Integrating Factors

A typical such equation is of the form

$$\frac{dy}{dx} + P(x)y = Q(x). \tag{2.1}$$

If the given equation is not in this form, you should rewrite it to conform to this form since, as you will soon see, the solution can be written down once we know the functions $P(x)$ and $Q(x)$. This equation is not separable. But we can employ a trick that occurs many times in differential equations. We rewrite the equation as $dy + P(x)\,y\,dx = Q(x)\,dx$ and multiply this by (as yet) an unknown function $H(x)$ so that the resulting equation

$$H(x)\,dy + H(x)P(x)y\,dx = H(x)Q(x)\,dx \tag{2.2}$$

consists of differentials only! The right side is obviously so. If the left side is to be a differential, then (by looking at the first term) it must be of the form $d\bigl(H(x)\cdot y\bigr)$. But by the product rule of derivatives,

$$d\bigl(H(x)\cdot y\bigr) = H\,dy + y\,dH.$$

Comparing this with the left hand side of equation (2.2), the second terms must agree, that is, $y\,dH = HPy\,dx$, and since $y \not\equiv 0$, we must have

$$dH = HP\,dx, \qquad \frac{dH}{H} = P\,dx.$$

Integrating the second equation, we immediately get

$$\ln H(x) = \int P(x)\,dx, \qquad H(x) = e^{\left(\int P\,dx\right)}. \tag{2.3}$$

Equation (2.2) now becomes $d(H(x)\cdot y) = H(x)Q(x)\,dx$, whose solution is therefore

$$H(x)y = \int H(x)Q(x)\,dx + c.$$

From (2.3) we finally get

$$ye^{\left(\int P\,dx\right)} = \int e^{\left(\int P\,dx\right)} \cdot Q(x)\,dx + c. \tag{2.4}$$

The function $H(x)$ is called an **integrating factor**. In this example, multiplication by an integrating factor has transformed it into a separable equation. We will have more occasions to deal with integrating factors. Note that using equation (2.4) we can write down the solution of equation (2.1) only involving the functions $P(x)$ and $Q(x)$:

$$y = e^{-\int P\,dx}\left[\int e^{\int P\,dx} \cdot Q(x)\,dx + c\right].$$

Example 2.3. *Solve* $y' + y = 1/(1 + e^{2x})$.

Solution: The equation is in the form of (2.1) with $P = 1$ and $Q = 1/(1+e^{2x})$. Hence, $e^{\int P\,dx} = e^x$ and the solution is

$$ye^x = \int \frac{e^x}{1 + (e^x)^2}\,dx + c.$$

The integral is evaluated by the substitution $t = e^x$ so that $ye^x = \int dt/(1+t^2) + c$. That is, $ye^x = \arctan t + c$ and finally we get $y = e^{-x}(\arctan e^x + c)$.

Example 2.4. *Solve* $x\,dy = (3x^2 + y)dx$.

Solution: Note that this is a first order equation, but is not separable. This equation is in differential form and we should first rewrite it in the form of (2.1):

$$\frac{dy}{dx} - \frac{y}{x} = 3x.$$

Here $P(x) = -1/x$ and $Q(x) = 3x$. Also $\int P\,dx = -\int(1/x)dx = \ln(1/x)$ and $e^{\int P\,dx} = 1/x$. We can write down the solution as

$$\frac{y}{x} = \int \frac{3x}{x}\,dx + c = 3x + c.$$

Hence $y = 3x^2 + cx$ is the general solution. Notice that once you write the given equation in the form of (2.1) it is easy to write down the solution.

Remark 1. You should note that in equation (2.1), x is the independent variable and y the dependent variable. Sometimes a linear equation may not appear in this form! In some of those cases if we rewrite the equation with y as the independent variable and x as the dependent variable (reversing the roles of x and y), the equation will look very similar to (2.1) and may appear in the form

$$\frac{dx}{dy} + P(y)x = Q(y).$$

Chapter 2. First Order Equations

In this case the integrating factor is $e^{\int P\,dy}$ and the solution would be

$$x = e^{-\int P\,dy}\left[\int e^{\int P\,dy}\cdot Q(y)\,dy + c\right].$$

Example 2.5. *Solve* $y + xy' = y'ye^y$.

Solution: This first order equation is not linear in y because of the term e^y, but it is linear in x. We rewrite it to conform to (2.1) but with y as the independent variable:

$$\frac{dx}{dy} = \frac{ye^y - x}{y} = e^y - \frac{x}{y}, \text{ that is, } \frac{dx}{dy} + \frac{x}{y} = e^y.$$

It is immediate that $P(y) = 1/y$ and $e^{\int P\,dy} = y$. Hence, the solution is

$$xy = \int ye^y\,dy + c = ye^y - e^y + c$$

using integration by parts. Thus, $x = e^y - e^y/y + c/y$.

Bernoulli's equation. The equation $y' + P(x)y = Q(x)y^n$ is called Bernoulli's equation. It is trivial to check that it is linear if $n = 0$ or $n = 1$. It does not appear to be linear when $n \geq 2$. However, with a simple substitution it can be converted to a linear equation! Divide by y^n to get

$$y^{-n}\frac{dy}{dx} + y^{1-n}P(x) = Q(x).$$

If we now substitute $u = y^{1-n}$, $du/dx = (1-n)y^{-n}dy/dx$, and after simplification,

$$\frac{du}{dx} + u(1-n)P(x) = (1-n)Q(x)$$

which is linear and is in the form of equation (2.1).

Example 2.6. *Solve the equation* $xy' + y = xy^2$.

Solution: The given equation can be rewritten as

$$\frac{dy}{dx} + \frac{y}{x} = y^2$$

which is Bernoulli's equation. Dividing by y^2 we get

$$\frac{1}{y^2}\frac{dy}{dx} + \frac{1}{y}\frac{1}{x} = 1.$$

If we let $u = 1/y$ so that $du/dx = \{-1/y^2\}(dy/dx)$, then the given equation transforms into

$$\frac{du}{dx} - \frac{u}{x} = -1$$

which is linear. Here $P = -1/x$, $e^{\int P dx} = 1/x$ and the solution of the transformed equation is

$$\frac{u}{x} = -\ln x + c, \text{ that is, } u = -x\ln x + cx.$$

Since $u = 1/y$, the solution of the original equation is $1 + xy\ln x = cxy$.

2.3 Exact equations

A first order equation can often be written in the form

$$M(x,y)\,dx + N(x,y)\,dy = 0. \tag{2.5}$$

This equation is said to be **exact** if the left hand side is the differential of a function $F(x,y)$ so that

$$dF(x,y) = M(x,y)\,dx + N(x,y)\,dy = 0 \tag{2.6}$$

and the solution is clearly $F(x,y) = c$ for some constant c. The problem then is to find F!

Given $y = f(x)$, we know its differential is defined as $df = f'(x)\,dx$. For a function $F(x,y)$ of two (or several) variables one needs to be careful in writing its differential. Suppose for a moment $x = g(t), y = h(t)$ are both themselves functions of another variable t. Then from Calculus we know $F'(t)$ exists and is given by

$$\frac{dF}{dt} = \frac{\partial F}{\partial x}\cdot\frac{dx}{dt} + \frac{\partial F}{\partial y}\cdot\frac{dy}{dt}.$$

In analogy with the one variable case, we can now write the differential dF of $F(x,y)$:

$$dF = \frac{\partial F}{\partial x}\cdot dx + \frac{\partial F}{\partial y}\cdot dy.$$

Hence, if equation (2.5) is exact and F exists as required, then we must have

$$dF = \frac{\partial F}{\partial x} \cdot dx + \frac{\partial F}{\partial y} \cdot dy = M(x,y)\, dx + N(x,y)\, dy = 0.$$

It follows by comparing the coefficients of dx and dy that we must have

$$\frac{\partial F}{\partial x} = M(x,y) \text{ and } \frac{\partial F}{\partial y} = N(x,y). \tag{2.7}$$

Since F is necessarily continuous, its mixed partials with respect to x and y must be equal:

$$\frac{\partial^2 F}{\partial x \partial y} = \frac{\partial^2 F}{\partial y \partial x}.$$

Hence, from equation (2.7) we finally have

$$\frac{\partial M}{\partial y} = \frac{\partial N}{\partial x}, \tag{2.8}$$

which gives us *a necessary (and sufficient) condition* for equation (2.5) to be exact. But let us first consider an example.

Example 2.7. *Solve* $2x \sin y\, dx + x^2 \cos y\, dy = 0$.

Solution: Here $M = 2x \sin y$ and $N = x^2 \cos y$. It is easy to verify that $\partial M/\partial y = 2x \cos y = \partial N/\partial x$, showing equation (2.8) is satisfied and the equation is indeed exact. Hence, there exists some function $F(x,y)$ whose differential $dF = 2x \sin y\, dx + x^2 \cos y\, dy$. But how do we find F?

Since $\partial F/\partial x = M(x,y) = 2x \sin y$ we can integrate this equation partially with respect to x (that is, treating y as a constant just here) and write

$$F(x,y) = \int M\, \partial x = \int 2x \sin y\, \partial x, \text{ (Caution: This notation is \textbf{not} standard!)}$$

that is $F(x,y) = x^2 \sin y + h(y)$, where $h(y)$ is a function *independent of x* only (think about this!). But from equation (2.7)

$$N(x,y) = \frac{\partial F}{\partial y} = x^2 \cos y + h'(y) = x^2 \cos y$$

from the given problem. Hence $h'(y) = 0, h(y) = c$ where c is a pure constant. The final solution is $F(x,y) = x^2 \sin y + c$.

Remark 2. This is a brute force method! It involves a partial integration followed by a partial derivative. The method always works but can be trying in complicated problems.

Grouping

Grouping involves combining the terms of an exact equation $M\,dx + N\,dy = 0$ in such a way that it is almost obvious that $M\,dx + N\,dy$ is an exact differential. In the last example again, it is obvious that

$$(2x\sin y)\,dx + (x^2\cos y)\,dy \equiv d(x^2\sin y),$$

so that the equation is $d(x^2\sin y) = 0$ and the solution is $x^2\sin y = c$ as before. One clue is that the very form of the equation $M\,dx + N\,dy = 0$ suggests that the left side is possibly the differential of a product. With practice this becomes very easy.

Example 2.8. *Solve* $(2y^2 - 4x + 5)\,dx + (2y - 4 + 4xy)\,dy = 0.$

Solution: The equation is exact since $\partial M/\partial y = 4y = \partial N/\partial x$. Now group the terms as follows

$$\underbrace{(-4x+5)\,dx}_{d(-2x^2+5x)} + \underbrace{(2y-4)\,dy}_{d(y^2-4y)} + \underbrace{(2y^2\,dx + 4xy\,dy)}_{d(2xy^2)} = 0$$

and clearly the solution is $-2x^2 + 5x + y^2 - 4y + 2xy^2 = c$.

Some important exact differentials

The following list of exact differentials would be quite useful in solving exact differential equations by grouping:

1. $d(xy) = y\,dx + x\,dy$

2. $d\left(\dfrac{x}{y}\right) = \dfrac{y\,dx - x\,dy}{y^2}$

3. $\left(\dfrac{y\,dx - x\,dy}{x^2 + y^2}\right) = \dfrac{d\left(\frac{x}{y}\right)}{1 + \left(\frac{x}{y}\right)^2} = d\left\{\arctan\left(\dfrac{x}{y}\right)\right\}.$

4. $d\left(\dfrac{y}{x}\right) = \dfrac{x\,dy - y\,dx}{x^2}$

Example 2.9. *Solve* $y\,dx - x\,dy + \ln x\,dx = 0.$

Solution: It is easy to see that this equation is not exact. But we rewrite it as

$$x\,dy - y\,dx - \ln x\,dx = 0,$$

and if we divide by x^2 it becomes

$$\underbrace{\frac{x\,dy - y\,dx}{x^2}}_{d(y/x)} - \underbrace{\frac{\ln x}{x^2}\,dx}_{d\left(\int x^{-2}\ln x\,dx\right)} = 0$$

The integral is evaluated by parts as follows:

$$\int x^{-2}\ln x\,dx = -x^{-1}\ln x + \int x^{-2}\,dx = -x^{-1}\ln x - 1/x + c.$$

Hence, the solution of the equation is

$$\frac{y}{x} = -\frac{\ln x}{x} - \frac{1}{x} + c \text{ or } y = -\ln x + cx - 1.$$

Integrating factors - Non-exact equations

In the last example, a non-exact equation became exact after multiplication by $\mu(x) = 1/x^2$. This is another instance of an *integrating factor* which we first encountered in Section 2.2. There is a vast theory on integrating factors. This method is often cumbersome as involves e^f where f may be either a function of x alone or of y alone. Often simpler methods may be more useful. Here we provide a couple of simple rules one could use in some cases:

Note that if the equation (2.8) is not satisfied,

$$\frac{\frac{\partial M}{\partial y} - \frac{\partial N}{\partial x}}{N} \neq 0.$$

Rule 1. *Assume that*

$$\frac{\frac{\partial M}{\partial y} - \frac{\partial N}{\partial x}}{N} = h(x) \tag{2.9}$$

where $h(x)$ is a function of x alone. In this case, $\mu = e^{\int h(x)\,dx}$ is an integrating factor.

Rule 2. *If*

$$\frac{\frac{\partial N}{\partial x} - \frac{\partial M}{\partial y}}{M} = g(y) \tag{2.10}$$

is a function of y alone, then $\mu = e^{\int g(y)\,dy}$ is an integrating factor.

Example 2.10. *Solve* $(x^2 + y^2 + 2x)\,dx + 2y\,dy = 0$.

Solution: Here $\partial M/\partial y = 2y$ and $\partial N/\partial x = 0$, so that

$$h(x) = \frac{\frac{\partial M}{\partial y} - \frac{\partial N}{\partial x}}{N} = 1$$

is a function of x alone. Hence, $\mu = e^x$ is an integrating factor and we obtain the equation

$$\underbrace{(e^x y^2\, dx + 2e^x y\, dy)}_{d(e^x y^2)} + \underbrace{e^x(x^2 + 2x)\, dx}_{d\left(\int (x^2+2x)e^x\, dx\right)} = 0.$$

Using integration by parts, then solution then becomes $e^x y^2 + x^2 e^x = c$.

2.4 Homogeneous equations

We say that a function $z = f(x, y)$ is **homogeneous** of degree n if it can be written in the form

$$f(x, y) = x^n g(v), \quad v = \frac{y}{x}.$$

For instance, $f(x, y) = x^3 y^2 + x^2 y^3 - xy^4$ is homogeneous of degree 5 since we can write

$$f(x, y) = x^5 \left\{ \frac{y^2}{x^2} + \frac{y^3}{x^3} - \frac{y^4}{x^4} \right\} = x^5 g(v)$$

where $g(v) = v^2 + v^3 - v^4$, $v = y/x$.

The differential equation (2.5) is said to be **homogeneous** of degree n if *both* $M(x, y)$ and $N(x, y)$ are homogeneous and of the degree n. This definition applies right now only to equations of type (2.5). Later we use the same term to call higher order equations as homogeneous if the right hand side is zero (they may not always be so!). This would cause no confusion as you will see.

It is much easier to determine if a polynomial $P(x, y)$ in the two variables x and y is homogeneous. Such a polynomial is homogeneous of degree n if every term in the polynomial has degree n, that is the sum of the powers of x and y in every term is n. In particular, an equation of the form

$$\frac{dy}{dx} = \frac{P(x, y)}{Q(x, y)},$$

where P and Q are polynomials, is homogeneous of degree n if both P and Q are homogeneous of degree n.

For example, in $(x+y)\, dx + (x-y)\, dy = 0$ both $M = (x+y)$ and $N = (x-y)$ are of the same degree 1 so differential equation is homogeneous of degree 1. The equation

Chapter 2. First Order Equations

$(x^3 + y^3)\,dx - xy^2\,dy = 0$, is homogeneous of degree 3. But $x^3\,dy = (x^2y - y^2)\,dx$, is not homogeneous since the degree of the term y^2 is only two while the others are of degree 3.

The substitution $y = vx$

When an equation is homogeneous, the substitution $y = vx$ is very useful. With this substitution, and assuming $M(x,y)$ and $N(x,y)$ are both of degree n, equation (2.5) can be written in derivative form as

$$\frac{dy}{dx} = -\frac{M(x,y)}{N(x,y)} = -\frac{x^n M(v)}{x^n N(v)} = -g(v). \tag{2.11}$$

for some function g. Further, by product rule,

$$y = vx \Rightarrow \frac{dy}{dx} = v + x\frac{dv}{dx}. \tag{2.12}$$

By (2.11) and (2.12), equation (2.5) can be transformed into

$$x\frac{dv}{dx} = g(v) - v,$$

which is separable.

Should we always write the differential equation $M(x,y)dx + N(x,y)dy = 0$ in the derivative form as we have done above? Not necessarily! We could make the substitutions

$$y = vx, \; dy = vdx + xdv$$

in the differential form to get

$$M(x,v)dx + N(x,v)(vdx + xdv) = 0,$$

that is,

$$(M(x,v) + vN(x,v))dx + xN(x,v)dv = 0$$

which would be separable. Generally though converting to the derivative form usually involves less algebraic simplification.

You should be aware that with the substitutions for y and dy/dx, equation (2.5) may be transformed into a separable equation, but the resulting equation may sometimes be more daunting and often can be solved by other methods.

Example 2.11. *Solve* $(x^3 + y^3)\,dx - xy^2\,dy = 0$.

Solution: We rewrite the given equation as

$$\frac{dy}{dx} = \frac{x^3 + y^3}{xy^2}$$

Using the substitutions from equation (2.12),

$$v + x\frac{dv}{dx} = \frac{1+v^3}{v^2}$$

and

$$x\frac{dv}{dx} = \frac{1+v^3}{v^2} - v = \frac{1}{v^2}.$$

This is a separable equation and leads to

$$\frac{dx}{x} = v^2 dv.$$

If we had not transformed the substitution into derivative form but made the substitutions $y = vx, dy = vdx + xdv$ in the differential form, we would get

$$(x^3 + v^3 x^3)dx - v^2 x^3(xdv + vdx) = 0,$$

and after canceling x^3 and simplifying we would get

$$(1 + v^3 - v^3)dx - xv^2 dv = 0,$$

that is,

$$\frac{dx}{x} = v^2 dv,$$

which is the same as before. Its solution is $\ln|x| = \{v^3/3\} + c$, which is equivalent to $3x^3 \ln|x| = y^3 + c_1 x^3$.

Integrating factor for Homogeneous Equations

The following rule applies only to homogeneous equations.

Rule 3. *If $Mx + Ny \neq 0$ and the equation is homogeneous, then*

$$\frac{1}{Mx + Ny} \text{ is an integrating factor of } M\,dx + N\,dy = 0.$$

Notice that unlike other integrating factors, there is no exponential involved in this

Chapter 2. First Order Equations

integrating factor! This may often trump the usual method for homogeneous equations.

Example 2.12. *Solve* $(x^2y - 2xy^2)\,dx - (x^3 - 3x^2y)\,dy = 0$.

Solution: Simplify by removing the common factor x to get

$$(xy - 2y^2)\,dx - (x^2 - 3xy)\,dy = 0.$$

This equation is homogeneous of degree 2 and

$$Mx + Ny = x^2y - 2xy^2 - x^2y + 3xy^2 = xy^2 \neq 0$$

and the rule applies. Hence, $1/(Mx+Ny) = 1/xy^2$ is an integrating factor. Multiply the last equation by $1/xy^2$ and rewrite to get

$$\left(\frac{1}{y} - \frac{2}{x}\right)dx - \left(\frac{x}{y^2} - \frac{3}{y}\right)dy = 0$$

$$\frac{dx}{y} - \frac{x\,dy}{y^2} - \frac{2\,dx}{x} + \frac{3\,dy}{y} = 0$$

$$\underbrace{\frac{y\,dx - x\,dy}{y^2}}_{d(x/y)} - \underbrace{\frac{2\,dx}{x}}_{2\,d(\ln x)} + \underbrace{\frac{3\,dy}{y}}_{3\,d(\ln y)} = 0,$$

which implies that

$$\frac{x}{y} + \ln\frac{y^3}{x^2} = c.$$

Example 2.13. *Solve* $(x - y)\,dx = (x + y)\,dy$.

Solution: This is homogeneous (M and N are of degree 1). We rewrite the equation as

$$\frac{dy}{dx} = \frac{x - y}{x + y}. \qquad (2.13)$$

Substituting $y = vx$, and using equation (2.12) we get

$$v + x\frac{dv}{dx} = \frac{1-v}{1+v}$$

$$x\frac{dv}{dx} = \frac{1-v}{1+v} - v = \frac{1-2v-v^2}{1+v}$$

$$\frac{dx}{x} = \frac{1+v}{1-2v-v^2}\,dv$$

$$\ln|x| = (-1/2)\ln|1-2v-v^2| + c$$

$$2\ln|x| + \ln|1-2v-v^2| = 2\ln c_1$$

$$x^2(1-2v-v^2) = c_1^2$$

$$x^2 - 2xy - y^2 = c_2.$$

In the last example, the substitution $y = vx$ is actually an overkill! If you observe carefully, the given equation is in fact *exact*! It can be solved very easily by grouping:

$$x\,dx - y\,dy = x\,dy + y\,dx$$

leading to $x^2 - y^2 = 2xy + c$, same as before! Also notice that the last rule for finding integrating factor does apply but the factor itself is not particularly simple! It pays to study the equation carefully before attempting a solution!

2.5 Applications

2.5.1 Introduction

In this section we consider various applications of the first derivative to a variety of interesting problems such as those that occur in physics, population biology, dilution and accretion (mixture), and in geometry, to orthogonal trajectories, envelopes, etc.

In the first of these we consider motions of objects under gravity. Examples of this kind are numerous. Differential equations are ideally suited to describe such motion. Some well known examples are the motions of planets in the solar system, the trajectory of a satellite shot into space, etc. Here we discuss the free fall of a stone under gravity, motion under gravity subject to air resistance (such as that of a parachute), etc. We also consider the motion of a projectile fired at a fixed angle on a level terrain and with given initial velocity. A typical example is that of the motion of a cannon ball. These models help in determining the maximum height reached, the total time of motion, and in the case of projectiles, the maximum range.

Chapter 2. First Order Equations

Our next set of applications involve two models in which the central theme is the rate of change of a physical quantity. Examples of this type abound. The rate at which a given quantity of a substance cools when placed in an environment which is cooler than itself, increase of population in a demographic area, radioactive decay, etc. Since the rate of change refers to the derivative, most such situations are modeled by a first order linear equation which is solved easily. Because the rate of change is usually proportional to the quantity left, the solution is invariably an exponential function.

In the mixture problems considered here, the setting is the following. We have a cistern containing a solvent and a chemical dissolved in it. In most cases the solvent is water and the chemical is salt. There is an *inlet pipe*, which lets in more solvent into the cistern (with or without the chemical), and an *outlet pipe* (also called drain) that drains the mixture from the cistern. To keep the mixture uniform in the cistern, it is consistently stirred. The problem is to calculate the amount of chemical in the cistern at any given time when one or both of the pipes are open. In more complicated type of mixture problems, we may have two or more cisterns with their own inlet and outlet pipes, and also with pipes connecting the cisterns. These systems lead to what are called *Systems of Equations* which we shall consider in Chapter 7.

In geometry we consider orthogonal trajectories. Here, given a family of curves $f(x, y, \alpha) = 0$, where α is a parameter and varies with each member of the family, we look for a curve or a family of curves each member of which cuts every member of the given family at right angles. In problems involving envelopes, again given a family of curves $f(x, y, \alpha)$, the aim is to find a curve(s) that is tangential to every member of the given family.

2.5.2 Motion of an object under gravity

In this section we will be concerned with motion of bodies under gravity such as those falling freely, falling against air resistance (called retarded fall) and of projectiles thrown at an angle from the ground on a level terrain. The starting point for all such analysis is Newton's second law of motion and the acceleration due to gravity. Recall that under Newton's second law of motion, the force F acting on an object equals its mass m times the acceleration a. Thus

$$F = ma. \tag{2.14}$$

It is customary to note the time by t, which is the independent variable, and velocity by v. With reference to coordinate axes that will be chosen, we will measure horizontal distance by x and vertical distance by y. The acceleration due to gravity g will be assumed to be 32 ft/sec per sec, that is 32 ft/sec^2.

1. Free fall motion (no air resistance)

Let us first consider the motion of an object falling freely under gravity. Let the line of fall be the positive direction of the y-axis, the point from which the fall takes place the origin. Let time be counted from the moment the fall takes place. Hence, the velocity at time t is $v = dy/dt$ and the downward acceleration is d^2y/dt^2. In particular equation (2.14) now becomes

$$m\frac{d^2y}{dt^2} = mg$$

from which

$$\frac{d^2y}{dt^2} = g. \tag{2.15}$$

Integrating,

$$v = \frac{dy}{dt} = gt + c_1,$$

where c_1 is a constant of integration. At time $t = 0$, the initial velocity $v(0) = 0$ since it is a free fall motion. Thus from the last equation, $c_1 = v(0) = 0$ and the last equation becomes

$$v(t) = gt. \tag{2.16}$$

Another integration yields

$$y = \frac{1}{2}gt^2 + c_2,$$

where c_2 is another constant of integration. Since $y(0) = 0$, $c_2 = 0$. Thus, the final equation of motion is

$$y = \frac{1}{2}gt^2. \tag{2.17}$$

From equations (2.16) and (2.17), we get the very useful formula

$$v = \sqrt{2gy} \tag{2.18}$$

and the total time of travel T to be

Chapter 2. First Order Equations

$$T = v(t)/g = \sqrt{\frac{2y}{g}}. \tag{2.19}$$

Example 2.14. *A ball is dropped from a tower 16 ft above the ground. When does it hit the ground? What is the velocity with which it strikes the ground?*

Solution: From equation (2.18), the final velocity is $v = 32$ ft/sec and from (2.19) $T = 1$ sec.

2. Retarded fall (with air resistance)

Let us now consider the case when a ball is dropped from a height as in the last case, but that it experiences an air resistance directly proportional to its velocity. This means as the body gains velocity it meets with greater air resistance. We can write the resistance $R(t)$ as

$$R(t) \propto v(t)$$

and if k is the constant of proportionality, $R(t) = kv$. In this case equation, (2.14) becomes

$$m\frac{d^2y}{dt^2} = mg - kv$$

from which

$$\frac{d^2y}{dt^2} = g - \frac{k}{m}\frac{dy}{dt}. \tag{2.20}$$

Equation (2.20) is not linear but is still easily solvable. Let $\mu = k/m, v = dy/dt$. Then (2.20) becomes

$$\frac{dv}{dt} = g - \mu v. \tag{2.21}$$

This is a linear equation in v and we can write down its solution as

$$ve^{\mu t} = \int ge^{\mu t}dt + c_3,$$

$$v = g/\mu + c_3 e^{-\mu t}.$$

At $t = 0$, $v = 0$, so $c_3 = -g/\mu$. Hence

$$v = \frac{g}{\mu}(1 - e^{-\mu t}), \tag{2.22}$$

which gives the velocity at any time t after the ball begins to fall. Because of the term $e^{-\mu t}$ the velocity decreases since $\mu > 0$. As $t \to \infty$, $e^{-\mu t} \to 0$ and $v = g/\mu$ is often called the *limiting velocity*.

Example 2.15. *Inside the earth, the force of gravity is not constant but varies as the distance from the center. If a tube is drilled from the North Pole on the surface of the earth to its center, and a rock is dropped in the tube, what will be its velocity when it reaches the center given that the radius of the earth is R?*

Solution: We assume earth's center to be the origin and the positive direction of the y-axis towards the Pole. At time t, the only force on the rock is due to gravity. Hence equation (2.15) becomes
$$\frac{d^2y}{dt^2} = -\mu y,$$
where μ is the constant of proportionality. The negative sign shows the rock is traveling in a direction opposite to the positive direction. We rewrite the last equation as
$$\frac{dv}{dt} = -\mu y.$$

Since $\dfrac{dv}{dt} = \dfrac{dv}{dy} \cdot \dfrac{dy}{dt} = v\dfrac{dv}{dy}$, the last equation can be further rewritten as
$$v\frac{dv}{dy} = -\mu y.$$

By separation of variables,
$$\frac{1}{2}v^2 = -\mu\frac{y^2}{2} + c$$
for some constant c. At $t = 0$, $y = R$ and $v = 0$, so that $c = \mu R^2/2$. It follows that
$$v^2 = \mu(R^2 - y^2).$$

At the center of the earth, $y = 0$ so that the velocity at the center if $R\sqrt{\mu}$. But since at the surface of the earth, we have $y = R$ and $|d^2y/dt^2| = g$ it follows that $\mu R = g$ and we can rewrite the velocity of the rock at the center of the earth as
$$v = R\sqrt{\frac{g}{R}} = \sqrt{gR}.$$

3. Motion of a projectile (no air resistance)

We now consider the motion of an object thrown from a point on the earth's surface. Extensions to the more general case when the object is thrown at a fixed height from the ground are quite easy.

Chapter 2. First Order Equations

Let the origin be the point from which the object is thrown, the y-axis the vertical line from the origin upwards and the x-axis the horizontal line through the origin so that the motion of the object is in the xy-plane. We assume that the object is thrown with initial velocity u at an angle α to the x-axis and the time t is measured from the moment the throw takes place.

During its motion, the only force acting on the object is due to gravity acting vertically. This force can be resolved along the x and y axes giving rise to the pair of equations of motion

$$m\frac{d^2y}{dt^2} = -mg, \quad m\frac{d^2x}{dt^2} = 0. \tag{2.23}$$

The negative sign shows that motion is taking place against gravity. From (2.23) we get

$$\frac{d^2y}{dt^2} = -g, \quad \frac{d^2x}{dt^2} = 0. \tag{2.24}$$

Integrating the equations in (2.24) we have

$$v_y(t) = \frac{dy}{dt} = -gt + c_1, \quad v_x(t) = c_2 \tag{2.25}$$

where v_x, v_y are the horizontal and vertical components of the velocity. From the initial conditions given, $v_y(0) = u\sin\alpha$, $v_x(0) = u\cos\alpha$ and using these the last equations become

$$v_y(t) = -gt + u\sin\alpha, \quad v_x(t) = u\cos\alpha. \tag{2.26}$$

Another integration of equations in (2.26) yields the vertical and horizontal distances traveled by the object at time t:

$$y(t) = -\frac{1}{2}gt^2 + ut\sin\alpha + c_3, \quad x(t) = ut\cos\alpha + c_4. \tag{2.27}$$

At $t = 0$ the object is on the ground so that $x(0) = y(0) = 0$ and using these the last equations now give us

$$y(t) = -\frac{1}{2}gt^2 + ut\sin\alpha, \quad x(t) = ut\cos\alpha. \tag{2.28}$$

Equations (2.26) and (2.28) give us all the information we need. We note that the horizontal velocity of object is constant ($u\cos\alpha$). To find the maximum height reached by the object, note that it moves upwards as long as $v_y(t) \neq 0$. At the highest point, $v_y(t) = -gt + u\sin\alpha = 0$, which gives us the time taken to reach the

highest point,
$$t_{\text{max height}} = \frac{u \sin \alpha}{g}.$$

Using this from (2.28) we get the maximum height reached
$$y_{\max} = \frac{u^2 \sin^2 \alpha}{2g}.$$

What is the maximum ground distance traveled by the object? Note that when the object is on the ground $y(t) = 0$. From equations (2.28) this happens if $t = 0$, that is initially, or when $t = (2u/g)\sin \alpha$. It follows from (2.28) that
$$x_{\max} = \frac{2u^2 \sin \alpha \cos \alpha}{g} = \frac{u^2 \sin 2\alpha}{g}.$$

In particular the object will have maximum horizontal range if thrown so that $\sin 2\alpha = 1$, that is, $\alpha = \pi/4$.

What is the trajectory of the object? To find the cartesian equation of the trajectory, we eliminate t from the two equations in (2.28). We have $t = x/(u\cos \alpha)$ and substituting this in the equation for y, we have
$$y = -\frac{1}{2}g\left(\frac{x}{u\cos \alpha}\right)^2 + u\sin \alpha \left(\frac{x}{u\cos \alpha}\right)$$

which after simplification gives
$$y = x\tan \alpha - \frac{gx^2}{2u^2 \cos^2 \alpha},$$

and this is the equation of a parabola.

Example 2.16. *A projectile is fired from the earth with a velocity of 160 ft/sec and at an angle of 45°. Find the range of the projectile and the amount of time it stays in the air.*

Solution: The projectile is up in the air as long as $y > 0$. It is on the ground when $y = 0$. From (2.28), $y = 0 \Rightarrow t = 0$ or $t = 2u\sin \alpha/g$. Here $u = 160, \alpha = \pi/4$ and so $t = 5\sqrt{2}$ seconds. The range is $x = u^2 \sin 2\alpha/g = 160^2/32 = 800$ feet.

2.5.3 Newton's law of cooling

Newton's law of cooling says simply that:

The rate of change of the temperature of a cooling body is proportional to the difference between the temperature of the body and the constant temperature of the medium surrounding the body.

An immediate consequence of the law is that the cooling body loses its heat more rapidly initially and this rate slows down with time.

Let us suppose that we have an object, say a cup of coffee, whose initial temperature is T_0 and it is placed in a room which is maintained at a temperature M_0 where $M_0 < T_0$. Let T be the current temperature of the body. Then by Newton's law of cooling,

$$\frac{dT}{dt} \propto (T - M_0),$$

that is,

$$\frac{dT}{dt} = k(T - M_0), \tag{2.29}$$

where k is a constant of proportionality. This is a first order equation which is separable and we can rewrite as

$$\frac{dT}{(T - M_0)} = k\,dt$$

and whose solution is

$$\ln|T - M_0| = kt + c,$$

with c being the constant of integration. At $t = 0$, $T = T_0$ so that $c = \ln|T_0 - M_0|$. Hence, the solution can be written as

$$\ln|T - M_0| = \ln|T_0 - M_0| + kt.$$

Also, since $T_0 > T > M_0$, we can drop the absolute values and write the solution to (2.29) as

$$T - M_0 = (T_0 - M_0)e^{kt}. \tag{2.30}$$

A moment's reflection shows that in most cases we really need e^k, not the actual value of k.

Example 2.17. *The temperature of a cup of coffee initially is $185°F$ and it is in a room maintained at $72°F$. Fifteen minutes later, the temperature is $150°F$. When will the coffee be at $100°F$?*

Solution: Let the temperature of the coffee at time t be $T°$F. We will measure t in hours. Using equation (2.30),

$$T - 72 = (185 - 72)e^{kt}, \qquad (2.31)$$

where we need to determine k (or e^k). Since $T = 150°$ when $t = 0.25$, we get from (2.31)

$$150 - 72 = 113\, e^{0.25k},$$

that is, $(e^k)^{0.25} = 78/113 \approx 0.690$. Hence, $e^k = (0.690)^4 \approx 0.227$.

To find when the temperature of the coffee would be $100°$, from (2.31) we have

$$100 - 72 = 113\, e^{kt},$$

that is, $0.227^t = 28/113 \approx 0.247$. Hence,

$$t = \ln 0.247 / \ln 0.227 = 0.943 \text{ hours } \approx 57 \text{ minutes}.$$

Example 2.18. *The police discover the body of a murdered young man at 10:30 a.m. in a condo kept at $72°F$. The coroner records the body temperature at $84°F$ and an hour later at $80°F$. When did the murder take place?*

Solution: Let us measure time in hours and count it from the moment the body is discovered. Since the initial temperature is $84°F$, by Newton's law of cooling, using (2.30)

$$(T - 72) = (84 - 72)e^{kt} = 12e^{kt}.$$

The body temperature at the end of one hour is $80°$ so that

$$(80 - 72) = 12e^k$$

from which $e^k = 8/12 = 2/3$. The normal temperature of a healthy human body is $98.6°F$. This must have been the temperature just prior to death. Hence

$$(98.6 - 72) = 12(e^k)^t.$$

Since $e^k = 2/3$ this gives us $26.6/12 = (2/3)^t$ from which

$$t = \frac{\ln(26.6/12)}{\ln(2/3)} = -1.963 \text{ hours},$$

that is 1 hour and 57 minutes before we started the clock. Hence, the murder took place around 8:33 a.m.

2.5.4 Malthus' law of population dynamics

We all know that population grows in general, but how fast does the population of a city grow? What will the population of the US be in 2025? Questions of this kind have been of interest to many scientists and the first person to propose a mathematical law was Rev. Thomas Robert Malthus, an English clergy man who laid out his findings in his 1798 writings.

Malthusian law says:

> *The rate of change of population is proportional to the actual population at any given time.*

Notice that this law is very similar in nature to Newton's law. Both laws predict that the rate of change of a quantity is in some sense proportional to the quantity remaining at a given time. The only difference is that Newton's law has to do with the *decrease* in heat while Malthus law has to do with *increase* in population.

Let the population at a given time t_0 be P_0 and at any time t later be $P(t)$. Then according to Malthus law,

$$\frac{dP}{dt} \propto P. \tag{2.32}$$

If k is the constant of proportionality, equation (2.32) becomes

$$\frac{dP}{dt} = kP. \tag{2.33}$$

This is a very simple equation whose solution is $\ln P = kt + c$, where c is the constant of integration. Using the initial condition that at $t = t_0, P = P_0$, we get

$$\ln P_0 = k\,t_0 + c.$$

We can then write the solution as

$$\ln P = kt + \ln P_0 - kt_0$$
$$= \ln P_0 + k(t - t_0),$$

that is,

$$P = P_0 e^{k(t-t_0)}. \tag{2.34}$$

Before we proceed further we should mention that Malthus law has proved remarkably accurate in predicting world population for certain periods and also for some species of mammals.

Example 2.19. *The world population in 1965 and in 1970 was 3.345 billions and 3.706 billions, respectively. What was the population in 1973?*

Solution: From equation (2.34), using the data for 1965 and 1970,

$$3.345 = 3.706 \, e^{k(1965-1970)},$$

that is,

$$3.345 = 3.706 \, e^{-5k}$$
$$e^k = (3.706/3.345)^{0.2} = 1.020.$$

To find the population in 1973, we have (again from equation (2.34)) that

$$P = 3.706 \, e^{k(1973-1970)} = 3.706 \, (e^k)^3 = 3.706(1.020)^3 = 3.932 \text{ billions}.$$

The actual population of the world in 1973 was 3.937 billions!

If the population of a city at time t_0 is P_0, it is apparent from equation (2.34) that the Malthus law predicts that the population of the city will grow exponentially without any limit. This is obviously not very realistic. In most cases, population growth is limited by available living space, decrease in food supply, etc. A different model has been proposed by the *logistic model*, also known as the *Verhulst-Pearl model*. According to this model, equation (2.33) is to be modified to:

$$\frac{dP}{dt} = kP\left(1 - \frac{P}{M}\right). \tag{2.35}$$

The only difference between this and the Malthus equation is the additional term $-kP^2/M$. This can be explained in the following way. The denominator M denotes a limiting factor. If the *decrease* in population per person is proportional to $-P/M$, then for the entire population it is proportional to $P \cdot (-P/M) = -P^2/M$. When $P \ll M$, that is, P is very small in comparison to M, the logistic model coincides with the Malthus model. In fact, it has been observed that the Malthus model is fairly accurate for world population for years past but not so for the distant future.

The solution of (2.35) is not as easy as that of (2.33), but not very difficult either. The variables are separable and we have

$$\frac{dP}{P\left(1-\frac{P}{M}\right)} = k\,dt.$$

Using partial fractions the last equation can be rewritten as

$$\left\{\frac{1}{P} + \frac{1/M}{1-(P/M)}\right\} dP = k\,dt,$$

which on integration yields

$$\ln P - \ln(1-P/M) = kt + \ln c,$$

$\ln c$ being the constant of integration written in this form for easier simplification. We rewrite the last equation in the form

$$\frac{P}{1-(P/M)} = ce^{kt}. \tag{2.36}$$

If we use the initial conditions that at time $t = 0$, the starting population is P_0, we have from the last equation

$$c = \frac{P_0}{1-(P_0/M)} = \frac{MP_0}{M-P_0}. \tag{2.37}$$

From (2.36), solving for P we get

$$P = (1-P/M)ce^{kt}$$
$$\Rightarrow P = \frac{Mce^{kt}}{M+ce^{kt}}, \tag{2.38}$$

as is easily verified. In equation (2.38), we substitute for c from (2.37) to get

$$P = \frac{\frac{MP_0}{M-P_0} Me^{kt}}{M + \frac{MP_0}{M-P_0} e^{kt}}$$
$$= \frac{e^{kt} MP_0}{(M-P_0) + P_0 e^{kt}}$$
$$= \frac{MP_0}{P_0 + (M-P_0)e^{-kt}}, \tag{2.39}$$

which is the solution of (2.35). A little laborious perhaps, but not hard.

If we let $t \to \infty$ in (2.39) we get $P = M$, the limiting size of the population.

Example 2.20. *The elk population in a small mountain area is given by the logistic equation*
$$\frac{dP}{dt} = 0.1\, P(t)\left(1 - \frac{P(t)}{300}\right).$$
If the initial elk population is 120, find P as a function of t. What is the population in ten years? When does the population double?

Solution: In this problem $M = 300, P_0 = 120, k = 0.1$. From equation (2.39),
$$P(t) = \frac{MP_0}{P_0 + (M - P_0)e^{-kt}} = \frac{300 \cdot 120}{120 + 180\, e^{-(0.1 \cdot 10)}} = \frac{600}{2 + 3e^{-1}} \approx 193$$
which is the population of the elk in 10 years. To find the time when the population doubles, we need t when $P = 2P_0 = 240$. From equation (2.39) we have
$$240 = \frac{300 \cdot 120}{(120 + 180 e^{-0.1t})}$$
from which $e^{0.1t} = 6$ or $t = 10 \ln 6 = 17.9$ years.

2.5.5 Mixture problems

Most mixture problems are of the following type.

Example 2.21. *A tank of volume V gallons is filled with brine (salt dissolved in water) containing k pounds of salt. At $t = 0$, brine containing c pounds of salt per gallon flows through an inlet valve at the rate of r gallons per minute. The fluid is kept uniform by constant stirring and flows out at the rate of s gallons per minute. How much salt is in the tank at $t = t_0$?*

Solution: Let $x = x(t)$ be the number of pounds of dissolved salt in the tank at any time $t \geq 0$. In this problem:

Concentration of salt in the cistern at time t is x/V pounds/gallon;

Concentration of brine entering the cistern is c pounds/gallon;

Brine is entering the tank at r gallons/min;

Brine is leaving the tank at s gallons/min.

Chapter 2. First Order Equations

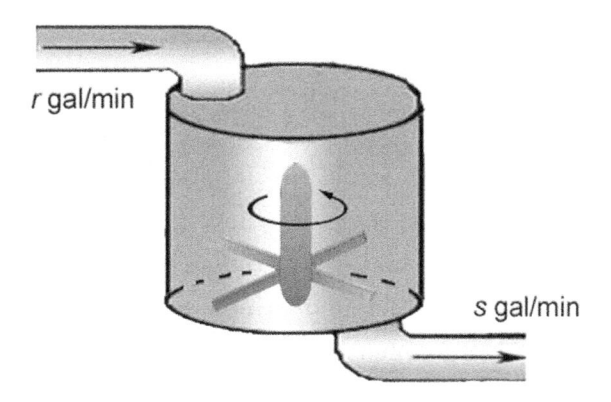

Figure 2.1: Tank model with constant stirring to keep the mixture uniform.

It is clear that the *input rate* of brine is $c \cdot r$ pounds/minute and the *output rate* is $x/V \cdot s$ pounds/minute. Almost all problems deal with the rate at which x changes with respect to time, that is, dx/dt. A moment's reflection leads us to what is usually referred to as the fundamental equation:

$$\frac{dx}{dt} = \text{Input rate} - \text{Output rate}. \tag{2.40}$$

In our present case this is,

$$\frac{dx}{dt} = cr - \frac{s}{V}x. \tag{2.41}$$

This is a linear equation and is easily solved.

Example 2.22. *A tank contains 1000 liters of brine containing 400 grams of salt. Fresh water runs into the tank at the rate of 8 liters/min. The solution is kept uniform by constant stirring and runs out of an outlet tube at the same rate. When will the amount of salt in the tank be half of what it started with?*

Solution: This is similar to Example 2.21 with $V = 1000$, $k = 400$, $c = 0$ since only fresh water flows in. Here $r = s = 8$. Thus, equation (2.41) becomes

$$\frac{dx}{dt} = 0 - \frac{8}{1000} \cdot x = -\frac{x}{125}.$$

Separating variables, we get

$$\frac{dx}{x} = -\frac{dt}{125} \tag{2.42}$$

whose solution is $x = Ce^{-t/125}$, where C is a constant. From the initial condition, at $t = 0$, $x = 400$ so that $C = 400$ and

$$x = 400e^{-t/125}. \tag{2.43}$$

To find out when the salt content would be 200 grams of salt (half of the original amount), we let $x = 200$ in (2.43) to get $t = 125(\ln 2) = 86.643$ minutes. We can avoid the constant of integration and get to the answer more quickly if we simply integrate equation (2.42). If t_0 is the amount of time it takes for x to change from 400 grams to 200 grams, then we must have

$$\int_{400}^{200} \frac{dx}{x} = \int_0^{t_0} -\frac{1}{125} dt \tag{2.44}$$

from which we immediately get

$$\ln \frac{1}{2} = -\frac{t}{125},$$

that is $t = 125 \ln 2$, as before!

Example 2.23. *A tank contains 100 gallons of fresh water. A brine solution is pumped in at 2 gallons/minute containing 1 lb of salt/gallon. The mixture is constantly stirred and runs out at 1 gallon/minute. How much salt is present when the tank has 150 gallons?*

Solution: Since 2 gallons are pumped in and only 1 gallon is pumped out, the tank gains 1 gallon of fluid each minute. At the end of time t, the amount of fluid in the tank is $100 + t$ gallons. If x is the amount of salt in the tank at time t, the density of the solution is $x/(100 + t)$ lbs/gallon. Thus, the input rate is $2 \cdot 1$ lbs/min while the output rate is $(x/(100+t)) \cdot 1$ lbs/min. The fundamental equation here becomes

$$\frac{dx}{dt} = 2 - \frac{x}{100 + t}.$$

Rewriting this equation as

$$\frac{dx}{dt} + \frac{x}{100 + t} = 2$$

we notice that it is linear. The integrating factor is

$$e^{\int \frac{dt}{100+t}} = 100 + t$$

and hence the solution is

$$x(100+t) = \int 2(100+t)dt$$
$$= (100+t)^2 + C.$$

(*verify!*), where C is an arbitrary constant. At $t = 0$, $x = 0$ since the tank contains only fresh water. Thus $C = -100^2$. Substituting this in the last equation and simplifying we get

$$x = \frac{t(200+t)}{100+t}.$$

Since the tank originally had 100 gallons, and it is gaining 1 gallon/minute, it follows that it will have 150 gallons of fluid when $t = 50$. Substituting this in the last equation for x, we obtain

$$x = \frac{50(200+50)}{100+50} = 83.33 \text{ gallons.}$$

2.5.6 Applications to Geometry

1. Orthogonal trajectories

1-parameter family of curves

The cartesian equation of a curve C usually involves the variables x, y and other constants that determine its size, shape and position. For example,

$$y = mx + c$$

is the equation of a family of lines, where m denotes the slope of a particular line and which goes through the point $(0, c)$. If we fix c, we get a *pencil* of lines all going through the point $(0, c)$. See Figure 2.2(a).

We can write the equation of this pencil of lines as $f(x, y, c, m) = y - mx - c = 0$. The constant m varies from line to line, but is fixed for a particular line. We call m a *parameter* and the pencil of lines is called a *single parameter* or *1-parameter family*. If, on the other hand, we fix m but let c vary, we get the 1-parameter family of parallel lines (since all have the same slope m) with varying y-intercepts, c. See Figure 2.2(b).

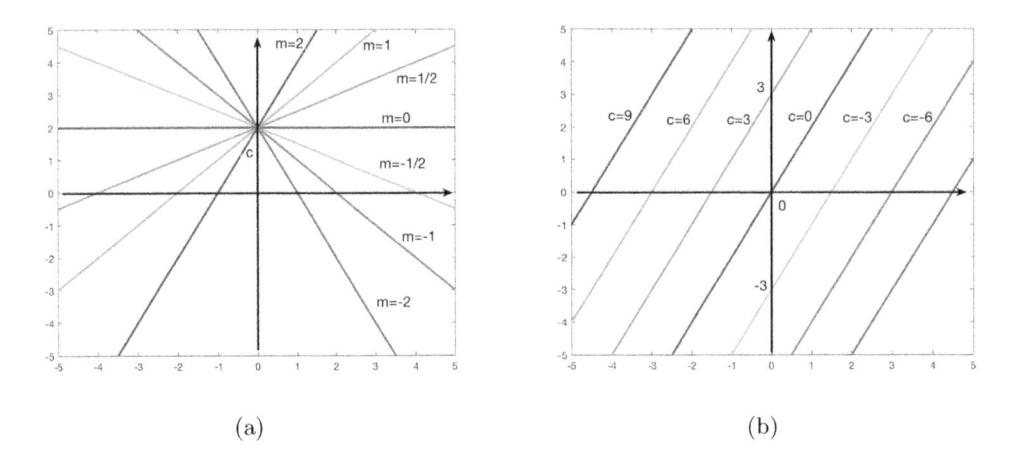

Figure 2.2: Family of lines $y = mx + c$. In (a) the parameter $c > 0$ is fixed and m varies, and in (b) the parameter $m > 0$ is fixed while c varies.

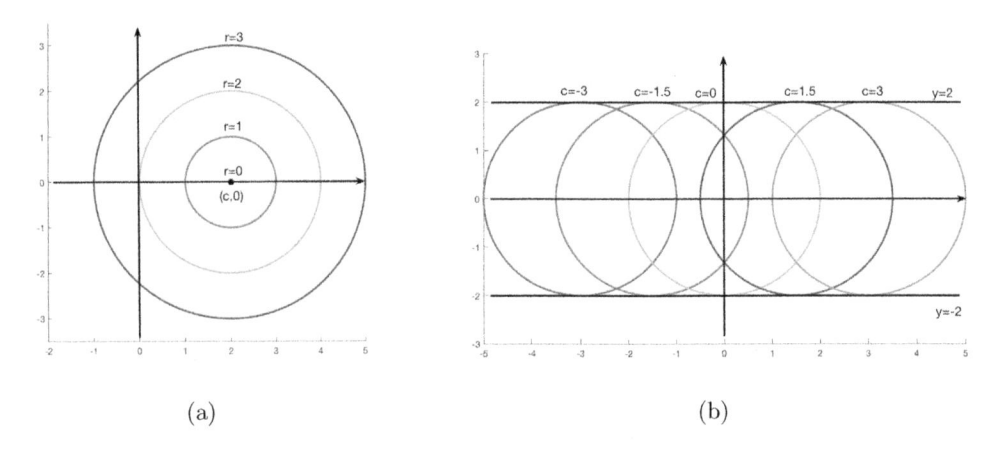

Figure 2.3: Family of circles $f(x, y, r, c) = (x - c)^2 + y^2 = r^2$. In (a) the center $(c, 0)$ with $c = 2$ is fixed and r varies, while in (b) $r = 2$ is fixed and c varies.

Similarly,
$$f(x, y, r, c) = (x - c)^2 + y^2 = r^2 \qquad (2.45)$$

represents a family of circles with radius r and centered at $(c, 0)$. The size of the circle is determined by r. If we now fix c so that it is a constant for all circles represented by (2.45), we get a 1-parameter family of *concentric circles* all centered at $(c, 0)$ with different radii. Here r is the parameter. If, on the other hand, we fix r and let c vary, we get the 1-parameter of circles, all of radius r, but centered at

Chapter 2. First Order Equations

various points on the x-axis. See Figure 2.3

Differential equation of a 1-parameter family

Suppose we have a 1-parameter family of curves given by

$$f(x, y, c) = 0. \tag{2.46}$$

It is likely that it was obtained from an *integral equation*, that is one obtained by integrating a differential equation. How do we find the original differential equation? If we differentiate the last equation with respect to x we get an equation of the form

$$g(x, y, y', c) = 0. \tag{2.47}$$

Since the differential equation we seek cannot have the parameter c in it, *we eliminate it from the last two equations* to get

$$F(x, y, y') = 0,$$

which is the differential equation we seek. *In all problems involving the differential equation of a 1-parameter family, this elimination is critical!*

Example 2.24. *Find the differential equation of the 1-parameter family of circles given by $x^2 + y^2 = r^2$.*

Solution: Differentiating the given equation we get $x + yy' = 0$ and this does not contain r. So there is nothing to eliminate and this is differential equation of the given family.

Example 2.25. *Find the differential equation of the 1-parameter family given by*

$$(x - c)^2 + y^2 = c^2. \tag{2.48}$$

Solution: This is a family of circles with center at $(c, 0)$ and radius c, that is, this is a family of circles for which the y-axis is the tangent at the origin. Differentiating (2.48), we obtain

$$2(x - c) + 2yy' = 0, \tag{2.49}$$

that is,

$$x + yy' = c. \tag{2.50}$$

The parameter c is still present and so we eliminate it using the given equation (2.48). Expanding the quadratic term in (2.48) and simplifying we have

$$x^2 + y^2 = 2cx,$$

whence it follows that

$$c = \frac{x^2 + y^2}{2x}.$$

Substituting it to (2.50) gives us

$$x + yy' = \frac{x^2 + y^2}{2x},$$

which after some simplification yields the differential equation

$$y' = \frac{y^2 - x^2}{2xy},$$

which is the differential equation of the given 1-parameter family.

Orthogonal trajectories

Two curves C_1 and C_2 which intersect at a point P are said to be *orthogonal* to each other at P if the tangents to C_1 and C_2 at P are orthogonal, that is, perpendicular to each other. Given a 1-parameter family C of curves, any curve that is orthogonal to every member of C is called an *orthogonal trajectory* of C. If two 1-parameter family of curves C_1 and C_2 have the property that every member of one family is orthogonal to every member of the other, C_1 and C_2 are said to be orthogonal trajectories of each other. Orthogonal trajectory problems occur in many physical fields. For example in electrical fields, equipotential lines and lines of current flow are orthogonal trajectories.

Suppose that C_1 and C_2 are orthogonal to each other, then the slopes of their tangents at the point of intersection P are negative reciprocal of each other. If we denote the slope of the tangent at P of C_i as y'_i, then we must have

$$y'_1 \cdot y'_2 = -1.$$

Given C_1 we can use the last equation to find the differential equation of its orthogonal trajectories, and hence the equation of the orthogonal trajectories themselves.

Example 2.26. *Find the orthogonal trajectories of the pencil of lines given by*

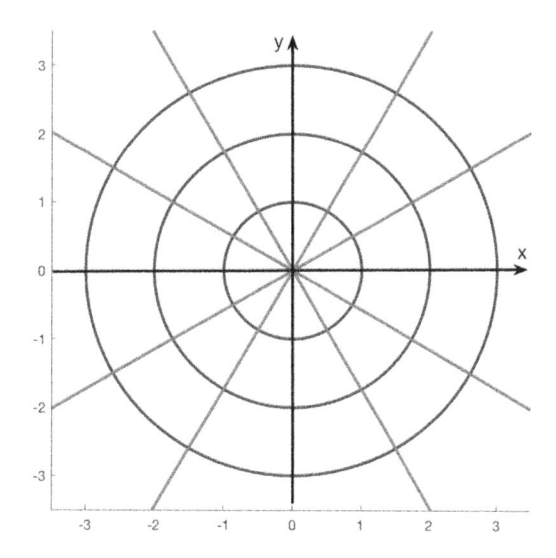

$$y = mx. \qquad (2.51)$$

Figure 2.4: The orthogonal trajectories of the lines $y = mx$ are the family of concentric circles $x^2 + y^2 = c^2$. Note that their tangents at the intersection points are orthogonal to each other.

Solution: Let C_1 be the pencil of lines $y = mx$. We want to find the equation of the family of curves C_2 that are orthogonal trajectories to C_1. The slopes of the tangents to C_1 are given by the derivative

$$y_1' = y' = m.$$

From (2.51), $m = y/x$, and therefore $y_1' = y/x$. Hence, the slope of the tangents to C_2 must be the negative reciprocal, that is, $y_2' = -x/y$. The differential equation of C_2 is then given by

$$y' = -\frac{x}{y}.$$

This is a separable equation, which can be written as $ydy = -xdx$. Integration yields

$$\int y dy = -\int x dx$$
$$\frac{1}{2}y^2 = -\frac{1}{2}x^2 + c_1$$
$$x^2 + y^2 = c^2,$$

where $c^2 = 2c_1$ is an arbitrary constant. This is a family of concentric circles centered at the origin. See Figure 2.4.

Example 2.27. *Find the orthogonal trajectories of the family of parabolas given by*

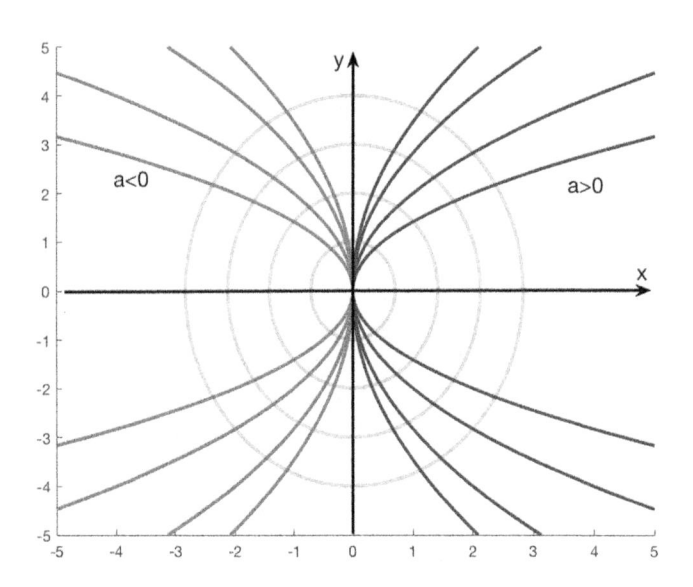

$$y^2 = 4ax. \tag{2.52}$$

Figure 2.5: The orthogonal trajectories of the family of parabolas $y^2 = 4ax$ are the family of ellipses $2x^2 + y^2 = c^2$.

Solution: Let C_1, C_2 be the given family of parabolas and its orthogonal trajectory, y_1', y_2' the slopes of their tangents, respectively. Differentiating the given equation we get

$$yy_1' = 2a.$$

From the given equation for C_1,
$$a = \frac{y^2}{4x}.$$

Eliminating a from the last two equations,
$$yy_1' = \frac{y^2}{2x},$$

that is,
$$y_1' = y/2x.$$

Since $y_1' \cdot y_2' = -1$,
$$y_2' = -\frac{2x}{y}$$

which leads to the differential equation
$$y' = -\frac{2x}{y},$$

that is,
$$yy' + 2x = 0$$

for C_2. Integrating this last equation we get the equation of the orthogonal trajectories to be
$$2x^2 + y^2 = c^2$$

or
$$\frac{x^2}{c^2/2} + \frac{y^2}{c^2} = 1$$

which if a family of ellipses. See Figure 2.5.

In finding orthogonal trajectories, cartesian coordinates (x, y) may not always be very useful. The differential equation of the orthogonal trajectories of a given family may not be easily integrable with the techniques available to us now. Consider the 1-parameter family of circles in Example 2.25. The differential equation of this family was shown to be
$$y' = \frac{y^2 - x^2}{2xy}.$$

Hence, the equation of the orthogonal trajectory of the family is
$$y' = -\frac{2xy}{y^2 - x^2},$$

that is,
$$y' = \frac{2xy}{x^2 - y^2}.$$
Unfortunately, the techniques at our disposal now cannot integrate this equation. However, we may be able to find the equation of the orthogonal trajectory in *polar coordinates* more easily!

Polar Coordinates

Let O be the pole, OI the initial line. Let C be a given curve with equation $f(r, \theta) = 0$. Let P, Q be points on C with polar coordinates (r, θ) and $(r + \delta r, \theta + \delta\theta)$, respectively. Let TPT' be the tangent at P. Extend OP to OM where $QM \perp OM$. Assume that the tangent TT' makes an angle ϕ with OM. See Figure 2.6.

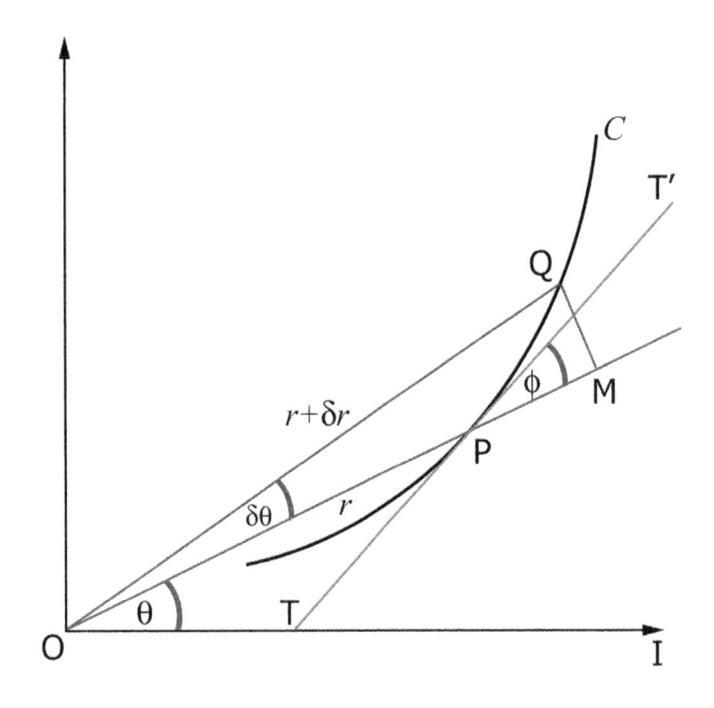

Figure 2.6: A curve C and its tangent in polar coordinates.

We assume that Q is close to P and thus δr and $\delta\theta$ are infinitesimals. We have

Chapter 2. First Order Equations

$$\tan \phi \approx \frac{QM}{PM} = \frac{QM}{OM - OP}$$
$$= \frac{(r + \delta r) \sin \delta\theta}{(r + \delta r) \cos \delta\theta - r}$$
$$= \frac{(r + \delta r) \sin \delta\theta}{\delta r \cos \delta\theta - r(1 - \cos \delta\theta)}$$
$$= \frac{(r + \delta r)\frac{\sin \delta\theta}{\delta\theta}}{\frac{\delta r}{\delta\theta} \cos \delta\theta - r\frac{\sin^2(\delta\theta/2)}{\delta\theta/2}}$$

dividing the numerator and denominator by $\delta\theta$. In the limit as $\delta\theta \to 0$, $\delta r \to 0$, note that

$$\frac{\sin \delta\theta}{\delta\theta} \to 1, \ \cos \delta\theta \to 1, \ \frac{\sin^2(\delta\theta/2)}{\delta\theta/2} = \frac{\sin(\delta\theta/2)}{\delta\theta/2} \cdot \sin(\delta\theta/2) \to 0, \ \frac{\delta r}{\delta\theta} \to \frac{dr}{d\theta},$$

and it follows that

$$\tan \phi = \frac{r d\theta}{dr}.$$

Now if C' is a family which is an orthogonal trajectory of C intersecting C at P, it is clear that the tangent to C' at P must make an angle ϕ' where

$$\phi' = \phi + \frac{\pi}{2}.$$

Hence,

$$\tan \phi' = \tan(\phi + \frac{\pi}{2}) = -\cot \phi = -\frac{dr}{r d\theta}.$$

Thus, to get the orthogonal trajectory C' of C all we need to do is to replace

$$\frac{r d\theta}{dr} \text{ by } -\frac{1}{r}\frac{dr}{d\theta}$$

or what is the same thing, replace

$$\frac{dr}{d\theta} \text{ by } -r^2 \frac{d\theta}{dr}.$$

If the differential equation for C is

$$f\left(r, \theta, \frac{dr}{d\theta}\right) = 0,$$

then that for C' would simply be

$$F\left(r, \theta, -r^2\frac{d\theta}{dr}\right) = 0.$$

Example 2.28. *Find the orthogonal trajectories of $r^n = a^n \sin(n\theta)$.*

Solution: Differentiating the given equation with respect to θ,

$$nr^{n-1}\frac{dr}{d\theta} = na^n \cos(n\theta),$$

$$\frac{dr}{d\theta} = \frac{nra^n \cos(n\theta)}{nr^n} = \frac{ra^n \cos(n\theta)}{a^n \sin(n\theta)},$$

using $r^n = a^n \sin(n\theta)$ from the given equation. Simplifying

$$\frac{dr}{d\theta} = r \cot(n\theta),$$

which is the differential equation of the given 1-parameter family. To find the differential equation of the orthogonal trajectories we replace $dr/d\theta$ by $-r^2 d\theta/dr$ in the last equation to get

$$-r^2\frac{d\theta}{dr} = r\cot(n\theta),$$

$$-r\frac{d\theta}{dr} = \cot(n\theta).$$

Hence,

$$-\frac{dr}{r} = \frac{\sin(n\theta)}{\cos(n\theta)} d\theta,$$

which upon integrating gives

$$\ln r - \frac{1}{n}\ln(\cos(n\theta)) = \ln c$$

for some constant c. Simplifying we finally get

$$r^n = c^n \cos(n\theta)$$

as the equation of the orthogonal trajectories.

Remark 3. You may be wondering why we did not use the angle the tangent makes with the initial line OI, usually denoted by ψ, in polar coordinates as we did in cartesian coordinates. The reason is that it is much more complicated to compute. Besides, the information about the tangent is more easily obtained by use of the angle

ϕ.

2. Envelopes

Given a 1-parameter family of curves

$$f(x, y, \alpha) = 0,$$

any curve(s) that *touches* every member of this family is called an *envelope* of the family. The name arises out of the following situation. Consider the 1-parameter family of circles given by

$$(x - \alpha)^2 + y^2 = r^2,$$

where r is a fixed constant and α is the parameter. The centers of all the circles of the family lie on the x-axis and all have a fixed radius. See Figure 2.3(b). It is easy to see from the picture that the circles of the given family are contained between the lines $y = \pm r$, that is the two lines form an *envelope* for all the circles. It is important to remember not all families of curves have envelopes! For instance, the family of concentric circles centered at a point and with any arbitrary radius does not have an envelope (see Figure 2.3(a)).

Definition 2.1. *Given a 1-parameter family of curves C_1, another family of curves C_2 is said to be the envelope of C_1 if:*

1. *at any point P of C_2, there is a unique member of C_1 that is tangent to C_2 at P, and*

2. *every member of C_1 is tangent to C_2 at a distinct point of C_2.*

Given a family of curves C_1 and also given that it has an envelope, how do we find the equation of the envelope? [1] If the equation of C_1 is given by

$$f(x, y, \alpha) = 0, \qquad (2.53)$$

we will find two parametric equations for the envelope. To begin with we can use equation (2.53) for one of the parametric equations. To find another, we proceed as follows.

---

[1] Here we present a heuristic method. The full theoretical definition, necessary and sufficient conditions for an envelope to exist are beyond the scope of this book.

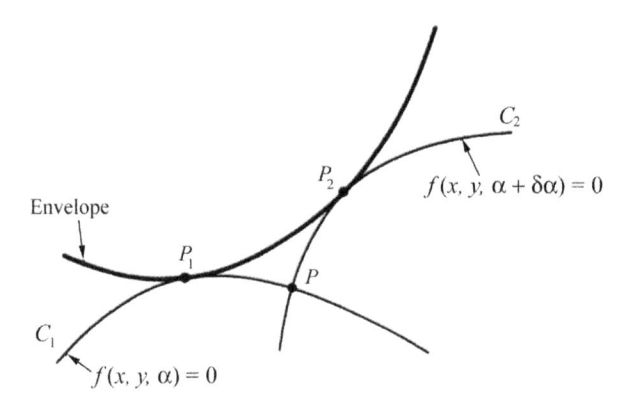

Figure 2.7: Two members C_1 and C_2 of a given family of curves touch the envelope at P_1 and P_2.

Let $\delta\alpha$ be very small and consider two members of the given family with equations $f(x, y, \alpha) = 0$ and $f(x, y, \alpha + \delta\alpha) = 0$, which touch the envelope at P_1 and P_2. See Figure 2.7. If P is their point of intersection, then at P,

$$f(x, y, \alpha) = 0 \text{ and } f(x, y, \alpha + \delta\alpha) = 0$$

since it lies on both curves. Then as $\delta\alpha \to 0$, both P and P_2 tend to P_1 and we have

$$\lim_{\delta\alpha \to 0} \frac{f(x, y, \alpha + \delta\alpha) - f(x, y, \alpha)}{\delta\alpha} \to 0.$$

Hence,
$$\frac{\partial f}{\partial \alpha}(x, y, \alpha) = 0$$

and this is the other parametric equation we were seeking. To find the equation of the envelope, we need to eliminate the parameter α from the two equations

$$f(x, y, \alpha) = 0, \quad \frac{\partial f}{\partial \alpha}(x, y, \alpha) = 0.$$

(Caution: This elimination may not always be possible!)

Example 2.29. *For the family of circles $(x - \alpha)^2 + y^2 = r^2$, where r is a fixed radius, prove that its envelope is the lines $y = \pm r$.*

Solution: Here r is fixed and α is the parameter. Let

$$f(x, y, \alpha) = (x - \alpha)^2 + y^2 - r^2 = 0. \tag{2.54}$$

Chapter 2. First Order Equations 61

Differentiating partially with respect to α and set it equal to 0,

$$\frac{\partial f}{\partial \alpha} = -2(x - \alpha) = 0,$$

gives us $x = \alpha$. Substituting it to (2.54) we have

$$y^2 = r^2$$

that is, $y = \pm r$.

Example 2.30. *Find the equation of the envelope of the family of lines*

$$y = mx + \frac{a}{m},$$

where $a \neq 0$ is a fixed constant.

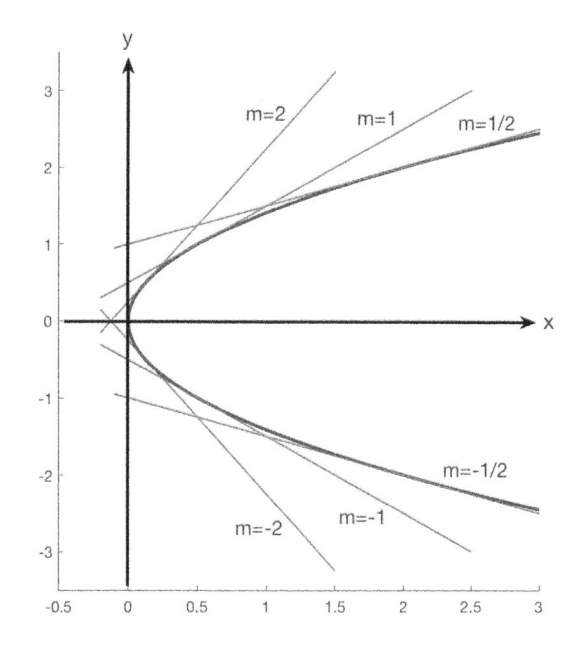

Figure 2.8: The envelope of the family of lines $y = mx + a/m$, where $a \neq 0$ is the parabola $y^2 = 4ax$.

Solution: Since a is fixed, the parameter here is m. Write the given equation as

$$f(x, y, m) = y - mx - \frac{a}{m} = 0 \qquad (2.55)$$

and differentiate it partially with respect to m to get

$$\frac{\partial f}{\partial m} = -x + \frac{a}{m^2} = 0,$$

that is $-m^2x + a = 0$. Solving for m, we have $m = \pm\sqrt{a/x}$. For the case $m = \sqrt{a/x}$, substituting it to (2.55) yields

$$y - x\sqrt{a/x} - \frac{a}{\sqrt{a/x}} = 0$$
$$y - \sqrt{ax} - \sqrt{ax} = 0$$
$$y = 2\sqrt{ax}. \qquad (2.56)$$

Likewise, for $m = -\sqrt{a/x}$, we get

$$y = -2\sqrt{ax}. \qquad (2.57)$$

From (2.56) and (2.57), the equation of the envelope is therefore $y^2 = 4ax$, which is a parabola with axis the x-axis and focus at $(a, 0)$. The case where $a > 0$ is shown in Figure 2.8.

Example 2.31. *Find the equation of the envelope, if it exists, of the family of lines* $f(x, y, m) = y - mx = 0$.

Solution: The parameter is m and we see from the given equation that

$$\frac{\partial f}{\partial m} = -x = 0$$

and it is impossible to eliminate m. Hence the given family has no envelope!

Example 2.32. *Find the envelope of the family of lines which are at a fixed distance p from the origin.*

Solution: Let C be a particular member from the family of lines. Let α be the angle that the perpendicular line segment from the origin to C makes with the x-axis. See Figure 2.9.

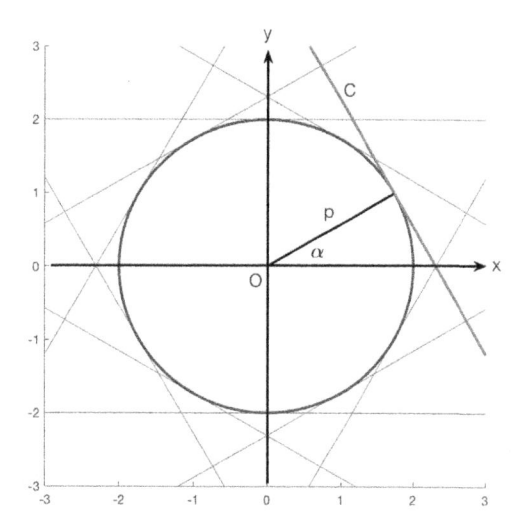

Figure 2.9: The envelope of the family of lines that are at distance p from the origin is the circle centered at the origin with radius p.

Then it is easy to see that the equation of the family of lines is given by

$$x \cos \alpha + y \sin \alpha = p, \tag{2.58}$$

where p is fixed and α is the parameter. (Note: This is often called the *normal form* of the equation of a line). Differentiating partially with respect to α we get

$$-x \sin \alpha + y \cos \alpha = 0. \tag{2.59}$$

We eliminate α from the last two equations as follows. Multiply (2.58) by $\cos \alpha$, and equation (2.59) by $\sin \alpha$ and subtract the two equations to get

$$x(\cos^2 \alpha + \sin^2 \alpha) = p \cos \alpha,$$

that is

$$x = p \cos \alpha. \tag{2.60}$$

Likewise, if we multiply (2.58) by $\sin \alpha$ and (2.59) by $\cos \alpha$ and add them together, we obtain

$$y = p \sin \alpha. \tag{2.61}$$

From (2.60) and (2.61), it follows that

$$x^2 + y^2 = p^2,$$

which we recognize as the equation of a circle centered at the origin and with radius p. See Figure 2.9.

Example 2.33. *Find the envelope of the family of lines of constant length ℓ whose extremities touch the coordinate axes.*

Solution: Let AB be a typical line of length ℓ and assume that the line segment from the origin perpendicular to AB, of length p, makes an angle α with the x-axis (see Figure 2.10).

The equation of AB in normal form is then

$$x \cos \alpha + y \sin \alpha = p$$

with two parameters α and p. We seem to have two parameters α and p, but it is easy to eliminate p first. We have

$$OA = \ell \cos \alpha, \quad OB = \ell \sin \alpha.$$

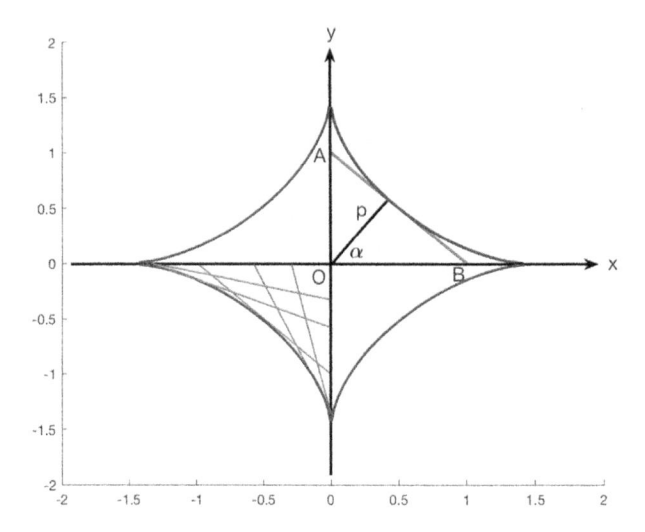

Figure 2.10: The envelope of the family of lines of constant length ℓ whose extremities touch the x and y axes is the hypocycloid $x^{2/3} + y^{2/3} = \ell^{2/3}$.

Hence,
$$p = OB\cos\alpha = \ell\sin\alpha\cos\alpha$$
and the equation of the line AB becomes
$$x\cos\alpha + y\sin\alpha = \ell\sin\alpha\cos\alpha, \qquad (2.62)$$
which now contains just the parameter α. We partially differentiate the last equation with respect to α:
$$-x\sin\alpha + y\cos\alpha = \ell\cos^2\alpha - \ell\sin^2\alpha. \qquad (2.63)$$

From the last two equations, multiply (2.62) by $\cos\alpha$, and (2.63) by $\sin\alpha$ and subtract to get
$$x(\cos^2\alpha + \sin^2\alpha) = \ell(\sin\alpha\cos^2\alpha - \sin\alpha\cos^2\alpha + \sin^3\alpha)$$
that is $x = \ell\sin^3\alpha$ and likewise $y = \ell\cos^3\alpha$, which are the parametric equations of the envelope. To find the cartesian equation, we can eliminate α to get the *hypocycloid*
$$x^{2/3} + y^{2/3} = \ell^{2/3}.$$

2.6 Exercises

1. Classify the following problems as separable, linear, exact, and/or homogeneous:

    (a) $(1-x)dy - (1+y)dx = 0$

    (b) $y - xy' = 2(y^2 + y')$

    (c) $xy' - ay = x + 1$

    (d) $y - x - xy\cot x + xy' = 0$

    (e) $e^y dx + (xe^y + 2y^2)dy = 0$

2. Use separation of variables to solve the following equations:

    (a) $(y^2 + 1)dy + (e^x + x)dx = 0.$

    (b) $\dfrac{dy}{dx} = \dfrac{xy}{1+x^2}$

    (c) $x^5 y' + y^5 = 0$

    (d) $y' - y\tan x = 0$

(e) $(y + yx^2 + 2 + 2x^2)dy = dx$

(f) $y'/(1+x^2) = x/y$ and $y = 3$ when $x = 1$

(g) $y' = x^2 y^2$ and the curve passes through $(-1, 2)$.

3. Solve the following linear equations:

(a) $\dfrac{dy}{dx} + \dfrac{4y}{x} = 6x^2.$

(b) $\dfrac{dy}{dx} + 3y = 4x^3 e^{-3x}.$

(c) $x\dfrac{dy}{dx} + \dfrac{2x+1}{x+1}y = x - 1.$

(d) $xdy + (xy + y - 1)dx = 0.$

(e) $ydx + (xy^2 + x - y)dy = 0.$ (*Use Remark 1*)

(f) $(\cos^2 x - y\cos x)dx - (1 + \sin x)dy = 0.$

(g) $\dfrac{dy}{dx} - \dfrac{y}{x} = \dfrac{-y^2}{x}.$

4. Verify that the following are exact equations. If they are, you may use the l..o..n..g method(!) or look for clever groupings where you can. *You must do the last two problems by long method only.*

(a) $(3x + x^2 + 2y)dx + (2x + y - \frac{1}{y^2})dy = 0.$

(b) $(2xy^2 + 2y) + (2x^2 y + 2x)\dfrac{dy}{dx} = 0.$

(c) $(2xy + x)dx + (x^2 + 3y^2)dy = 0.$

(d) $\left(\dfrac{y}{x} + 6x\right)dx + (\ln x - 2)dy = 0$ with $x > 0$.

(e) $(6xy + 2y^2)dx + (3x^2 + 4xy)dy = 0.$

(f) $\dfrac{dy}{dx} = -\dfrac{ax + by}{bx + cy}$ with a, b, c, d constants.

(g) $(y\sec^2 x + \sec x \tan x)dx + (\tan x + \sec^2 y)dy = 0.$

(h) $\left(\dfrac{3s^2 - 2}{t}\right)ds + \left(\dfrac{2s - s^3}{t^2}\right)dt = 0.$

(i) $2xydx + x^2 dy - 3dx + 4ydy = 0.$

(j) $(y\sin 2x + y^3 \sin x)dx + (\sin^2 x - 3y^2 \cos x)dy = 0.$

(k) This is a toughie!

$$\left(-\dfrac{1+y}{x^2}\right)dx + \left(\dfrac{y^2 - x}{xy^2}\right)dy = 0.$$

(l) $(6xy + 2y^2 - 5)dx + (3x^2 + 4xy - 6)dy = 0$.

5. Verify that the following equations are not exact and solve them as directed.

   (a) Show that $1/x^2$ as well as $1/y^2$ are integrating factors of the equation $ydx - xdy = 0$ and use them to solve the equation. Are the two solutions same?

   (b) Use problem (a) to solve the equation $ydx - xdy + \ln x = 0$.

   (c) Find an integrating factor for $(x^2 + y^2 + 2x)dx + 2ydy = 0$.

   (d) Find an integrating factor for the equation $ydx + (2x + e^y)dy = 0$ and solve it.

6. Solve the following homogeneous equations:

   (a) $(x^3 - 3xy^2)dx + 2x^2ydy = 0$.

   (b) $(xy + y^2)dx - x^2dy = 0$.

   (c) $\dfrac{dy}{dx} = \dfrac{y(\ln y - \ln x + 1)}{x}$.

   (d) Example 2.11 is solved in the text as a homogeneous equation. Find an integrating factor to make it exact and solve the equation.

   (e) $xy' = y - 2xe^{-y/x}$.

   (f) $dy/dx = (y^3 + 3x^2y)/(x^3 + 3xy^2)$.

   (g) $y' = (x^3 + xy^2)/x^2y$.

   (h) $(x^2 + y^2)dx = xydy$.

7. Solve the following equations by any method of your choice.

   (a) $\tan y \; \sec^2 x \, dx + \tan x \; \sec^2 y \, dy = 0$

   (b) $y^2 + x^2 y' = xyy'$

   (c) $\dfrac{dy}{dx} + y \cos x = \dfrac{1}{2} \sin 2x$

   (d) $(y^2 e^x + 2xy)dx - x^2 dy = 0$

   (e) $(x^2 + y^2)(xdx + ydy) = a^2(xdy - ydx)$

   (f) $(x^3 + y^3)dx - 3xy^2 dy = 0$

   (g) $x\sqrt{1 + y^2} + yy'\sqrt{1 + x^2} = 0$

   (h) $(x^2y - 2xy^2)dx = (x^3 - 3x^2y)dy$

   (i) $\dfrac{dy}{dx} + \dfrac{3x^2 y}{1 + x^3} = \dfrac{\sin^2 x}{1 + x^3}$

(j) $y'' + y' = 1$

(k) $y - x\dfrac{dy}{dx} = y^2 + \dfrac{dy}{dx}$

(l) $y' - y\tan x = (\sin x \cos^2 x)/y^2$

(m) $(1-x^2)y' - xy = x^2y^2$

(n) $2xdy + 2ydx = xydy$

(o) $(1+xy^2)dx + (1+x^2y)dy = 0$

(p) $x\dfrac{dy}{dx} - (1+x)y = xy^2$

8. A stone is thrown upward from the ground with an initial velocity of 128 ft/sec. Assuming no other forces on the stone except the force of gravity, find

   (a) the maximum height it reaches

   (b) time taken to reach the maximum height

   (c) the amount of time the stone stays in the air.

9. Assume that the radius of the earth is R and a space shuttle takes off from the surface of the earth and keeps on traveling. What was the initial velocity of the shuttle?

10. A projectile is fired with a velocity of 96 ft/sec on a level terrain. Given that it reaches its maximum height in 2 seconds, find

    (a) the initial angle of projection

    (b) the maximum height reached

    (c) its range from the point where it is fired from.

11. *"A woman has just fallen from a 17th story window. In high school physics they teach you that falling bodies accelerate at a speed of 32 ft/sec². So she would have fallen 32 feet in the first second, another 64 feet in the next second, then 96 feet in the third. Since she fell something like two hundred feet, I can't suppose she could have spent more than four seconds in the actual act of falling."*

    There are four errors in the physics of this paragraph (as well as one correct statement). What are the four errors?

12. A frozen pizza is brought home from a grocery store and placed in a freezer maintained at zero degrees. After 15 minutes, its temperature is 15 degrees

Chapter 2. First Order Equations   69

and after 30 minutes it is 7.5 degrees. What was the original temperature of the pizza when it was placed in the freezer? Can you first guess the answer?!

13. Suppose that in a culture of yeast, the quantity of active ferment increases at a rate proportional to itself. If the quantity doubles in three hours, by what ratio will it increase in 15 hours?

14. If the number of bacteria in a quart of milk doubles in four hours, in how much time will the number be multiplied by 10? Assume that the rate of growth be proportional to the number of bacteria present.

15. A tank contains 500 liters of brine with 250 grams of salt in the solution. Pure water runs into the tank at the rate of 15 liters/minute and the mixture, constantly stirred, is drained out at the same rate. How much salt remains in the tank after 3 hours?

16. A cistern contains 50 gallons of brine with 10 pounds of salt. Another brine solution containing 2 pounds of salt per gallon is pumped into the cistern at 3 gallons per minute and the mixture runs out at the same rate. If the cistern is constantly stirred, find the amount of salt in the cistern after t minutes.

17. A room is 20 ft long, 30 ft wide and 12 ft high. It has been found it is contaminated with carbon dioxide whose strength is 0.09%. Find the percentage of carbon dioxide in the room after 18 minutes if air containing only 0.02% is pumped into the room at 2000 cubic ft/min.

18. A tank contains 100 gallons of brine with 300 pounds of salt. It is desired to reduce the amount of salt. To do this, 3 gallons of fresh water are pumped into the tank each minute. At the same time, an outlet value drains the tank at the same rate. When will the tank contain 200 pounds of salt?

19. An aquarium contains 10 gallons of polluted water. To clean the aquarium, fresh water is pumped in at 5 gallons per minute and drained at the same rate. How long will it take to reduce the pollutants to half of its initial level?

20. Find the differential equation of the 1-parameter family of confocal parabolas (i.e. all having the same focus) whose equation is given by

$$y^2 = 4a(x + a).$$

Show that there is no change when dy/dx is replaced by $-dx/dy$. What does this mean? Draw a sketch.

21. Find the orthogonal trajectories of the following 1-parameter families of curves:

    (a) $2x^2 + 3y^2 = a^2$.

    (b) $y = ae^{2x}$.

    (c) $y = \sqrt{2x + a}$.

    (d) $x^3 - 3xy^2 = a$.

22. Show that the orthogonal trajectories of the 1-parameter family of curves given by $y = cx^5$ is the 1-parameter family of ellipses $x^2 + 5y^2 = c^2$, $x \neq 0, y \neq 0$.

23. Recall that in polar coordinates, $x = r\cos\theta$ and $y = r\sin\theta$. Use this to show that the polar equation of the family of circles given by $(x - c)^2 + y^2 = c^2$ (Example 2.25) is $r = 2c\cos\theta$. Hence prove that the equation of its orthogonal trajectory is $r = 2a\sin\theta$, for some constant a.

24. Find the orthogonal trajectories of the lemniscates $r^2 = a^2 \cos 2\theta$.

25. Find the envelope, if any, of each of the following families of curves:

    (a) $(x - a)^2 + y^2 = 4a$.

    (b) $(x + y - c)^2 = 4xy$.

    (c) $y = mx + am^2$, where m is the parameter and a is constant.

    (d) $x\cos^3\theta + y\sin^3\theta = c$, where θ is the parameter and c is constant.

    (e) $y = mx + \sqrt{a^2m^2 + b^2}$, where m is the parameter, a and b are constants.

Chapter 3

Higher Order Homogeneous Linear Equations

3.1 Introduction

We now proceed to the study of differential equations that are still linear but possibly of higher order. A typical equation is of the form

$$a_0(x)\frac{d^n y}{dx^n} + a_1(x)\frac{d^{n-1} y}{dx^{n-1}} + \ldots + a_{n-1}(x)\frac{dy}{dx} + a_n(x)y = Q(x), \tag{3.1}$$

where the coefficients $a_0(x), a_1(x), a_2(x), \ldots, a_n(x)$, and $Q(x)$ are continuous functions of x. When $Q(x) = 0$, equation (3.1) is said to be *homogeneous*. Notice that the word *homogeneous* has a different meaning in the context of first order equations.

The notation used in equation (3.1) is laborious to write (and to typeset!) and we will use the following equivalent forms often:

$$a_0(x)y^{(n)} + a_1(x)y^{(n-1)} + \ldots + a_{n-1}(x)y' + a_n(x)y = Q(x),$$
$$a_0(x)D^n y + a_1(x)D^{n-1} y + \ldots + a_{n-1}(x)Dy + a_n(x)y = Q(x). \tag{3.2}$$

In the second form (3.2) we have used the **differential operator** notation D:

$$D \equiv \frac{d}{dx}, \quad D^2 \equiv \frac{d^2}{dx^2}, \ldots, D^n \equiv \frac{d^n}{dx^n}$$

We will find the differential operator notation to be particularly useful when dealing with *Operator methods* in Chapter 4.

In the following examples,

71

(i) $y''' + 3y' + 2y = 0$

(ii) $5\dfrac{d^2y}{dx^2} - 3\dfrac{dy}{dx} + 2y = \sin x$

(iii) $xD^2y - (2x+1)Dy + (x+1)y = e^x/x^2$,

(i) is of third order, homogeneous with constant coefficients, (ii) is of second order, nonhomogeneous with constant coefficients, and (iii) is of second order, nonhomogeneous and with variable coefficients. The difficulty of solving such equations increases roughly in the order of the equations given above.

The following theorem is important for what follows.

Theorem 3.1. *Given the equation*

$$a_0(x)D^ny + a_1(x)D^{n-1}y + \ldots + a_{n-1}(x)Dy + a_n(x)y = 0, \tag{3.3}$$

if $y = f(x)$ and $y = g(x)$ are two of its solutions, then so are $y = f(x) + g(x)$ and $y = cf(x)$ for any arbitrary constant c.

Proof: The proof simply exploits the properties of the derivative, that is, $D(f(x) + g(x)) = D(f(x)) + D(g(x))$ and $D(cf(x)) = cD(f(x))$. Indeed using the fact that $f(x)$ and $g(x)$ are solutions of the given equation, we have from the given equation

$$a_0(x)D^n(f) + a_1(x)D^{n-1}(f) + \ldots + a_n(x)(f) = 0 \tag{3.4}$$

and

$$a_0(x)D^n(g) + a_1(x)D^{n-1}(g) + \ldots + a_n(x)(g) = 0. \tag{3.5}$$

Adding equations (3.4) and (3.5) we get

$$a_0(x)D^n(f+g) + a_1(x)D^{n-1}(f+g) + \ldots + a_n(x)(f+g) = 0$$

and this shows that $f + g$ is also a solution of (3.3). Multiplying both sides of (3.4) by any real number c, we get

$$ca_0(x)D^n(f) + ca_1(x)D^{n-1}f + \ldots + ca_n(x)f = 0$$

and this is the same as

$$a_0(x)D^n(cf) + a_1(x)D^{n-1}(cf) + \ldots + a_n(x)(cf) = 0$$

Chapter 3. Higher Order Homogeneous Linear Equations   73

showing that cf is also a solution of (3.3). □

Remark 4. As a consequence of the last theorem, if $f_1, f_2, \ldots, f_k$ are solutions of (3.3), then so is $\sum_{j=1}^{k} c_j f_j(x)$ for arbitrary constants $c_1, \ldots, c_k$. (If you are familiar with basic Linear Algebra (see Appendix A), you will recognize that Theorem 3.1 simply says that the set $\mathcal{V}$ of all solutions of equation (3.3) is a vector space over the set of real numbers!)

We need a few more tools before we start solving homogeneous linear equations. (You may find the material in Appendix A: Review of Basic Linear Algebra useful for what follows.)

Definition 3.1. *The functions $f_1(x), f_2(x), \ldots, f_n(x)$ are said to be linearly dependent if there exist constants $c_1, c_2, \ldots, c_n$, not all zero such that*

$$c_1 f_1(x) + c_2 f_2(x) + \ldots + c_n f_n(x) = 0.$$

Otherwise they are called linearly independent.

This definition simply says that if the functions $f_1(x), f_2(x), \ldots, f_n(x)$ are linearly dependent, then one of them can be written as a *linear combination* of the others. Since not all the constants are zero, let us assume that one of them, say c_1, is not zero. Then we can write

$$f_1 = -\frac{c_2}{c_1} f_2 + \cdots + -\frac{c_n}{c_1} f_n.$$

For linearly independent functions any linear combination of the form $c_1 f_1 + \ldots + c_n f_n = 0$ implies that it is the trivial linear combination with all c_is necessarily zero.

This definition is however not particularly useful in testing for linear independence. What we need is the notion of the *Wronskian*.

Definition 3.2. *The Wronskian of the functions $f_1(x), f_2(x), \ldots, f_n(x)$ is the determinant*

$$W(f_1, \ldots, f_n) = \begin{vmatrix} f_1 & f_2 & f_3 & \cdots & f_n \\ f_1' & f_2' & f_3' & \cdots & f_n' \\ \vdots & \vdots & \vdots & \cdots & \vdots \\ f_1^{(n-1)} & f_2^{(n-1)} & f_3^{(n-1)} & \cdots & f_n^{(n-1)} \end{vmatrix}.$$

We omit the proof of the following important theorem.

Theorem 3.2. *The functions $f_1(x), \ldots, f_n(x)$ are linearly independent if their Wronskian $W(f_1, \ldots, f_n) \neq 0$.*

Remark 5. Theorem 3.2 is useful if we have three or more functions, but is also laborious to apply! If we only have two functions, say f_1, f_2, we can check their linear independence much more quickly. The two functions are linearly *dependent* if there exist constants c_1, c_2, not both zero, such that

$$c_1 f_1(x) + c_2 f_2(x) = 0.$$

Let us assume that $c_1 \neq 0$. Then the last equation can be rewritten as

$$f_1(x) = -\frac{c_2}{c_1} f_2(x), \text{ or equivalently } \frac{f_1(x)}{f_2(x)} = c,$$

for some constant c. This says their ratio must be a constant function. If this is not the case, f_1 and f_2 are linearly independent. This is often much simpler to verify.

Example 3.1. *Show that e^{ax} and e^{bx} are linearly independent unless $a = b$.*

Solution: It is easy to see that $e^{ax}/e^{bx} = e^{(a-b)x}$ is a constant only if $a - b = 0$, that is, $a = b$.

Example 3.2. *Show that $\cos x$ and $\sin x$ are linearly independent.*

Solution: Their Wronskian is

$$\begin{vmatrix} \cos x & \sin x \\ -\sin x & \cos x \end{vmatrix} = \cos^2 x + \sin^2 x = 1 \neq 0.$$

Hence, they are linearly independent. Otherwise also note that $\cos x / \sin x = \cot x$ which is not a constant. This is a much easier proof of their linear independence.

Theorem 3.3. *Let $f_1, f_2, \ldots, f_n$ be n linearly independent solutions of*

$$a_0(x)D^n y + a_1(x)D^{n-1}y + \ldots + a_{n-1}(x)Dy + a_n(x)y = 0, \ a_0 \neq 0.$$

Then any solution of this equation is of the form

$$y = c_1 f_1(x) + c_2 f_2(x) + \ldots + c_n f_n(x),$$

where $c_1, c_2, \ldots, c_n$ are arbitrary constants.

Theorem 3.3 is an extremely powerful theorem. It says that for a homogeneous linear equation of degree n all we need are n linearly independent solutions to find *any* of its solutions. (If you have had a course in Linear Algebra, you will recognize that Theorems 3.1 and 3.3 claim that the set of solutions of the general homogenous linear equation of order n is a vector space over the set of real numbers and is of dimension n.)

For example, you can easily verify that $f_1(x) = x$ and $f_2(x) = x^2 - 1$ are two solutions of $(x^2+1)y'' - 2xy' + 2y = 0$. Their Wronskian is $\begin{vmatrix} x & x^2 - 1 \\ 1 & 2x \end{vmatrix} = x^2 + 1$, which is not a constant; hence they are linearly independent. Hence all of the solutions of the given equation are given by $y = c_1 x + c_2(x^2 - 1)$ where c_1 and c_2 are arbitrary constants.

In Chapter 1 we studied the Initial Value Problem associated with the first order equation and the Picard's theorem. The following theorem is its extension for homogeneous linear equations of higher order. The proof is not important for our purposes, only its use.

Theorem 3.4. *Consider the equation*

$$a_0(x)D^n y + a_1(x)D^{n-1}y + \cdots + a_{n-1}(x)Dy + a_n(x)y = 0,$$

where $a_0(x), \ldots a_n(x)$ are continuous functions of x on some real interval $I = [a, b]$ and $a_0(x) \neq 0$ for any $x \in I$. Let x_0 be any arbitrary point in I and let $c_0, c_1, \ldots, c_{n-1}$ be arbitrary constants. Then there exists a unique solution $f(x)$ of the given equation such that $f(x_0) = c_0, f'(x_0) = c_1, \ldots, f^{(n-1)}(x_0) = c_{n-1}$.

Corollary 3.1.1. *In the special case when $a_0(x), \ldots, a_n(x)$ are all constant functions, for any real number x_0 and arbitrary constants $c_0, c_1, \ldots, c_{n-1}$, there exists a unique solution satisfying the initial conditions given in the above theorem.*

As an illustration of the use of the above Corollary, consider the IVP:

Example 3.3. *Given that e^x, xe^x are two solutions of $y'' - 2y' + y = 0$, find the solution y such that $y(0) = 1, y'(0) = 2$.*

Solution: First of all since $xe^x/e^x = x$ is not a constant, the two given solutions are linearly independent. Thus any solution of the given equation is of the form $y = c_1 e^x + c_2 x e^x$. Clearly, $y'(x) = c_1 e^x + c_2 x e^x + c_2 e^x$. Applying the initial conditions given, $y(0) = c_1 = 1, y'(0) = c_1 + c_2 = 2$. Hence, $c_1 = 1, c_2 = 1$ and the required solution is $y = e^x + xe^x$.

3.2 Solution of the homogeneous linear equations

For the rest of this chapter we will be concerned with the case when (3.1) is homogeneous and the functions $a_0(x), a_1(x), \ldots, a_n(x)$ are constants. In light of Theorem 3.3, to solve such an equation we need to find n linearly independent solutions of (3.1) to find its general solution.

Consider the following example.

Example 3.4. *Solve*
$$y'' - 5y' + 6y = 0. \tag{3.6}$$

Solution: It is easy to see that y'' is a linear combination of y' and y. But $y = e^{mx}$ has the property that

$$D(e^{mx}) = me^{mx}, \quad D^2(e^{mx}) = m^2 e^{mx}, \ldots, D^k(e^{mx}) = m^k e^{mx},$$

that is, the derivatives of y are constant multiples of y. If we write (3.6) using differential operator and substitute $y = e^{mx}$, we get

$$(D^2 - 5D + 6)y = 0$$
$$(m^2 - 5m + 6)e^{mx} = 0,$$

and since e^{mx} is not identically zero,

$$m^2 - 5m + 6 = 0,$$

which is a quadratic equation and referred to as the ***auxiliary equation***. Its roots are $m = 2, 3$. Hence e^{2x} and e^{3x} are both solutions of (3.6). It is obvious that they are linearly independent (Remark 5). By Theorem 3.3, the general solution to the given equation is $y = c_1 e^{2x} + c_2 e^{3x}$.

Example 3.5. *Solve* $(D^2 - 1)y = 0$.

Solution: The equation is same as $y'' - y = 0$. The auxiliary equation is $m^2 - 1 = 0$, and its roots are $m = \pm 1$. Hence, the solutions are e^x and e^{-x}, which are linearly independent. The general solution is given by $y = c_1 e^x + c_2 e^{-x}$.

It is clear from the last example that the solution of a homogeneous linear equation very much depends on the roots of the auxiliary equation. In the two examples above, the roots were real and distinct giving rise to two linearly independent solutions leading to the general solution. In those examples, the auxiliary equation was quadratic. But the roots of a quadratic equation need not be distinct, not even real! We consider these cases next.

3.2.1 Special case: Auxiliary equation has equal roots

If the auxiliary equation has a pair of equal roots, the corresponding solutions are identical and hence *linearly dependent* by Remark 5. What do we do? This is best explained by an example.

Example 3.6. *Solve the equation $y'' - 4y' + 4y = 0$.*

Solution: The auxiliary equation is $m^2 - 4m + 4 = 0$ with roots $m = 2, 2$. The corresponding solutions are e^{2x} and e^{2x}. We rewrite the given equation using the operator D as

$$(D^2 - 4D + 4)y = (D-2)(D-2)y = 0. \qquad (3.7)$$

It may appear that we have treated $(D^2 - 4D + 4)$ as an algebraic polynomial (which is true!) but it makes sense as a differential operator as well:

$$\begin{aligned}(D^2 - 4D + 4)y &= \frac{d^2 y}{dx^2} - 4\frac{dy}{dx} + 4y \\ &= \frac{d}{dx}\left\{\frac{dy}{dx} - 2y\right\} - 2\left\{\frac{dy}{dx} - 2y\right\} \\ &= \left\{\frac{d}{dx} - 2\right\}\left\{\frac{dy}{dx} - 2y\right\} \\ &= \left\{\frac{d}{dx} - 2\right\}\left\{\frac{d}{dx} - 2\right\}y \\ &= (D-2)(D-2)y.\end{aligned}$$

From (3.7), we make a change of variables by letting $(D-2)y = u$

$$(D-2)\underbrace{(D-2)y}_{u} = 0 \Rightarrow \begin{cases} (D-2)u = 0 \\ (D-2)y = u \end{cases}$$

Note that the first equation $(D-2)u = 0$ is homogeneous with auxiliary equation

$m - 2 = 0$. Hence, $u = e^{2x}$. Now we solve the second equation

$$(D - 2)y = u = e^{2x} \text{ or what is the same thing } \frac{dy}{dx} - 2y = e^{2x},$$

which is linear, discussed in the last chapter. Its solution is clearly

$$ye^{-2x} = \int e^{-2x} \cdot e^{2x} dx = \int dx = x. \tag{3.8}$$

It follows that $y = xe^{2x}$ is another solution of the given equation (verify!) and the two solutions e^{2x}, xe^{2x} are obviously linearly independent. Hence, the general solution is

$$y = c_1 e^{2x} + c_2 x e^{2x}. \tag{3.9}$$

Remark 6. You may be wondering why we did not include a constant of integration in equation (3.8). The reason is that including constants of integration leads to the same solution as in (3.9). To see this, let us solve the given equation including constants of integration. First observe that the solution of $(D - 2)u = 0$ leads to $du/dx = 2u$ from which $u = c_1 e^{2x}$. Next substituting for u, we get the linear equation $y' - 2y = c_1 e^{2x}$ whose solution is $ye^{-2x} = \int e^{-2x} c_1 e^{2x} dx = c_1 x + c_2$, which leads to $y = c_1 x e^{2x} + c_2 e^{2x}$, which is no different from (3.9).

Remark 7. It is worth noting from the previous example that when the auxiliary equation has a root $m = \alpha$ that repeats, the corresponding (linearly independent) solutions are $e^{\alpha x}, xe^{\alpha x}, x^2 e^{\alpha x}, \ldots$, and so on. This fact will be of much use to us in Chapter 4 when dealing with the *Method of Undetermined Coefficients*.

3.2.2 Special case: Auxiliary equation has complex roots

Consider the following equation: $(D^2 - 4D + 5)y = 0$. The auxiliary equation is $m^2 - 4m + 5 = 0$, whose roots are $m = 2 \pm i$ with corresponding solutions $y_1 = e^{(2+i)x} = e^{2x} e^{ix}$, and $y_2 = e^{(2-i)x} = e^{2x} e^{-ix}$. But these are complex solutions. How do we find linearly independent real solutions?

It is convenient to think of the constants $c_1, \ldots, c_n$ in Theorem 3.3 to include complex numbers as well (or what is the same thing, to think of the solution space $\mathcal{V}$ of the given equation as a vector space over the complex numbers $\mathbb{C}$). Since sums and differences of solutions are also solutions, we use Euler's formula, $e^{i\theta} = \cos\theta + i\sin\theta$.

Then we can write y_1, y_2 as

$$y_1 = e^{2x}(\cos x + i \sin x)$$
$$y_2 = e^{2x}(\cos x - i \sin x).$$

Adding and subtracting these equations we get the solutions,

$$u_1 = y_1 + y_2 = 2e^{2x} \cos x$$
$$u_2 = y_1 - y_2 = 2ie^{2x} \sin x.$$

Since a constant multiple of a solution is also a solution (remember we are using complex numbers also for constants) we get

$$v_1 = (1/2)u_1 = e^{2x} \cos x, \quad v_2 = (1/2i)u_2 = e^{2x} \sin x$$

as solutions as well. However, v_1, v_2 are real solutions. They are also linearly independent since $v_1/v_2 = \cot x$ is not a constant (Remark 5) and hence the general solution of $(D^2 - 4D + 5)y = 0$ is $y = e^{2x}(c_1 \cos x + c_2 \sin x)$. You should verify this satisfies the given equation! With some practice you should be able to write down the general solution of such equations with ease.

Example 3.7. *Solve the equation* $y'''' + 3y''' + 4y'' + 3y' + y = 0$.

Solution: The auxiliary equation is $m^4 + 3m^3 + 4m^2 + 3m + 1 = 0$. By inspection, we see that $m = -1$ is a root of the equation (the coefficients of odd powers of m are equal to the coefficients of the even powers of m). Hence, $(m + 1)$ is a factor of the left side of the auxiliary equation. We divide the auxiliary equation by $(m + 1)$ and write

$$m^4 + 3m^3 + 4m^2 + 3m + 1 = (m + 1)(m^3 + 2m^2 + 2m + 1).$$

We see once again that $(m + 1)$ is a factor of $m^3 + 2m^2 + 2m + 1$. We divide the latter by $(m + 1)$ and write

$$m^4 + 3m^3 + 4m^2 + 3m + 1 = (m + 1)^2(m^2 + m + 1).$$

Hence, the roots of the auxiliary equation are $m = -1, -1, (-1 \pm i\sqrt{3})/2$, where the complex roots being the roots of $m^2 + m + 1 = 0$. The general solution of the given equation is

$$y = c_1 e^{-x} + c_2 x e^{-x} + e^{-\frac{1}{2}x}\left(c_3 \cos \frac{\sqrt{3}}{2}x + c_4 \sin \frac{\sqrt{3}}{2}x\right).$$

Remark 8. When the given differential equation is of order 2, the auxiliary equation is simply a quadratic equation which can be solved by either factoring or using the quadratic formula. For higher order equations, one still attempts to factor the auxiliary equation. We suggest you try $m = 1$ (the sum of the coefficients should be zero) or $m = -1$ as in the example above. If these don't work, try if $m = \pm 2$ are solutions by actual substitution.

Remark 9. If you are wondering what would happen if the complex roots, say $m = \alpha \pm i\beta$ repeat (in a fourth order equation $(D^4 + 2D^2 + 1)y = 0$), Remark 7 should enable you to guess that the general solution would be of the form

$$y = e^{\alpha x}(c_1 \cos \beta x + c_2 \sin \beta x) + x e^{\alpha x}(c_3 \cos \beta x + c_4 \sin \beta x).$$

We shall prove this is indeed the case when we discuss the *Operator Methods*. But most problems one faces with are usually of the second degree and this complicated situation rarely occurs!

3.3 Applications

In this section we consider several applications of the material we have studied so far. In the first two applications (Sections 3.3.1-3.3.2), our object of interest is a curve that often occurs in daily life. The goal is to find the cartesian equation of the curve when we model it using mathematics. The modeling procedure is pretty similar in both applications. At an arbitrary point P on the curve, we use the fact that if the tangent at P makes an angle ψ with the horizontal, then $\tan \psi = dy/dx$, the derivative at the point. In each case, our model leads to a second order differential equation satisfied by the equation of the curve.

The rest of the applications in this section deal with objects that have natural tendency to vibrate around an equilibrium position, oscillating back and forth about the point of equilibrium. Well known examples are the pendulum of a clock, a spring balance, and the string of a musical instrument when plucked. Of course in most cases the object comes to its position of rest due to external forces. When the

Chapter 3. Higher Order Homogeneous Linear Equations

external forces are negligible, the motion is called *free undamped motion*. Otherwise it is called *damped motion*. In this section we shall see that the mathematical model that describes this motion leads to a second order linear differential equation as well.

3.3.1 Catenary

Can you guess the shape assumed by a rope or cable, of uniform density, suspended between two points, and hanging under its own weight? If you guessed it would be a parabola, you would be in good company - Galileo thought as much. But then you would be wrong as was he! The curve is called a *catenary* (the Latin word for chain is *catena*).

The catenary occurs freely in nature. In a spider's web, the woven silk is several parallel elastic catenaries. In many parks, a simple chain fence consists of a chain hanging from two identical posts. Many suspension bridges are of this type. The correct equation for the catenary was obtained by Gottfried Leibniz, Christiaan Huygens, and Johann Bernoulli in 1691.

Consider a chain hanging from two identical posts. To derive the cartesian equation for the catenary, let us choose a vertical through the lowest point O of the chain as the y-axis. The position of the x-axis will be determined later. We will assume that the curve has uniform density, that is, the weight of a unit length of the chain is a constant, say μ.

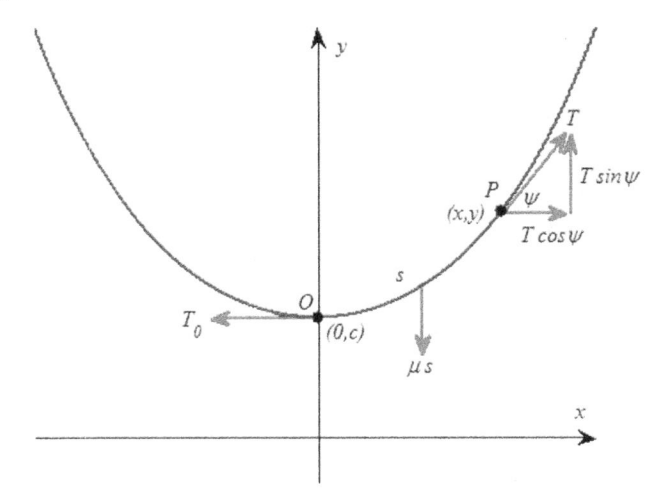

Figure 3.1: Catenary

Consider a point $P(x, y)$ on the curve. Let s be the length of the arc OP. The portion OP of the chain is in equilibrium under the action of three forces: The horizontal tension of the chain T_0, the weight of the chain μs and the variable tension of the chain at the point P which acts along the tangent PT (due to the flexibility of the chain). See Figure 3.1.

Let ψ be the angle PT makes with the x-axis. Then because of the equilibrium of the chain, we have
$$T_0 = T\cos\psi, \quad \mu s = T\sin\psi.$$

Recall from calculus that $\tan\psi = y'$. It follows from these equations that
$$\frac{dy}{dx} = y' = \tan\psi = \frac{\mu s}{T_0}.$$

Let us write $c = T_o/\mu$ so that the last equation can be written as
$$cy' = s.$$

Differentiating with respect to x,
$$cy'' = \frac{ds}{dx} = \sqrt{1+(y')^2}.$$

This is a second order equation but the y term is absent! We can integrate it as follows. Let $z = y'$. Then the last equation can be written as
$$c\frac{dz}{dx} = \sqrt{1+z^2},$$

that is,
$$\frac{dz}{\sqrt{1+z^2}} = \frac{dx}{c}. \tag{3.10}$$

Integrating equation (3.10) gives us
$$\frac{x}{c} = \int \frac{dz}{\sqrt{1+z^2}} + c_1, \tag{3.11}$$

where c_1 is a constant of integration. The integral in (3.11) is a standard integral. To evaluate it, substitute $z = \tan\theta$ to get

$$\int \frac{dz}{\sqrt{1+z^2}} = \int \frac{\sec^2\theta \, d\theta}{\sqrt{1+\tan^2\theta}} = \int \sec\theta \, d\theta = \ln|\sec\theta + \tan\theta| = \ln|z + \sqrt{1+z^2}|.$$

Hence, from equation (3.11),

$$\frac{x}{c} = \ln|z + \sqrt{1+z^2}| + c_1.$$

When $x = 0$, $\psi = 0$, so that $\tan\psi = y' = z = 0$. Hence, $c_1 = 0$. Thus,

$$\frac{x}{c} = \ln|z + \sqrt{1+z^2}|. \qquad (3.12)$$

From (3.12) we get

$$e^{x/c} = |z + \sqrt{1+z^2}| = z + \sqrt{1+z^2}$$

and $\quad e^{-x/c} = \dfrac{1}{e^{x/c}} = |z - \sqrt{1+z^2}| = -(z - \sqrt{1+z^2}).$

It follows that,

$$y' = z = \frac{e^{x/c} - e^{-x/c}}{2}.$$

Integrating once more,

$$y = c\,\frac{e^{x/c} + e^{-x/c}}{2} + c_2,$$

where c_2 is a constant of integration. Remember that the position of $x-axis$ is still not defined. We now choose the x-axis to be c units below O so that $x = 0 \Rightarrow y = c$. It follows that $c_2 = 0$ and the equation of the catenary is

$$y = c\,\frac{e^{x/c} + e^{-x/c}}{2}.$$

Recall from calculus that the *hyperbolic cosine*, $\cosh x$ is defined as

$$\cosh x = \frac{e^x + e^{-x}}{2}.$$

Using this the equation of the catenary can written more succinctly as

$$y = c\cosh\left(\frac{x}{c}\right).$$

3.3.2 Curve of pursuit

Suppose that a mouse is running away from a cat in a straight line and the cat is chasing him. What path does the cat pursue? Will the cat catch the mouse or would the mouse get away? Problems of this kind are usually called *curves of pursuit*.

Assume the usual coordinate axes and assume that the mouse is at the point $(x_0, 0)$

with $x_0 > 0$, and that the cat is at the origin when it first spots the mouse. We will assume that the mouse runs along vertically along the line $x = x_0$. Let us call the curve followed by the cat as C. See Figure 3.2.

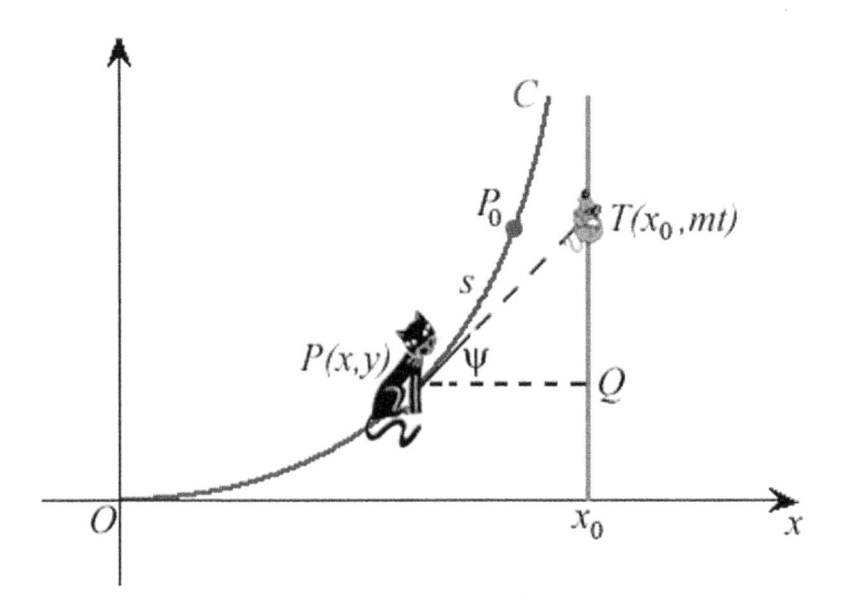

Figure 3.2: Curve of pursuit

We will assume both the cat and the mouse run at constant speeds c and m respectively. At time t, the cat is at some point $P(x,y)$ on C while the mouse is at the point $T(x_0, mt)$. Since the cat always keeps the mouse in his sight, PT is the tangent to C at point P. Let PQ be perpendicular to the y-axis. In $\triangle QPT$,

$$\angle QPT = \psi, \quad \tan \psi = \frac{TQ}{PQ} = \frac{mt - y}{x_0 - x}.$$

But $\tan \psi = y'$ so that

$$\frac{dy}{dx} = y' = \frac{mt - y}{x_0 - x},$$

from which we get

$$(x_0 - x)y' = mt - y. \tag{3.13}$$

The cat is not running along a straight line but along the curve C. If the length of the arc $P_0P = s$, then $s = ct$. It follows that

$$\frac{ds}{dt} = c, \tag{3.14}$$

Chapter 3. Higher Order Homogeneous Linear Equations 85

the speed of the cat. We have three variables x, y, t and since we need the Cartesian equation of C, let us eliminate t. We differentiate equation (3.13) *with respect to x* to get

$$-y' + (x_0 - x)y'' = m\frac{dt}{dx} - y'$$
$$(x_0 - x)y'' = m\frac{dt}{dx} \qquad (3.15)$$

Now $dx/dt = (dx/ds) \cdot (ds/dt)$ by chain rule. From calculus,

$$\frac{ds}{dx} = \pm\sqrt{1 + (y')^2}.$$

From (3.14) and (3.15) we now get

$$(x_0 - x)y'' = \frac{m}{c}\sqrt{1 + (y')^2}. \qquad (3.16)$$

To avoid cumbersome notation, let $r = m/c$. As we have done before, we set $z = y'$ in (3.16) to get $(x_0 - x)z' = r\sqrt{1 + z^2}$, which we rewrite as

$$\frac{dz}{\sqrt{1 + z^2}} = \frac{r\,dx}{(x_0 - x)}. \qquad (3.17)$$

This is the differential equation satisfied by C and is very similar to the one we saw in the case of the catenary. We can evaluate the integral on the left as usual by substituting $z = \tan\theta$, etc., (the details are left as an exercise) to get

$$\ln|y' + \sqrt{1 + (y')^2}| = -r\ln|x_0 - x| + c_1. \qquad (3.18)$$

To determine the constant of integration c_1, we note that when $x = 0$, we have $y' = z = 0$. Hence, $c_1 = r\ln x_0$. Substituting this in (3.18) and dropping the natural log, we can now rewrite (3.18) as

$$y' + \sqrt{1 + (y')^2} = \left(\frac{x_0}{x_0 - x}\right)^r. \qquad (3.19)$$

To solve for y' we use the same trick as in the case of the catenary by noticing that

$$\frac{1}{y' + \sqrt{1 + (y')^2}} = -(y' - \sqrt{1 + (y')^2}) = \left(\frac{x_0}{x_0 - x}\right)^{-r}. \qquad (3.20)$$

Subtracting (3.20) from (3.19) we have,

$$2y' = \left(\frac{x_0}{x_0 - x}\right)^r - \left(\frac{x_0}{x_0 - x}\right)^{-r},$$
$$= \left(1 - \frac{x}{x_0}\right)^{-r} - \left(1 - \frac{x}{x_0}\right)^r. \tag{3.21}$$

Case 1: $r \neq 1$

We integrate both sides of equation (3.21) to get

$$2y = \frac{x_0}{1+r}\left(1 - \frac{x}{x_0}\right)^{1+r} - \frac{x_0}{1-r}\left(1 - \frac{x}{x_0}\right)^{1-r} + c_2, \tag{3.22}$$

where c_2 is the constant of integration. Using the fact that $x = 0 \Rightarrow y = 0$, we get

$$0 = \frac{x_0}{1+r} - \frac{x_0}{1-r} + c_2$$

from which $c_2 = 2rx_0/(1 - r^2)$. We can therefore rewrite (3.22) as

$$y = \frac{1}{2}\left\{\frac{x_0}{1+r}\left(1 - \frac{x}{x_0}\right)^{1+r} - \frac{x_0}{1-r}\left(1 - \frac{x}{x_0}\right)^{1-r}\right\} + \frac{rx_0}{1-r^2}, \tag{3.23}$$

and this gives the Cartesian coordinates of C when $r \neq 1$.

Case 2: $r = 1$

In this case equation (3.21) reduces to

$$2y' = \frac{x_0}{x_0 - x} + \frac{x}{x_0} - 1.$$

Integrating the last equation,

$$2y = \left\{-x_0 \ln|x_0 - x| + \frac{x^2}{2x_0} - x\right\} + c_3.$$

By using the fact that $x = 0 \Rightarrow y = 0$ once more, we get $c_3 = x_0 \ln x_0$. Substituting this and simplifying the last equation becomes

$$y = \frac{1}{2}\left\{x_0 \ln \frac{x_0}{(x_0 - x)} + \frac{(x_0 - x)^2}{2x_0} - \frac{x_0}{2}\right\}, \tag{3.24}$$

and this gives the equation of C when $r = 1$.

Now that we have found the Cartesian equation for C, let us answer some of the questions we asked in the opening paragraph.

1. *Will the cat catch the mouse?*

   If $r < 1$, then $m < c$. In this case, the cat is faster. For the cat to catch the mouse, we must have $x = x_0$. Substituting this in equation (3.23), we get
   $$y = \frac{rx_0}{1-r^2} = \frac{mcx_0}{c^2 - m^2}.$$
   This shows that the cat would indeed catch the mouse at the point $R = (x_0, mcx_0/(c^2 - m^2))$. What if the cat is extremely fast in comparison to the mouse? In this case $r = m/c$ is negligible, that is, $r = 0$. In this case, equation (3.23) gives $y = 0$, that is, the cat will catch the mouse the moment he sees him!

2. *Can the mouse ever escape?*

   If $r = 1$, that is $m = c$, the speeds of the cat and mouse are equal. As the cat tries to approach the mouse $x \to x_0$. If we take the limit of the right side of equation (3.24) as $x \to x_0$, we notice that $y \to \infty$, that is, the mouse will leave the cat in the dust behind him! The cat cannot catch the mouse in this case.

3.3.3 Simple harmonic motion

Undamped free motion is sometimes also called *oscillator motion*. The following example best describes the principles involved.

Suppose that a point P moves along the circumference of a circle of radius a centered at the origin in *counter-clockwise* direction with constant angular velocity ω radians per second. Let Q be the foot of the perpendicular from P on the x-axis. Let $P(x, y)$ be the position of P at any time t, $P_0(x_0, y_0)$ its initial position, and $Q_0(x_0, 0)$ the corresponding initial position of Q. Let δ be the angle OP_0 makes with the x-axis. See Figure 3.3.

It is obvious that OP makes the angle $\omega t + \delta$ with the x-axis. Hence, $x = a\cos(\omega t + \delta)$.

If we measure the angles with respect to the y-axis instead, that is, OP_0 makes the angle δ with the positive y-axis, then OP makes the angle $\omega t + \delta$ with the y-axis. In this case, $x = a\sin(\omega t + \delta)$. See Figure 3.4.

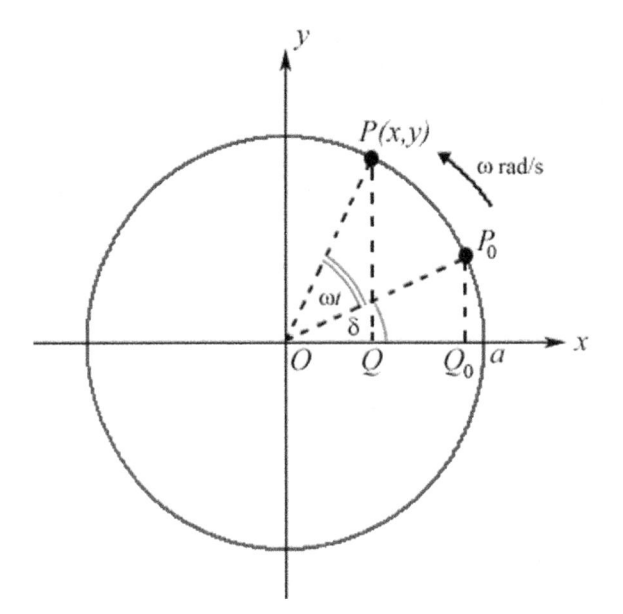

Figure 3.3: A diagram illustrating the principle of simple harmonic motion. The phase angle δ is measured with respect to the x-axis.

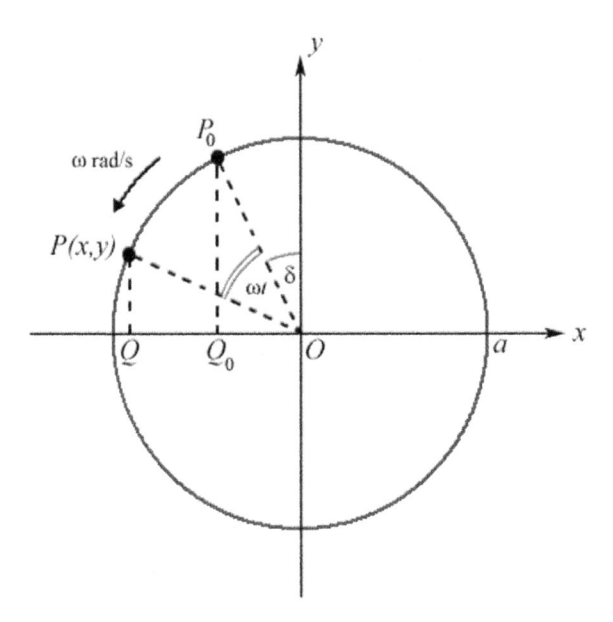

Figure 3.4: A diagram illustrating the principle of simple harmonic motion. The phase angle δ is measured with respect to the y-axis.

Thus, the position of Q at any time t, is described by either of the equations

$$x = a\cos(\omega t + \delta),$$
$$x = a\sin(\omega t + \delta). \qquad (3.25)$$

As P moves, Q starting from Q_0, moves to the left. As P and Q continue to move, their positions coincide at $(-a, 0)$. As P continues to move, Q reverses direction and moves to the right towards the origin, the positions of P and Q coinciding again, this time at $(a, 0)$. Then Q reverses direction and starts moving to the left. As P ends at P_0, Q returns to Q_0.

As P revolves around the circle, Q moves back and forth along the x-axis, changing directions at the endpoints. The motion of Q is said to be an *undamped simple harmonic motion*.

Since the maximum value of cosine (or sine) is 1, it follows from (3.25) that $|x| \leq a$. We call O the *equilibrium position* of Q and a its *amplitude*. Note that the amplitude is always considered positive. The angle δ is often called the *phase angle*. In equations (3.25) if $t = 2n\pi/\omega$, where n is an integer, then P has completed n revolutions or equivalently Q has completed n oscillations. The *time for one oscillation* of Q is called its *period* and denoted by T. Thus,

$$T = \frac{2\pi}{\omega}.$$

The reciprocal f of T, which is the *number of oscillations or cycles per unit of time* is called the *frequency* of Q. It is important to note that if T is measured in seconds, f is measured as radians/sec. Sometimes f may be specified as *radians/sec* and in this case we can convert it to cycles/sec by using the fact that one cycle equals 2π radians.

It is easy to verify (exercise!) that the function $x(t)$ given by either of the equations (3.25) satisfies the differential equation

$$\frac{d^2x}{dt^2} + \omega^2 x = 0, \qquad (3.26)$$

which is the differential equation satisfied by Q. Notice the special form of the equation: *It is a second order homogeneous equation where the first derivative term is missing and the coefficient of the dependent variable is positive.*

Conversely, if the position $x(t)$ of a moving object satisfies an equation of the form of (3.26), we can show it is executing a simple harmonic motion, that is, $x(t)$ must be of the form given by equations (3.25). To see this, consider the equation

$$\frac{d^2x}{dt^2} + sx = 0, \quad s > 0. \tag{3.27}$$

Using the methods of this chapter, we can write the solution to (3.27) as

$$x = c_1 \cos \sqrt{s}t + c_2 \sin \sqrt{s}t, \tag{3.28}$$

where c_1, c_2 are constants.

Let $c = \sqrt{c_1^2 + c_2^2}$. Then (3.28) becomes

$$x = c\left(\frac{c_1}{c} \cos \sqrt{s}t + \frac{c_2}{c} \sin \sqrt{s}t\right). \tag{3.29}$$

Let μ be an angle such that $\tan \mu = c_1/c_2$, so that $\sin \mu = c_1/c$, $\cos \mu = c_2/c$. Then (3.29) can be written as

$$x = c\left(\sin \mu \cos \sqrt{s}t + \cos \mu \sin \sqrt{s}t\right), \tag{3.30}$$

or

$$x = c \sin(\sqrt{s}t + \mu). \tag{3.31}$$

You should verify that had we interchanged c_1 and c_2 in (3.28) and replaced μ by $-\mu$, then the solution of (3.27) could be written as

$$x = c \cos(\sqrt{s}t + \mu). \tag{3.32}$$

Both (3.31) and (3.32) are similar to equations (3.25) showing that the motion is indeed a simple harmonic motion with amplitude c and period $2\pi/\sqrt{s}$.

To summarize, a simple harmonic motion can be described by either of the equations (3.25), or equivalently by the differential equation (3.26). The period is readily readable from any of these equations.

Equation (3.26) provides the period ω, but not the amplitude c. To uniquely determine the solution given by equations (3.25), from Theorem 3.1 of this chapter, we need two initial conditions that specify $x(t_0)$ and $x'(t_0)$. Often $t_0 = 0$.

Example 3.8. *An object executes a simple harmonic motion with frequency 6 radians/sec. It starts at the origin (its equilibrium position) with initial velocity 5 ft/sec. Find (a) its period, (b) the differential equation satisfied by the object, (c) the equation of motion, (d) its amplitude, and (e) the phase angle.*

Solution: Here $f = 6$ radians/sec $= 6/2\pi = 3/\pi$ cycles/sec, hence the period $T = 2\pi/\omega = \pi/3$ sec. Clearly, $\omega = 6$ radians/sec, and the differential equation satisfied by the object is

$$\frac{d^2 x}{dt^2} + 36x = 0.$$

For the equation of motion, let us pick the first equation in (3.25). Then

$$x = c\cos(6t + \delta), \quad v = \frac{dx}{dt} = -6c\sin(6t + \delta).$$

At $t = 0$ we have

$$x = 0 = c\cos\delta, \quad v = 5 = -6c\sin\delta.$$

Since $c > 0$, from the first equation we have $\delta = \pm\pi/2 \Rightarrow \sin\delta = \pm 1$. From the second equation, $\sin\delta < 0$, that is $\delta = -\pi/2$. It follows that the amplitude $c = 5/6$ ft, the phase angle $\delta = -\pi/2$ radians, and the equation of motion is

$$x = \frac{5}{6}\cos\left(6t - \frac{\pi}{2}\right).$$

1. Hooke's law

Assume that a toy cart of mass m is attached to a wall by means of a spring. When the cart is at rest at the point O, there are no forces acting on it except its weight. We choose O for the origin, and initially $x = 0$. When the cart is displaced by a distance x from O, away from the wall, then the spring's tension exerts a restoring force F_x (see Figure 3.5). According to Hooke's law, this force is proportional to x, that is,

$$F_x \propto x, \text{ or } F_x(x) = -kx. \tag{3.33}$$

The negative sign shows that the force acts in the negative direction; in fact F_x always acts against the motion and hence has a sign opposite to that of x. The constant of proportionality $k > 0$ is a measure of the stiffness of the spring. If the spring is very stiff, i.e. k is large, common sense tells us that there will be little or no vibration.

The only force that influences the motion of the cart is the restorative force of the spring. By Newton's second law of motion, the force F_x acting on the cart equals the product of its mass and acceleration. Hence, from (3.33),

$$F_x = m\frac{d^2 x}{dt^2} = -kx,$$

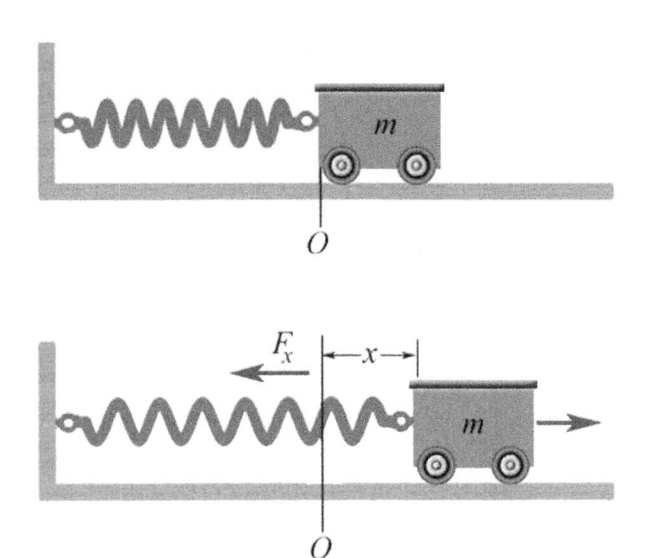

Figure 3.5: Mass-spring oscillator

from which
$$\frac{d^2x}{dt^2} + \frac{k}{m}x = 0.$$

It is immediate that the cart executes a simple harmonic motion whose equation of motion is
$$x = c\cos(\sqrt{k/m}\, t + \delta). \tag{3.34}$$

It is clear that the cart has an amplitude c, period T and frequency f, which by substituting for ω, we have
$$T = 2\pi\sqrt{\frac{m}{k}}, \quad f = \frac{1}{T} = \frac{1}{2\pi}\sqrt{\frac{k}{m}}.$$

The expression for T shows that if the mass of the cart is large or the stiffness of the spring is light, then T is larger, that is it takes more time to complete one period (as we noticed earlier) and the frequency f is correspondingly smaller.

From (3.34), since $|x| \leq c$, the cart oscillates around O with maximum displacement $\pm c$. If we write $\omega = \sqrt{k/m}$, it follows from (3.34) that the velocity v of the cart is given by
$$v = \frac{dx}{dt} = -c\omega\sin(\omega t + \delta) \tag{3.35}$$

and when $|x| = c$, that is at the end points, $|\cos(\omega t + \delta)| = 1$, that is, $|\sin(\omega t + \delta)| = 0$.

At the end points, where $x = \pm c$, the speed of the cart is $s = |dx/dt| = 0$.

When the cart is at the origin, from (3.34), $\cos(\omega t + \delta) = 0$ and $\sin(\omega t + \delta) = \pm 1$. Hence, at the origin the cart has its maximum speed $s = c\omega$.

The motion of the cart is thus clear. Once it is pulled to the right and let go (with no initial velocity), it moves towards the wall with increasing speed reaching the maximum at the origin. The speed then reduces becoming zero at the left end point. The cart then moves to the right, again reaching its maximum speed at the origin and moving to the right with reducing speed.

We can simplify (3.34) in specific cases if we know $x(t)$ and $v(t)$ for some $t = t_0$. Suppose for instance that at $t = 0$, the cart is pulled through a distance x_0 and let go with no initial velocity $v = 0$. Substituting these values in (3.34) and (3.35) we get,

$$x_0 = c\cos\delta, \quad 0 = -c\omega\sin\delta,$$

from which $\delta = 0$, $c = x_0$. Hence in this particular case, the equation of motion is

$$x = x_0 \cos\omega t = x_0 \cos\sqrt{k/m}\,t.$$

2. Simple pendulum

We now consider the motion of simple pendulum, consisting of a "pendulum bob" attached to one end of a rod. The other end of the rod is attached to a fixed point C in such a way that the pendulum is free to move in an oscillatory motion.

Let the length of the rod be ℓ and the mass of the bob be m. Assume that the bob is pulled to the right through a small angle and let go. Let $P(x,y)$ be the coordinates of the bob at any time t, and θ the angle the pendulum makes with the vertical. The bob moves along the arc of a circle centered at C with radius ℓ. Let CO be the vertical line through C such that $CO = \ell$. The length of the arc PO is $s = \ell\theta$. The only force acting on the bob is its weight $w = mg$ and it acts downwards. We resolve this force into two forces: One component along CP and another perpendicular to it. The latter is tangential to the circular arc PO. The force along CP is $mg\cos\theta$ and the one at right angle to it is the force $F = mg\sin\theta$. It is clear that F acts along the tangent to the arc PO and is the only *restorative force* trying to move the pendulum to the equilibrium position CO.

As we saw in the previous case (of the cart attached to the wall), F and θ have opposite signs. When the pendulum moves counterclockwise, F moves clockwise and vice versa. The velocity v of the pendulum acts tangentially to the arc PO.

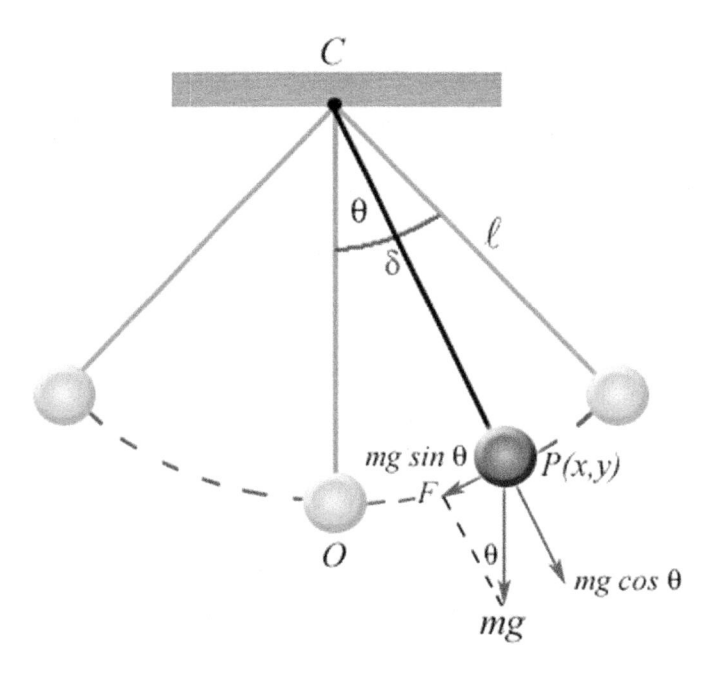

Figure 3.6: Simple pendulum

By Newton's second law,
$$F = m\frac{dv}{dt} = -mg\sin\theta,\qquad(3.36)$$
the negative emphasizing F and θ (and hence $\sin\theta$) have opposite signs. We have
$$v = \frac{ds}{dt},\quad s = \ell\theta,\quad \frac{dv}{dt} = \ell\frac{d^2\theta}{dt^2}.$$
It follows from equation (3.36) that
$$\ell\frac{d^2\theta}{dt^2} + g\sin\theta = 0,\qquad(3.37)$$
which is the equation satisfied by the pendulum. Equation (3.37) does not define a simple harmonic motion! But we know that
$$\sin\theta = \theta - \frac{\theta^3}{3!} + \cdots,$$
and for small values of θ, $\sin\theta \approx \theta$. Hence, we can rewrite (3.37) as
$$\frac{d^2\theta}{dt^2} + \frac{g}{\ell}\theta = 0,\qquad(3.38)$$

Chapter 3. Higher Order Homogeneous Linear Equations 95

which now describes a simple harmonic motion. If we write the solution to (3.38) as

$$\theta = c\cos(\sqrt{g/\ell}\, t + \delta), \tag{3.39}$$

its amplitude is c with phase angle δ. Its period T and its frequency f are given by

$$T = 2\pi\sqrt{\ell/g}, \quad f = \frac{1}{T} = \frac{1}{2\pi}\sqrt{g/\ell}. \tag{3.40}$$

3. Simple pendulum (continued)

Assume that the pendulum is pulled through an angle α at $t = 0$. If α is not small, θ need not be small enough for us to approximate $\sin\theta$ by θ.

Let $\omega = d\theta/dt$ be the angular velocity of the bob. If we multiply both sides of equation (3.37) by $d\theta/dt$ we get

$$\ell\frac{d\theta}{dt}\frac{d^2\theta}{dt^2} + g\sin\theta\frac{d\theta}{dt} = 0,$$

and integrating the last equation it follows that

$$\ell\left(\frac{d\theta}{dt}\right)^2 - 2g\cos\theta = c_1,$$

for some constant c_1. At $t = 0$, $\theta = \alpha, \omega = d\theta/dt = 0$. It follows that $c_1 = -2g\cos\alpha$. Substituting this in the last equation and taking square roots we obtain

$$\left(\frac{d\theta}{dt}\right)^2 = \frac{2g}{\ell}(\cos\theta - \cos\alpha),$$

that is,

$$\omega = \frac{d\theta}{dt} = \pm\left(\sqrt{2g/\ell}\,\right)\sqrt{\cos\theta - \cos\alpha}.$$

Hence,

$$dt = \pm\left(\sqrt{\ell/2g}\,\right)\frac{d\theta}{\sqrt{\cos\theta - \cos\alpha}}.$$

We integrate the last equation to finally obtain

$$t(\theta) = \pm\left(\sqrt{\ell/2g}\,\right)\int_\alpha^\theta \frac{d\eta}{\sqrt{\cos\eta - \cos\alpha}}.$$

To find the period T of the pendulum, we notice that as the pendulum swings from $\theta = -\alpha$ to $\theta = \alpha$, it covers one half of the period. Thus,

$$\frac{T}{2} = \left(\sqrt{\ell/2g}\right) \int_{-\alpha}^{\alpha} \frac{d\eta}{\sqrt{\cos\eta - \cos\alpha}}. \tag{3.41}$$

Further, $\cos\eta$ is an even function so it follows that

$$T = 2\sqrt{2}\left(\sqrt{\ell/g}\right) \int_{0}^{\alpha} \frac{d\eta}{\sqrt{\cos\eta - \cos\alpha}}. \tag{3.42}$$

Alas, as elegant as formula (3.42) is, the integral is not easy to evaluate. The rest of what follows should give you an idea of how mathematicians tackle problem of this kind. We use the double angle formula from trigonometry, $\cos\theta = 1 - 2\sin^2(\theta/2)$, etc., to rewrite (3.42) as

$$\begin{aligned} T &= 2\left(\sqrt{\ell/g}\right) \int_{0}^{\alpha} \frac{d\eta}{\sqrt{\sin^2(\alpha/2) - \sin^2(\eta/2)}} \\ &= 2\left(\sqrt{\ell/g}\right) \int_{0}^{\alpha} \frac{d\eta}{\sqrt{u^2 - \sin^2(\eta/2)}}, \end{aligned} \tag{3.43}$$

where $u = \sin(\alpha/2)$. If we make the substitution

$$\sin\frac{\eta}{2} = u\sin\phi,$$

we note that as η goes from 0 to α, then ϕ goes from 0 to $\pi/2$ and

$$\frac{1}{2}\cos\frac{\eta}{2} d\eta = u\cos\phi \, d\phi.$$

Substituting this in (3.43) gives us

$$T = 4\left(\sqrt{\ell/g}\right) \int_{0}^{\pi/2} \frac{u\cos\phi \, d\phi}{\cos(\eta/2)\sqrt{u^2 - u^2\sin^2\phi}},$$

which finally simplifies to

$$T = 4\left(\sqrt{\ell/g}\right) \int_{0}^{\pi/2} \frac{d\phi}{\sqrt{1 - u^2\sin^2\phi}}. \tag{3.44}$$

The integral in (3.44) cannot be evaluated in terms of elementary functions. It is called an ***elliptic integral of the first kind*** and occurs frequently in physics and in evaluating the circumference of an ellipse. Tables of elliptic integrals have been computed for values of u.

Chapter 3. Higher Order Homogeneous Linear Equations

It can be shown (the details are beyond the scope of these notes) that

$$T = 2\pi\sqrt{\ell/g}\left\{1 + \frac{u^2}{2^2} + \frac{(1\cdot 3)^2}{(2\cdot 4)^2}u^4 + \cdots\right\} \qquad (3.45)$$

and this gives the **actual period of the pendulum**.

For example, if $\alpha = 6°$, then $u = \sin 3° = 0.0523, k^2 = 0.002739$ and from (3.45)

$$T(\text{true value}) = 2\pi\sqrt{\ell/g}\left\{1 + \frac{0.002739}{4} + \frac{9}{64}\cdot(0.002739)^2 + \ldots\right\}$$

from which

$$T \approx 2\pi\sqrt{\ell/g}\,(1.0006858).$$

The value given by equation (3.45) of course is $T \approx 2\pi\sqrt{\ell/g}$. You should note that as the pendulum completes several periods, the error is no longer negligible.

3.4 Exercises

1. For each of the following equations, state if it is linear and if so whether it is homogeneous.

   (a) $y^{(4)} + 2n^2 y'' + n^4 y = \cos mx$.

   (b) $\dfrac{d^2y}{dx^2} + 2\left(\dfrac{dy}{dx}\right)^2 + 3y = 0$.

   (c) $(D^2 - 8D + 9)y = 0$.

   (d) $(D^3 + 3D^2 + 3D + 1)y = 0$.

   (e) $(D^2 - a^2)^2 y = 2e^{ax}$.

2. Determine whether the following sets are linearly independent:

   (a) $\{e^{2x}, e^{-2x}\}$

   (b) $\{1, x, x^2\}$

   (c) $\{\sin x, \cos x, 2\sin x + 3\cos x\}$

   (d) $\{x, 2+x, 1-x^2\}$

3. The auxiliary equations of some homogeneous linear equations are given below. Find their general solutions.

   (a) $m^2 + 4m + 3 = 0$.

   (b) $(m-1)(m+1)(m^2+4) = 0$.

(c) $(m^2 + 4m + 5)(m-2)^2(m+3) = 0$.

(d) $(m^2 + 4)^2 = 0$.

4. Find the general solution to each of the following equations.

    (a) $y'' - 3y' + 2y = 0$.
    (b) $4y'' - 7y' + 3y = 0$.
    (c) $2y'' + y' - 3y = 0$.
    (d) $y'' - 2y' + y = 0$.
    (e) $y'' + 4y' + 4y = 0$.
    (f) $y''' + 3y'' + y' + 3y = 0$.
    (g) $(D^3 - 6D^2 + 5D + 12)y = 0$.
    (h) $16y'' + 32y' + 25y = 0$.
    (i) $(8D^3 + 12D^2 + 6D + 1)y = 0$. (Hint: $e^{-1/2x}$ is one of the solutions)
    (j) $y''' = y'$.
    (k) $(D^3 - 5D^2 + 9D - 5)y = 0$.
    (l) $(D^2 - 4)^2 y = 0$.

5. Solve the following initial value problems:

    (a) $(D^2 - 6D + 25)y = 0$, $y(0) = -3$, $y'(0) = -1$.
    (b) $(D^2 + 4D + 3)y = 0$, $y(0) = 1$, $y'(0) = 1$.
    (c) $y'' - 2y' + y = 0$, $y(0) = 0$, $y'(0) = 1$.
    (d) $y''' + ay'' + by' + cy = 0$, $y(0) = y'(0) = y''(0) = 0$.
    (e) $16\dfrac{d^2y}{dx^2} + 32\dfrac{dy}{dx} + 25y = 0$, $y(0) = 0, y'(0) = 1$.
    (f) $D^3 y = 0$, $y(0) = 0, y'(0) = 1$.

6. Find the general solution to the fourth order linear homogeneous differential equation with constant coefficients if one solution is $xe^{2x}\cos x$.

7. Find a general solution to a fourth order linear homogeneous differential equation with constant coefficients if one solution is $x^3 e^{-x}$. Write down the corresponding differential equation.

8. Find the general solution to the equation $y^{(4)} - 7y''' + 13y'' + 3y' - 18y = 0$ if one solution is xe^{3x}.

9. Consider a rope of negligible density ($\mu = 0$) hanging from two points at equal heights from the ground. What is the shape of the curve the rope forms?

10. A simple pendulum of length 5 feet is released from a position of 1 radian. Find

    (a) the position of the pendulum as a function of time
    (b) the amplitude, period and frequency
    (c) the velocity (both linear and angular) with which the pendulum crosses the equilibrium position.

11. A clock pendulum is regulated so that it crosses the equilibrium position every 2 seconds. What is the length of the pendulum?

12. An object weighting 4 lbs is attached to the end of helical spring which stretches it by 6 inches. The spring oscillates and when it comes to rest, the object is pulled an additional 6 inches and let go. Show that it executes a simple harmonic motion. Find its

    (a) equation of motion
    (b) period
    (c) frequency
    (d) amplitude

Chapter 4

Nonhomogeneous Linear Equations

4.1 Introduction

In this chapter we continue our study of higher order linear equations which are not necessarily homogeneous, but whose coefficients are constants (higher order linear equations with variable coefficients will be considered in Chapter 5). A typical such equation of order n is of the form

$$a_0\, y^{(n)} + a_1\, y^{(n-1)} + \ldots + a_{n-1}\, y' + a_n\, y = Q(x), a_0 \neq 0, \tag{4.1}$$

where $a_0, a_1, \ldots a_n$ are constants and $Q(x)$ is a function continuous for all real values. In the D operator notation, equation (4.1) can be written as

$$(a_0 D^n + a_1 D^{n-1} + \ldots + a_{n-1} D + a_n) y = Q(x) \tag{4.2}$$

and we will employ this notation throughout this chapter (for the ease of writing as well as other advantages that will be apparent as we proceed). Notice that the left side of (4.2) is simply a polynomial in D of degree n and so we can write (4.2) as

$$p_n(D) y = Q(x), \tag{4.3}$$

When the degree of $p(D)$ is clear from the context we will often omit the subscript n. For example, the equation

$$2\frac{d^3y}{dx^3} + 3\frac{d^2y}{dx^2} + \frac{dy}{dx} + y = \sin x$$

can be written more simply as

$$p(D)y = \sin x, \text{ where } p(D) \equiv 2D^3 + 3D^2 + D + 1.$$

The following theorem is fundamental for the rest of this chapter.

Theorem 4.1. *Let $f(x), g(x)$ be two different solutions of equation (4.3). Then $f(x) = h(x) + g(x)$, where $h(x)$ is the solution of the homogeneous equation*

$$p_n(D) = 0. \tag{4.4}$$

Proof: Since $f(x), g(x)$ are solutions of equation (4.3),

$$p_n(D)(f(x)) = Q(x),$$
$$p_n(D)(g(x)) = Q(x).$$

By subtracting the second equation from the first we get

$$p_n(D)(f(x) - g(x)) = 0.$$

Then $h(x) = f(x) - g(x)$ is a solution of the homogeneous equation (4.4) and it is clear that $f(x) = h(x) + g(x)$. $\square$

Recall from Theorem 3.3 of Chapter 3 that the general solution $h(x)$ of the homogeneous equation (4.4) is of the form

$$h(x) = c_1 f_1(x) + c_2 f_2(x) + \ldots + c_n f_n(x),$$

where $c_1, c_2, \ldots, c_n$ are arbitrary constants and $f_1, f_2, \ldots, f_n(x)$ are linearly independent solutions of (4.4). As a consequence, we now have from Theorem 4.1,

Theorem 4.2. *Let $q(x)$ be any solution of (4.3). Then the general solution of (4.3) is given by*
$$y = c_1 f_1(x) + c_2 f_2(x) + \ldots + c_n f_n(x) + q(x),$$
where $c_1, c_2, \ldots, c_n$ are arbitrary constants and $f_1, f_2, \ldots, f_n(x)$ are linearly independent solutions of the homogeneous equation $p_n(D)y = 0$.

Chapter 4. Nonhomogeneous Linear Equations

Theorem 4.2 is a very powerful theorem that provides a way to find *all* solutions of (4.3). It tells us that to solve the nonhomogeneous linear equation (4.3), find a *particular solution* of (4.3) (usually denoted by y_p) and add the general solution of (4.4) (often denoted by y_c and called the *complementary part*). Thus the general solution y of (4.3) is of the form

$$y = y_c + y_p.$$

Equation (4.4) is often referred to as the *homogeneous part* of equation (4.3) and we already know from Chapter 3 how to find its solution y_c. The difficult part of solving (4.3) thus is to find y_p.

Consider the following example.

Example 4.1. *Verify that $y = \frac{1}{12}e^x$ is a solution of $y'' + 5y' + 6y = e^x$. Use this to find the general solution of the given equation.*

Solution: We have $(\frac{1}{12}e^x)'' + 5(\frac{1}{12}e^x)' + 6(\frac{1}{12}e^x) = \frac{1}{12}e^x + \frac{5}{12}e^x + \frac{6}{12}e^x = e^x$ and this verifies that $y = \frac{1}{12}e^x$ is indeed a solution of the given equation. The homogeneous part of the given equation is $y'' + 5y' + 6y = 0$ whose solution $y_c = c_1 e^{-2x} + c_2 e^{-3x}$. Since we know that $y_p = \frac{1}{12}e^x$, the general solution of the given equation is $y = c_1 e^{-2x} + c_2 e^{-3x} + \frac{1}{12}e^x$.

Remark 10. We do not include in y_p any term that already appears in y_c. Why? Because such a term, say $f(x)$ satisfies $p_n(D)y = 0$ and therefore cannot possibly satisfy equation (4.3) viz., $p_n(D)y = Q(x)$. We further note that y_p is linearly independent from y_c. If not, $y_p = ky_c$ for some constant k. But then ky_c is a solution of $p_n(D)y = 0$ (by Theorem 3.1 of Chapter 3) and hence y_p is a solution of $p_n(D)y = 0$ and therefore cannot satisfy $p_n(D)y = Q(x)$.

Initial Value Problem. There is an analog of Theorem 3.4 of Chapter 3 for the nonhomogeneous linear equation $p_n(D)y = Q(x)$. It is applicable to the more general case when the coefficients $a_0, a_1, \ldots, a_n$ are variable and are functions of x.

Theorem 4.3. *Consider the nonhomogeneous equation*

$$a_0(x)D^n y + a_1(x)D^{n-1}y + \ldots + a_{n-1}(x)Dy + a_n(x)y = Q(x),$$

where $a_0(x), \ldots, a_n(x)$ and $Q(x)$ are continuous functions of x on some real interval $I = [a, b]$ and $a_0(x) \neq 0$ for any $x \in I$. Let x_0 be any arbitrary point in I and let

$c_0, c_1, \ldots, c_{n-1}$ be arbitrary constants. Then there exists a unique solution $f(x)$ of the given equation such that $f(x_0) = c_0, f'(x_0) = c_1, \ldots, f^{(n-1)}(x_0) = c_{n-1}$.

To illustrate Theorem 4.3, let us consider the following example.

Example 4.2. *Solve the IVP:* $(D^2 + 4)y = x \sin x$, $y(\pi/2) = 0, y'(\pi/2) = 1$ *given that it has a particular solution* $y = \frac{1}{3}x \sin x - \frac{2}{9} \cos x$.

Solution: The auxiliary equation is $m^2 + 4 = 0$, hence $y_c = c_1 \cos 2x + c_2 \sin 2x$. Since we are given that $y_p = \frac{1}{3}x \sin x - \frac{2}{9} \cos x$, the general solution of the given equation is
$$y = c_1 \cos 2x + c_2 \sin 2x + \frac{1}{3}x \sin x - \frac{2}{9} \cos x.$$
$$y' = -2c_1 \sin 2x + 2c_2 \cos 2x + \frac{1}{3}x \cos x + \frac{1}{3} \sin x + \frac{2}{9} \sin x.$$

We apply the initial conditions to get
$$y(\pi/2) = 0 \Rightarrow c_1 = \pi/6,$$
$$y'(\pi/2) = 1 \Rightarrow c_2 = -\frac{2}{9}.$$

Hence, the required solution is $y = \frac{\pi}{6} \cos 2x - \frac{2}{9} \sin 2x + \frac{1}{3}x \sin x - \frac{2}{9} \cos x$.

The rest of this chapter is devoted to finding a particular solution of the equation $p_n(D)y = Q(x)$. There are two methods, *the Method of Undetermined Coefficients* and *the Method of Differential Operators*. These will be covered in Section 2 and Section 3, respectively. Of the two, the first is perhaps easier to understand but is decidedly laborious while the second is more elegant and powerful but requires careful understanding.

The following theorem called the *Superposition Principle* can sometimes prove helpful. It does not simplify the solution of a given equation but helps organize our work regardless of the method used.

Theorem 4.4. *(Superposition Principle)*
Let $p(D)$ be a polynomial in D, $f(x)$ be a solution of $p(D)y = U(x)$, and $g(x)$ a solution of $p(D)y = V(x)$. Then $f(x) + g(x)$ is a solution of $p(D)y = U(x) + V(x)$.

Proof: The Superposition Principle says in an equation such as (4.3), where the right side $Q(x)$ is the sum of several terms, we can split it into several subproblems and combine their solutions to find a solution of the given equation. The proof simply depends on the properties of derivative. Since $D(f(x) + g(x)) =$

$Df(x) + Dg(x)$, $D^2(f(x) + g(x)) = D^2f(x) + D^2g(x)$, and so on, it is easy to see that $p(D)(f(x) + g(x)) = p(D)f(x) + p(D)g(x) = U(x) + V(x)$. □

The process of finding y_p may become very involved. The superposition principle simply says to make several problems by splitting the right side and solve each of them. As you can see, the amount of work is still the same but perhaps it is better organized.

As an illustration of the above principle, consider the equation

$$(D^4 + D^2)y = 3x^2 + 4\sin x.$$

We will learn later in this chapter that a solution of $(D^4 + D^2)y = 3x^2$ is $f(x) = \frac{1}{4}x^4 - 3x^2$ (verify!) and a solution of $(D^4 + D^2)y = 4\sin x$ is $g(x) = 2x\cos x$ (verify!). Hence, a solution of the given equation is $f(x) + g(x) = \frac{1}{4}x^4 - 3x^2 + 2x\cos x$.

4.2 Method of Undetermined Coefficients

In the method of Undetermined Coefficients (UC), one writes down y_p as a linear combination of functions

$$y_p = A_1 f_1(x) + A_2 f_2(x) + \ldots + A_m f_m(x),$$

for some integer m, and where the functions $f_1, f_2, \ldots, f_m$ are obtained by:

(i) Carefully examining all the functions that appear in y_c and $Q(x)$.

(ii) The coefficients $A_1, A_2, \ldots, A_m$ are determined (hence the name of the method) by substituting y_p for y in (4.3). This gives rise to m equations to determine the constants $A_1, A_2, \ldots, A_m$.

As you might guess, the method is often laborious!

If you observe equation (4.3), it is evident that $Q(x)$ is a linear combination of y_p and its *linearly independent derivatives*. Indeed, y_c, the solution of the homogeneous part of (4.3), is a linear combination of functions that have finitely many linearly independent derivatives.

It follows that the UC method can be used only if $Q(x)$ consists of functions that have finitely many linearly independent derivatives as well.

This of course restricts the use of the method to a small class of functions: exponentials (e^{mx}), basic circular functions ($\sin ax$, $\cos ax$) and polynomials (x^n). Indeed,

e^{mx} has no linearly independent derivative, both $\sin ax, \cos ax$ have just one each, and x^n has n linearly independent derivatives, namely $1, x, x^2, \ldots, x^{n-2}, x^{n-1}$, omitting the constants (verify these assertions!). Luckily these are the functions that appear most in applications. On the other hand, $1/x$ has derivatives $1/x^2, 1/x^3, \ldots$ (omitting constants) which are all linearly independent. When $Q(x)$ involves functions such as $1/x, \tan x$, etc., that have infinitely many linearly independent derivatives, one has to take recourse to other methods some of which will be considered in the next chapter.

Remark 11. In what follows, we say that the equation

$$p_n(x) = k_0 x^n + k_1 x^{n-1} + \ldots + k_n = 0$$

has a root $x = a$ of *multiplicity r* if

1. a is a root of the equation, and

2. a occurs as a root r times.

In this case $(x - a)^r$ is a factor of the left side of the equation. For example, given the differential equation $y'' - 6y' + 9y = 0$, its auxiliary equation $m^2 - 6m + 9 = (m-3)^2 = 0$ has the multiple root $m = 3$ whose multiplicity is $r = 2$.

4.2.1 How the UC method works

In the UC method, one builds a possible function y_p by considering every term $q(x)$ that appears in $Q(x)$ and examines it with the terms in y_c. We first determine which of the following three cases $q(x)$ belongs to and start adding terms to y_p accordingly. *Caution: Be sure to check all the three cases given below before deciding which one applies! Different terms in $Q(x)$ may belong to different cases and the y_ps corresponding to each must be included.*

Case 1:
$$\begin{cases} q(x) = x^k f(x), \ k \geq 0 \\ f(x) \text{ is not a term in } y_c \end{cases}$$

In this case y_p includes a linear combination of $q(x)$ and all of its linearly independent derivatives.

Observe that when $k = 0$, Case 1 says $q(x) = f(x)$ is not a member of y_c.

Chapter 4. Nonhomogeneous Linear Equations 107

Example 4.3. *Without solving the equation*

$$y'' + 3y' + 2y = 2x^2,$$

find the form of y_p for it.

Solution: The auxiliary equation is $m^2 + 3m + 2 = 0$ and the roots are -1 and -2. Hence,

$$y_c = c_1 e^{-x} + c_2 e^{-2x}.$$

The only choice for $q(x)$ is $q(x) = x^2 = x^2 \cdot 1$ so that $k = 2$ and $f(x) = 1$ (excluding the constant coefficients) and $f(x) = 1$ is not a term in y_c. Thus, Case 1 applies and y_p is simply a linear combination of x^2 and all of its linearly independent derivatives (omitting the constant coefficients), namely x and 1. Thus,

$$y_p = Ax^2 + Bx + C.$$

The constants A, B, C will have to be determined later.

Example 4.4. *Same as in Example 4.3 for the equation*

$$y'' - 2y' - 3y = 2e^x - 10\sin x.$$

Solution: Here the auxiliary equation is $m^2 - 2m - 3 = 0$, $m = 3, -1$ so that

$$y_c = c_1 e^{3x} + c_2 e^{-x}.$$

Here there are two choices for $q(x)$, namely $q(x) = e^x$ and $q(x) = \sin x$. In both cases $k = 0$, and neither $q(x) = e^x$ nor $q(x) = \sin x$ is a term of y_c. Thus Case 1 applies and y_p consists of a linear combination of e^x and its linearly independent derivatives and similarly for $\sin x$. But the derivative of e^x is itself so that it has no linearly independent derivative (why?). The only linearly independent derivative of $\sin x$ is $\cos x$ (why?). Hence,

$$y_p = Ae^x + B\sin x + C\cos x,$$

where the constants A, B, C are yet to be determined.

Example 4.5. *A student wrote that the form of y_p for the equation $(D^2 - D)y = x$ as $y_p = Ax$ arguing that $q(x) = x$ is not in y_c. Is she correct?*

Solution: Here the homogeneous part is $(D^2 - D)y = 0$, the auxiliary equation is $m^2 - m = 0$, and hence
$$y_c = c_1 + c_2 e^x.$$
Here $q(x) = x$ is of the form $q(x) = x^1 \cdot 1$. But $f(x) = 1$ is in y_c and hence Case 1 does not apply! Thus the form of y_p as written is incorrect. We will return to this example shortly.

Case 2:

$$\begin{cases} q(x) = x^k f(x), \ k \geq 0 \\ f(x) \text{ is a term in } y_c \\ f(x) \text{ does not arise from a multiple root of the auxiliary equation} \end{cases}$$

In this case y_p is a linear combination of $x^{k+1} f(x)$ and all of its linearly independent derivatives (ignoring constant coefficients).

The reason for this rule should be clear. In the simple case when $k = 0$ and $q(x)$ appears in y_c, then it is a solution of the homogeneous part (4.4). In Remark 7 Chapter 3, when dealing with repeated roots of the auxiliary equation, we handled this as follows. If $m = a$ repeats r times and the solution corresponding to $m = a$ is $f(x)$, then we added to y_c the following terms $f(x), x f(x), x^2 f(x), \ldots, x^{r-1} f(x)$.

Let us consider some examples.

Example 4.6. *Without solving the equation find the form of y_p for the equation in Example 4.5.*

Solution: As we saw earlier, we have $y_c = c_1 + c_2 e^x$, $q(x) = x^1 \cdot 1$, $f(x) = 1$ is in y_c but does not arise from a multiple root of the auxiliary equation. Thus Case 2 applies. Here $k = 1$ and therefore y_p consists of a linear combination of x^{1+1} and its linearly independent derivatives $x, 1$. But we can drop 1 as it is included in y_c. Thus $y_p = Ax^2 + Bx$.

Example 4.7. *Without solving the equation*
$$(D^2 - 3D + 2)y = 2x^2 + e^x, \tag{4.5}$$
find the form of y_p for it.

Solution: The auxiliary equation is $m^2 - 3m + 2 = 0$ with roots $m = 1, 2$, which are

not multiple roots. Hence,
$$y_c = c_1 e^x + c_2 e^{2x}.$$

Next we start building y_p.

First consider the term $q_1(x) = x^2 = x^2 \cdot 1$ of $Q(x)$. Since 1 is not in y_c, Case 1 applies. Hence we include a linear combination of x^2 and its linearly independent derivatives x and 1.

Next consider the term $q_2(x) = e^x$ in $Q(x)$. This is of the form $x^0 f(x)$ where $f(x) = e^x$ is a term in y_c and belongs to Case 2. We therefore include a linear combination of $x^{0+1} e^x = xe^x$ and its only linearly independent derivative, e^x. But the latter is already in y_c and need not be included (Remark 10). Thus, the final form of y_p is
$$y_p = \underbrace{Ax^2 + Bx + C}_{I} + \underbrace{Exe^x}_{II},$$
where the terms in group I come from $q_1(x) = x^2$ and those in group II from $q_2(x) = e^x$. This example shows that different terms in $Q(x)$ can belong to different cases! Note also that the constants A, B, C and E will have to be determined and we avoid using D to denote a constant as it is reserved for differential operator.

Example 4.8. *Find an appropriate form of y_p for the equation*
$$(D^2 - 5D + 6) y = xe^{2x}.$$

Solution: Here $y_c = c_1 e^{2x} + c_2 e^{3x}$. The only term $q(x)$ is xe^{2x}, which is of the form $x^k f(x)$ with $k = 1$ and $f(x) = e^{2x}$ is a term in y_c. Hence, $q(x)$ belongs to Case 2 and y_p is a linear combination of $x^{(1+1)} e^{2x} = x^2 e^{2x}$ and its linearly independent derivatives, that is of, xe^{2x} and e^{2x}. But e^{2x} is already a term in y_c, thus need not be included (Remark 10). The particular solution is then given by
$$y_p = Ax^2 e^{2x} + Bxe^{2x}.$$

Case 3:

$$\begin{cases} q(x) = x^k f(x), \ k \geq 0 \\ f(x) \text{ is a term in } y_c \\ f(x) \text{ arises from a root of the auxiliary equation with multiplicity } r \end{cases}$$

In this case y_p will be a linear combination of $x^{k+r} f(x)$ and all of its linearly independent derivatives.

Remark 12. For Case 3, two things must happen:

(i) The auxiliary equation has a root $m = a$ with multiplicity r,

(ii) $f(x)$ is a solution corresponding to the root $m = a$ and $q(x) = x^k f(x), \ k \geq 0$.

Example 4.9. *Solve the equation*

$$(D^4 + D^2)y = 3x^2 + 4\sin x.$$

Solution: The auxiliary equation is $m^4 + m^2 = 0$ with roots $m = 0, 0, \pm i$. The root $m = 0$ is of multiplicity 2 ($r = 2$) and the function corresponding to this solution is $f(x) = 1$. Here

$$y_c = (c_1 + c_2 x) + c_3 \sin x + c_4 \cos x.$$

First consider $q_1(x) = x^2$. We can write this either as $x^k f(x)$, where $k = 2$ and $f(x) = 1$ is in y_c. Hence, y_p will include $x^{k+r} f(x) = x^{2+2} 1 = x^4$ and all of its linearly independent derivatives, namely $x^3, x^2, x, 1$. But x and 1 are already in y_c and therefore need not be included in y_p. So far we have

$$y_p = Ax^4 + Bx^3 + Cx^2.$$

Alternatively, we can also think of $q_1(x) = x^2$ as $x^k f(x)$, where $k = 1$ and $f(x) = x$ is in y_c. From this point of view, y_p will consist of $x^{k+r} f(x) = x^{1+2}(x) = x^4$, just as before.

Finally consider $q_2(x) = \sin x$. This belongs to Case 2 since $\sin x = x^0 f(x)$, where $f(x) = \sin x$ is in y_c. Hence, we also need to include a linear combination of the derivatives of $x^{0+1} f(x)$, that is of $x \sin x, x \cos x, \sin x, \cos x$. However, the last two need not be included since they are included in y_c. Thus,

$$y_p = (Ax^4 + Bx^3 + Cx^2) + x(E\sin x + F\cos x).$$

Example 4.10. *Find the form of particular solution y_p for the equation*

$$(D-2)^2 y = x^2 e^{2x}.$$

Solution: The auxiliary equation is $(m-2)^2 = 0$ and $m = 2, 2$. Thus, the root $m = 2$ has multiplicity 2 also. Hence,

$$y_c = c_1 e^{2x} + c_2 x e^{2x}.$$

Consider $q(x) = x^2 e^{2x}$, the only term in $Q(x)$. There are two possibilities. We can write this as $x^k f(x)$ with $k = 2, f(x) = e^{2x}$, where $f(x)$ of course is a term in y_c. Alternatively, we can also write $q(x) = x^k f(x), k = 1, f(x) = xe^{2x}$, $f(x)$ is a term in y_c. Since $q(x)$ belongs to Case 3, considering the first point of view we should include $x^{k+r} f(x) = x^{2+2} e^{2x} = x^4 e^{2x}$ and all of its linearly independent derivatives, namely $x^3 e^{2x}, x^2 e^{2x}, xe^{2x}, e^{2x}$. But the last two are in y_c and need not be included. You should verify you get the same result from the alternative point of view also. Thus,

$$y_p = (Ax^4 + Bx^3 + Cx^2)e^{2x}.$$

4.2.2 Determining coefficients

In the previous section we learned how to construct y_p with coefficients yet to be determined. In this section we shall see how one uses y_p to find the coefficients and thus write down the solution of (4.3). All one does is to actually substitute y_p for y in the left side of (4.3) and compare the coefficients of like terms on the left and right. This gives rise to a set of linear equations in an equal number of unknowns and they are solved by the usual method.

The process is best learned through some examples.

Example 4.11. *Solve the equation in Example 4.3: $y'' + 3y' + 2y = 2x^2$.*

Solution: From Example 4.3,

$$y_c = c_1 e^{-x} + c_2 e^{-2x} \quad \text{and} \quad y_p = Ax^2 + Bx + C$$

and hence,
$$y_p' = 2Ax + B, \quad y_p'' = 2A.$$

Substituting in the original equation we get

$$\begin{aligned} y_p'' + 3y_p' + 2y_p &= 2A + 3(2Ax + B) + 2(Ax^2 + Bx + C) \\ &= 2Ax^2 + (6A + 2B)x + (2A + 3B + 2C) \\ &= 2x^2. \end{aligned}$$

Comparing the coefficients of x^2, x and the constant terms, we have

$$2A = 2, \quad 6A + 2B = 0, \quad 2A + 3B + 2C = 0,$$

from which $A = 1, B = -3, C = 7/2$ and the complete solution is

$$\begin{aligned} y &= y_c + y_p \\ &= c_1 e^{-x} + c_2 e^{-2x} + x^2 - 3x + 7/2. \end{aligned}$$

Example 4.12. *Solve the equation in Example 4.7:* $(D^2 - 3D + 2)y = 2x^2 + e^x$.

Solution: We found that

$$y_c = c_1 e^x + c_2 e^{2x} \quad \text{and} \quad y_p = Ax^2 + Bx + C + Exe^x.$$

Hence,

$$\begin{aligned} Dy_p &= 2Ax + B + Exe^x + Ee^x \\ D^2 y_p &= 2A + Exe^x + 2Ee^x \\ (D^2 - 3D + 2)y_p &= 2Ax^2 + (2B - 6A)x + (2A - 3B + 2C) - Ee^x \\ &= 2x^2 + e^x \end{aligned}$$

and it follows that $A = 1, B = 3, C = \frac{7}{2}, E = -1$. Hence,

$$y_p = x^2 + 3x + \frac{7}{2} - xe^x$$

and the complete solution is $y = c_1 e^x + c_2 e^{2x} + x^2 + 3x + \frac{7}{2} - xe^x$.

Example 4.13. *Solve the equation in Example 4.8:* $(D^2 - 5D + 6)y = xe^{2x}$.

Chapter 4. Nonhomogeneous Linear Equations

Solution: From Example 4.8,

$$y_c = c_1 e^{2x} + c_2 e^{3x} \quad \text{and} \quad y_p = Ax^2 e^{2x} + Bxe^{2x}.$$

We thus get

$$Dy_p = 2Ax^2 e^{2x} + (2A + 2B)xe^{2x} + Be^{2x}$$
$$D^2 y_p = 4Ax^2 e^{2x} + (8A + 4B)xe^{2x} + (2A + 4B)e^{2x}$$
$$(D^2 - 5D + 6)\, y_p = -2Axe^{2x} + (2A - B)e^{2x}$$
$$= xe^{2x}$$

from which it follows that $A = -\frac{1}{2}$ and $B = -1$ and the complete solution is $y = c_1 e^{2x} + c_2 e^{3x} - \frac{1}{2}x^2 e^{2x} - xe^{2x}$.

Example 4.14. *Solve the equation in Example 4.9:* $(D^4 + D^2)\, y = 3x^2 + 4\sin x$.

Solution: As we found earlier,

$$y_c = (c_1 + c_2 x) + c_3 \sin x + c_4 \cos x$$
$$y_p = (Ax^4 + Bx^3 + Cx^2) + x(E\sin x + F\cos x).$$

Computing the derivatives of y_p,

$$Dy_p = (4Ax^3 + 3Bx^2 + 2Cx) + (E\sin x + F\cos x) + x(E\cos x - F\sin x)$$
$$D^2 y_p = (12Ax^2 + 6Bx + 2C) + 2(E\cos x - F\sin x) + x(-E\sin x - F\cos x)$$
$$D^3 y_p = (24Ax + 6B) + 3(-E\sin x - F\cos x) + x(-E\cos x + F\sin x)$$
$$D^4 y_p = 24A + 4(-E\cos x + F\sin x) + x(E\sin x + F\cos x)$$
$$(D^4 + D^2)\, y_p = (12Ax^2 + 6Bx + (2C + 24A)) + 4(-E\cos x + F\sin x) + x(E\sin x + F\cos x)$$
$$+ 2(E\cos x - F\sin x) - x(E\sin x + F\cos x)$$
$$= (12Ax^2 + 6Bx + (2C + 24A)) - 2(E\cos x - F\sin x)$$
$$= 3x^2 + 4\sin x$$

from which we get $A = \frac{1}{4}, B = 0, C = -3, E = 0, F = 2$ and

$$y_p = \frac{1}{4}x^4 - 3x^2 + 2x\cos x$$

and the complete solution is

$$y = (c_1 + c_2 x) + c_3 \sin x + c_4 \cos x + \frac{1}{4}x^4 - 3x^2 + 2x \cos x.$$

Example 4.15. *Solve the equation* $y'' + a^2 y = \cos ax$.

Solution: It is easy to see that $y_c = c_1 \cos ax + c_2 \sin ax$. To find y_p, here $q(x) = \cos ax = x^0 f(x)$ where $f(x) = \cos ax$ is a term in y_c. Hence, this is Case 2 and accordingly we assume

$$y_p = x(A \cos ax + B \sin ax).$$

Then it is easy to verify that

$$y_p'' = x(-a^2 A \cos ax - a^2 B \sin ax) + 2(-aA \sin ax + aB \cos ax)$$
$$y_p'' + a^2 y_p = 2(-aA \sin ax + aB \cos ax) = \cos ax.$$

Hence, $A = 0, B = 1/2a$ and

$$y_p = (x/2a) \sin ax.$$

Had the right hand side $Q(x)$ of the given equation been $\sin ax$, we would have $y_p = -(x/2a) \cos ax$. Thus,

$$y_p = \frac{x}{2a} \begin{Bmatrix} -\cos ax \\ +\sin ax \end{Bmatrix} \text{ according as } Q(x) = \begin{Bmatrix} \sin ax \\ \cos ax \end{Bmatrix} \tag{4.6}$$

Final Comments: The UC method is not difficult since it involves in carefully writing the correct form of y_p, but it is cumbersome, laborious and tiring. This is the bane of the method. In the next section we will learn how other methods would handle such problems more simply and elegantly. These methods automatically determine the correct form for y_p and then proceed to find the coefficients! Nevertheless when $Q(x)$ consists of polynomials of degree no higher than two, the method of coefficients would be hard to beat.

4.3 Differential Operator Method

In this section we will still be concerned with determining y_p but we will be using the method of *Differential Operators*. This is both an elegant as well as far simpler

Chapter 4. Nonhomogeneous Linear Equations   115

method than the UC method. Unlike the latter, the Operator method *automatically* finds the correct form of y_p and computes the coefficients with usually a lot less labor. *This material is usually not found in most standard texts!*

The operator $D \equiv \frac{d}{dx}$ is versatile in the sense that it represents the process of taking the derivative and at the same time can be manipulated as if it were an algebraic symbol! For example, we can think of D as an ordinary algebraic symbol and write

$$(D+3)(D+2) \equiv (D^2 + 5D + 6).$$

As a derivative operator, for any twice differentiable function $y = f(x)$,

$$\begin{aligned}(D+3)(D+2)y &= (D+3)(Dy + 2y) \\ &= (D+3)(y' + 2y) \\ &= Dy' + 2Dy + 3y' + 6y \\ &= y'' + 5y' + 6y \\ &= (D^2 y + 5Dy + 6y) \\ &= (D^2 + 5D + 6)y.\end{aligned}$$

It follows that D may be treated as just a symbol and at the same time acts as derivative operator (***Caution:*** *Only if the coefficients are constants!*). Note further that since the coefficients are all constants,

$$(D+3)(D+2) \equiv (D+2)(D+3),$$

that is, the factors commute. This is an important fact.

4.3.1 Meaning of the operator $\frac{1}{p(D)}$

Just as multiplication and division are "opposite" operations in the sense one nullifies the action of the other, so are D and $1/D$. Since D represents taking the derivative, *we can interpret $1/D$ as the opposite of taking derivative, that is, it represents integration.* Thus,

$$\frac{1}{D} x = \int x \, dx = x^2/2 + c.$$

Returning to equation (4.1) to fix ideas, let us assume that

$$p(D) = (D^2 + aD + b),$$

so that equation (4.1) can be written as

$$p(D)y = (D^2 + aD + b)y = Q(x).$$

If we treat $p(D)$ as a polynomial in the differential operator D, operating on both sides by $1/p(D)$, the *inverse operator of $p(D)$* (note that we still don't know its meaning other than that it nullifies the action of $p(D)$ in the sense $p(D)\{1/p(D)\} = I$, where I is the identity operator), we get

$$y_p = \frac{1}{p(D)} Q(x). \tag{4.7}$$

In the rest of this chapter we will investigate the meaning of the right hand side of (4.7) for various functions $Q(x)$.

Note: *From now on, we will think of $1/p(D)$ as the operator which does the opposite of $p(D)$, that is, they are inverse operators in the sense*

$$\left\{p(D)\frac{1}{p(D)}\right\}y = \left\{\frac{1}{p(D)}p(D)\right\}y = y.$$

Remark 13. For any constant a, we have $D(ay) = aDy$, $D^2(ay) = aD^2y$, etc., and in general,

$$D^k(ay) = a(D^k y) \quad \text{and} \quad p(D)ay = ap(D)y.$$

This property holds for inverse operators also, that is,

$$\frac{1}{p(D)}ay = a\frac{1}{p(D)}y.$$

To see this, operate on both sides by $p(D)$. On the left hand side we get ay at once and on the right,

$$p(D)\left\{a\frac{1}{p(D)}y\right\} = a\left\{p(D)\frac{1}{p(D)}\right\}y = ay$$

as well. **Hence constants can be pulled outside of inverse operators!**

4.3.2 Exponential rule $Q(x) = e^{kx}$

It is easy to verify that $De^{kx} = ke^{kx}$, $D^2 e^{kx} = k^2 e^{kx}$, etc., so that

$$p(D)e^{kx} = (D^2 + aD + b)e^{kx} = (k^2 + ak + b)e^{kx} = p(k)e^{kx}. \tag{4.8}$$

Operating on both sides by $1/p(D)$ and remembering we can pull out all constants, we have from (4.8)

$$\frac{1}{p(D)} p(D) e^{kx} = \frac{1}{p(D)} p(k) e^{kx}$$

$$e^{kx} = p(k) \frac{1}{p(D)} e^{kx}$$

and dividing both sides by $p(k)$ which is simply a constant, we get the important rule:

$$\boxed{\frac{1}{p(D)} e^{kx} = \frac{1}{p(k)} e^{kx}, \ p(k) \neq 0.} \tag{4.9}$$

Example 4.16. *Solve the equation $y'' + 5y' + 6y = 10e^{3x}$.*

Solution: Here $k = 3$. The auxiliary equation is $m^2 + 5m + 6 = 0$ so that the complementary solution is $y_c = c_1 e^{-2x} + c_2 e^{-3x}$. Using the operator method and rule (4.9),

$$y_p = \frac{1}{(D^2 + 5D + 6)} 10 e^{3x} = \frac{10}{(3^2 + 5 \cdot 3 + 6)} e^{3x} = \frac{e^{3x}}{3},$$

and the complete solution is $y = c_1 e^{-2x} + c_2 e^{-3x} + \frac{e^{3x}}{3}$.

Remark 14. The exponential rule fails if k is a root of the auxiliary equation $p(k) = 0$. This means $(D - k)$ is a factor of $p(D)$. This is taken care of in the next section.

4.3.3 Exponential shift $Q(x) = e^{kx} V(x)$

From the last section we see that the exponential rule (4.9) fails when we deal with $\frac{1}{p(D)} e^{kx}$, but $p(k) = 0$. This is taken care of by the *exponential shift*.

Consider now the equation

$$p(D) y = e^{kx} V(x),$$

where the right hand side has the additional factor $V(x)$ besides the exponential.

We note that

$$D(e^{kx}V) = ke^{kx}V + e^{kx}DV = e^{kx}(D+k)V$$
$$\begin{aligned}D^2(e^{kx}V) &= D \cdot \{D(e^{kx}V)\}\\ &= D\{e^{kx}(D+k)V\}\\ &= ke^{kx}(D+k)V + e^{kx}(D+k)DV\\ &= e^{kx}(D+k)(D+k)V\\ &= e^{kx}(D+k)^2V\end{aligned}$$

and in general
$$p(D)(e^{kx}V) = e^{kx}p(D+k)V,$$

which is usually referred to as the **exponential shift**. We are however interested in the inverse operation $\frac{1}{p(D)}e^{kx}V(x)$. Let us write

$$V_1 = \left\{\frac{1}{p(D+k)}\right\}V$$

so that $p(D+k)V_1 = V$. Then using the exponential shift, we get

$$p(D)(e^{kx}V_1) = e^{kx}p(D+k)V_1 = e^{kx}V.$$

Operating on both sides by $1/p(D)$,

$$\boxed{\frac{1}{p(D)}e^{kx}V(x) = e^{kx}\frac{1}{p(D+k)}V(x).} \qquad (4.10)$$

This means that we can move e^{kx} to the left of $\dfrac{1}{p(D)}$ as long as we replace D by $D+k$.

Caution: *One should be careful when using the exponential shift. It is important to remember that*

$$\frac{1}{p(D)}e^{kx}V \neq e^{kx}\frac{1}{p(k)}V.$$

That is, one cannot replace D by k. The correct usage is to replace D by $D+k$.

Remark 15. The following observations are very useful:

$$\frac{1}{p(D)}e^{kx} = e^{kx}\frac{1}{p(D+k)}1, \qquad \frac{1}{(aD+b)^n}\cdot 1 = \frac{1}{b^n} \quad \text{provided } b \neq 0.$$

Chapter 4. Nonhomogeneous Linear Equations   119

The first is obvious. To see the second, note that

$$\frac{1}{(aD+b)} \cdot 1 = \frac{1}{(aD+b)} e^{0x} = \frac{e^{0x}}{a(0)+b} = \frac{1}{b}.$$

By repeated application of this fact, the second equation follows.
We consider the following example.

Example 4.17. *Find a particular solution y_p of*

$$y'' - 5y' + 6y = e^{2x}.$$

Solution: We have

$$\begin{aligned}
y_p &= \frac{1}{D^2 - 5D + 6} e^{2x} \\
&= \frac{1}{(D-2)(D-3)} e^{2x} \\
&= \frac{1}{(2-3)} \frac{1}{(D-2)} e^{2x} \quad \text{(using exponential rule (4.9))} \\
&= -e^{2x} \frac{1}{((D+2)-2)} \cdot 1 \quad \text{(using exponential shift (4.10))} \\
&= -e^{2x} \frac{1}{D} \cdot 1 \\
&= -e^{2x} \int 1 \, dx \\
&= -xe^{2x}.
\end{aligned}$$

To appreciate the power of the exponential shift consider the following example.

Example 4.18. *Solve the equation of Example 4.10:*

$$(D-2)^2 y = x^2 e^{2x}.$$

Solution: As before $y_c = (c_1 x + c_2)e^{2x}$. Using the UC method, we would have to solve three equations. But using the method developed so far in this chapter,

$$y_p = \frac{1}{(D-2)(D-2)} x^2 e^{2x},$$
$$= e^{2x} \frac{1}{D} \frac{1}{D} x^2 \quad (\textit{using exponential shift (4.10)})$$
$$= e^{2x} \frac{1}{D} \int x^2 dx,$$
$$= e^{2x} \int \frac{x^3}{3} dx,$$
$$= \frac{x^4 e^{2x}}{12},$$

which is much faster.

Remark 16. If k is a root of $p(D)$ with multiplicity r, then $(D-k)^r$ is a factor of $p(D)$. Suppose $p(D) = \phi(D)(D-k)^r$. Then

$$\frac{1}{p(D)} e^{kx} = \frac{1}{\phi(D)} \frac{1}{(D-k)^r} e^{kx} = \frac{1}{\phi(D)} e^{kx} \frac{1}{D^r} \cdot 1 = \frac{e^{kx}}{\phi(k)} \frac{x^r}{r!}.$$

Example 4.19. Solve
$$y''' - 3y'' + 3y' - y = e^x.$$

Solution: We can rewrite the equation as $(D^3 - 3D^2 + 3D - 1)y = e^x$. The auxiliary equation has three equal roots, viz., 1,1,1 (i.e. 1 has multiplicity 3). Hence

$$y_c = (c_1 x^2 + c_2 x + c_3) e^x.$$

Also

$$y_p = \frac{1}{(D-1)^3} e^x$$
$$= e^x \frac{1}{D^3} \cdot 1$$
$$= \frac{x^3 e^x}{3!}.$$

The complete solution is

$$y_c = (c_1 x^2 + c_2 x + c_3) e^x + \frac{x^3}{3!} e^x.$$

Chapter 4. Nonhomogeneous Linear Equations

You should also try the UC method to solve this equation.

4.3.4 $Q(x)$ is a polynomial

This is one case where the operator method can get bogged down and in some cases it may be more easily done by the UC method if the number of equations to be solved is small.

Consider the equation $p(D)y = Q(x)$ where $Q(x)$ is a polynomial in x. To fix ideas, let us consider the equation

$$(D^2 - 4D + 3)y = x^2.$$

It is immediate that $y_c = c_1 e^x + c_2 e^{3x}$. Recall from calculus that

$$\frac{1}{1-x} = 1 + x + x^2 + x^3 + \ldots, \quad \frac{1}{1+x} = 1 - x + x^2 - x^3 + \ldots$$

To find y_p, we have

$$\begin{aligned}
y_p &= \frac{1}{D^2 - 4D + 3} x^2 \\
&= \frac{1}{(D-1)(D-3)} x^2 \\
&= -\frac{1}{2}\left\{\frac{1}{D-1} - \frac{1}{D-3}\right\} x^2 \\
&= \frac{1}{2}\left\{\frac{1}{1-D} - \frac{1}{3-D}\right\} x^2 \\
&= \frac{1}{2}\left\{(1 + D + D^2) - \frac{1}{3}(1 + D/3 + D^2/9)\right\} x^2 \\
&= \frac{1}{2}\left\{(2/3) + (8/9)D + (26/27)D^2\right\} x^2 \\
&= \frac{1}{2}\left\{(2/3)x^2 + (16/9)x + (52/27)\right\} \\
&= (1/3)x^2 + (8/9)x + (26/27).
\end{aligned}$$

It is really not necessary to split $\frac{1}{D^2-4D+3}$ into partial fractions before expanding them in powers of D. Alternately we can use the power series method without really splitting $\frac{1}{D^2-4D+3}$ as shown below

$$y_p = \frac{1}{D^2 - 4D + 3} x^2$$
$$= \frac{1}{(D-1)(D-3)} x^2$$
$$= \left(\frac{1}{D-1}\right)\left(\frac{1}{D-3}\right) x^2$$
$$= \frac{1}{3}\left(\frac{1}{1-D}\right)\left(\frac{1}{1-\frac{D}{3}}\right) x^2 \quad \text{(getting the denominators in the form } 1 \pm kD\text{)}$$
$$= \frac{1}{3}\left(\frac{1}{1-D}\right)\{1 + D/3 + D^2/9\} x^2$$
$$= \frac{1}{3}\left(\frac{1}{1-D}\right)\{x^2 + 2x/3 + 2/9\}$$
$$= \tfrac{1}{3}\{1 + D + D^2\}\{x^2 + 2x/3 + 2/9\}$$
$$= \tfrac{1}{3}\{(x^2 + 2x/3 + 2/9) + (2x + 2/3) + 2\}$$
$$= \tfrac{1}{3}x^2 + \tfrac{8}{9}x + \tfrac{26}{27}$$

as before. In fact there are all kinds of variations possible. We don't have to factor at all! Write the denominator as $3\{1 + \frac{D^2-4D}{3}\}$ and get

$$y_p = \frac{1}{3\{1 + \frac{D^2-4D}{3}\}} x^2$$
$$= \frac{1}{3}\left(1 - \frac{D^2-4D}{3} + \frac{D^4-8D^3+16D^2}{9}\right) x^2$$
$$= \frac{1}{3}\left(1 + \frac{4D}{3} + \frac{13D^2}{9}\right) x^2 \quad \text{(dropping all powers of D higher than 2)}$$
$$= \tfrac{1}{3}x^2 + \tfrac{8}{9}x + \tfrac{26}{27},$$

which is the same as before.

Remark 17. Notice that there is a need to rewrite a term such as $(D-3)$ in the form $-3(1 - \frac{D}{3})$ before applying the series expansion. Also, in the expansion of $\frac{1}{1-D}$ and $\frac{1}{-3(1-\frac{D}{3})}$ into power series, we only need take terms up to D^2 since $D^3 x^2 = 0, D^4 x^2 = 0$, etc.

Remark 18. If the right side is a polynomial, which method should one use? UC method or the operator method? It depends upon the form of $p(D)$. If $p(D)$ involves only factors such as $(D\pm 1), (D\pm 2)$, etc., where the coefficient of D is 1, the operator method would be still be useful. With factors of the form $aD \pm b$ it would be cumbersome and the UC method may be preferable. In any case if the right side

Chapter 4. Nonhomogeneous Linear Equations 123

involves cubic or higher order polynomials, the operator method should probably be the method of choice.

Remark 19. Sometimes however, you can use both methods. You can start with the operator method and switch over to the coefficients method if that appears simpler. This is particularly true when the right side contains terms such as $x^2 e^x$.

Example 4.20. *Solve the equation* $y'' + y = 1 - x^2 e^{-x}$.

Solution: Obviously, $y_c = c_1 \cos x + c_2 \sin x$.
To find y_p, we first use the Superposition Principle to split the given problem into two subproblems,

$$(i) \ \ y'' + y = 1, \quad (ii) \ \ y'' + y = -x^2 e^{-x}.$$

For the first subproblem, by observation, the particular solution is $y_p(i) = 1$. To find the particular solution $y_p(ii)$ for the second subproblem, if we apply the UC method, we would have to assume $y_p(ii) = Ax^2 e^{-x} + Bxe^{-x} + Ce^{-x}$, which is obviously very laborious! Instead we start with the operator method first. We have

$$y_p(ii) = \frac{1}{D^2 + 1}(-x^2 e^{-x})$$
$$= -\frac{1}{D^2 + 1}(x^2 e^{-x})$$
$$= -e^{-x}\frac{1}{(D-1)^2 + 1}x^2 \ \ (\text{by exponential shift})$$
$$= -e^{-x}\frac{1}{D^2 - 2D + 2}x^2.$$

One can now continue with the operator method by rewriting

$$D^2 - 2D + 2 = 2\left(1 + \frac{D^2 - 2D}{2}\right),$$

etc., and expanding in powers of $\dfrac{D^2 - 2D}{2}$. Instead, observe that $\dfrac{1}{D^2 - 2D + 2}x^2$ is simply the particular solution of the equation

$$(D^2 - 2D + 2)y = x^2$$

and can be found more easily by the undetermined coefficients method. Indeed, let

$$y = Ax^2 + Bx + C$$
$$y' = 2Ax + B$$
$$y'' = 2A.$$

Substituting,
$$2Ax^2 + (2B - 4A)x + (2A - 2B + 2C) = x^2$$

from which we get $A = C = \frac{1}{2}, B = 1$ so that

$$\frac{1}{D^2 - 2D + 2}x^2 = \frac{1}{2}(x^2 + 2x + 1).$$

Hence, the solution of the original problem is

$$y = y_c + y_p(i) + y_p(ii)$$
$$= c_1 \cos x + c_2 \sin x + 1 - e^{-x}(x^2 + 2x + 1)/2.$$

4.3.5 $Q(x)$ is a circular function: $Q(x) = \sin x, \cos x$

We now consider the equation

$$p(D)y = Q(x) \tag{4.11}$$

where $Q(x) = \sin ax$ or $\cos ax$. Let us assume $Q(x) = \sin ax$. We easily see that

$$D(\sin ax) = a \cos ax$$
$$D^2(\sin ax) = -a^2 \sin ax$$
$$D^3(\sin ax) = -a^3 \cos ax$$
$$D^4(\sin ax) = (D^2)^2(\sin ax) = (-a^2)^2 \sin ax = a^4 \sin ax$$

and so on. It follows that

$$p(D^2)\sin ax = p(-a^2)\sin ax$$

and likewise

$$p(D^2)\cos ax = p(-a^2)\cos ax.$$

Chapter 4. Nonhomogeneous Linear Equations 125

This gives us the important formula

$$\boxed{\frac{1}{p(D^2)} \begin{Bmatrix} \sin ax \\ \cos ax \end{Bmatrix} = \frac{1}{p(-a^2)} \begin{Bmatrix} \sin ax \\ \cos ax \end{Bmatrix}} \qquad (4.12)$$

Hence in finding y_p for equation (4.3), all we need to do is to replace D^2 by $(-a^2)$. In particular, we replace $D^{2n} = (D^2)^n$ by $(-a^2)^n$

Remark 20. Equation (4.12) can fail when $p(-a^2) = 0$, which happens when $D^2 + a^2$ is a factor of $p(D^2)$ and in which case $\sin ax$ and $\cos ax$ are part of the complementary solution. The easiest way to handle this is through the UC method (equation (4.6)).

In the notation of differential operators we can rewrite equation (4.6) as

$$\frac{1}{D^2 + a^2} \begin{Bmatrix} \cos ax \\ \sin ax \end{Bmatrix} = \frac{x}{2} \int \begin{Bmatrix} \cos ax \\ \sin ax \end{Bmatrix} dx. \qquad (4.13)$$

(For an elegant way of treating circular functions using operator methods, see Appendix B: Operator Methods with Complex Coefficients)

4.3.6 Substitution for D^2

In solving the equation $p(D)y = Q(x)$ where $Q(x)$ is a sine, cosine or both, when do we substitute $-a^2$ for D^2? Actually this can be done any time. Suppose that

$$p(D) = g(D^2) + h(D),$$

where $h(D)$ consists of all odd powers of D. Then from

$$p(D)\sin ax = g(D^2)\sin ax + h(D)\sin ax$$
$$= (h(D) + g(-a^2))\sin ax,$$

it follows that

$$\frac{1}{p(D)}\sin ax = \frac{1}{h(D) + g(-a^2)}\sin ax,$$

showing that we can substitute $-a^2$ for D^2 at any time.

After the substitution for the even powers of D, this leaves only *odd* powers of D

in $p(D)$, but this can be further simplified. We can write

$$p(D) = D\,g(D^2) + c,$$

where g contains only even powers of D. Then

$$p(D)\sin ax = (D\,g(D^2) + c)\sin ax$$
$$= (D\,g(-a^2) + c)\sin ax$$

so that

$$\frac{1}{p(D)}\sin ax = \frac{1}{D\,g(-a^2) + c}\sin ax$$
$$= \frac{1}{g(-a^2)D + c}\sin ax$$

and this is of the form

$$\frac{1}{pD+q}\sin ax,$$

where p and q are constants. But this is taken care of by the trick

$$\frac{1}{pD+q}\sin ax = \frac{1}{pD+q}\cdot\frac{pD-q}{pD-q}\sin ax$$
$$= \frac{pD-q}{p^2D^2-q^2}\sin ax$$
$$= \frac{pa\cos ax - q\sin ax}{p^2(-a^2)-q^2}.$$

Example 4.21. *Find a particular solution for the equation $(D^3+D^2+D)y = \sin 2x$.*
Solution:

$$y_p = \frac{1}{D^3+D^2+D}\sin 2x$$
$$= \frac{1}{D^2\cdot D + D^2 + D}\sin 2x$$
$$= \frac{1}{(-4)D - 4 + D}\sin 2x$$

$$= \frac{1}{-3D-4}\sin 2x$$
$$= \frac{-3D+4}{9D^2-16}\sin 2x$$
$$= \frac{-3D+4}{-36-16}\sin 2x$$
$$= \frac{6\cos 2x - 4\sin 2x}{52}$$
$$= \frac{3\cos 2x - 2\sin 2x}{26}.$$

4.4 Exercises

1. Using the method of undetermined coefficients, find a suitable form for the particular solution for each of the following. *Do not evaluate the coefficients!*

   (a) $y'' + 4y' + 4y = x^2$.

   (b) $y'' + 4y' + 4y = 2e^x$.

   (c) $y'' - 3y' + 2y = 2e^{3x}$.

   (d) $y'' + y = \sin x$.

   (e) $y'' + 2y' + y = x^2 e^x$.

   (f) $y''' + y' = x \sin x + x$.

   (g) $y'' - 4y' + 4y = e^{2x}$.

   (h) $y'' + y = \cos^2 x$ (Hint: use double angle formula).

   (i) $y'' + y' - 2y = xe^{-2x}$.

   (j) $y'' + 4y' + 4y = -x^2 e^{-2x}$.

2. Solve the following problems using the method of undetermined coefficients.

   (a) $y'' - 3y' + 2y = 2e^{3x}$.

   (b) $y' + y = 2\cos x$.

3. Find the particular solutions to the following problems using the operator method.

   (a) $y^{(4)} = e^{3x}$.

   (b) $y' - 2y = xe^{2x}$.

   (c) $y' + y = e^x + 2\cos x$.

(d) $y'' + 4y' + 4y = -x^2 e^{-2x}$.

(e) $y'' - 4y = e^{2x} \cos x$.

(f) $(D^2 - 1)y = x^4$.

4. Solve problems (a)-(g) using the method of undetermined coefficients. Solve *all* problems using the operator method.

   (a) $y'' + 3y' - 10y = 6e^{4x}$

   (b) $y'' + 10y' + 25y = 14e^{-5x}$

   (c) $y'' - y' - 6y = 20e^{-2x}$

   (d) $y'' + y = 2\cos x$

   (e) $y'' - 2y' + y = 6e^x$

   (f) $y'' + y' = 10x^4 + 2$

   (g) Use the Superposition Principle to solve
   $$y'' + 4y = 4\cos 2x + 6\cos x + 8x^2 - 4x.$$
   (Hint: Solve the three subproblems $p_2(D)y = 4\cos 2x$, $p_2(D)y = 6\cos x$, $p_2(D)y = 8x^2 - 4x$, where $p_2(D)y = y'' + 4y$.)

   (h) $y'' - 4y = e^{2x}$.

   (i) $y'' + 4y' + 4y = 10x^3 e^{-2x}$

   (j) $(D^2 - 1)y = e^{-x}$.

   (k) $y'' - y' + y = x^3 - 3x^2 + 1$

   (l) $y'' - 4y' + 3y = x^3 e^{2x}$.

   (m) $y''' - 8y = 16x^2$.

   (n) $(D - 2)^3 y = e^{2x}$

   (o) $(D - 2)^2 y = e^{2x} \sin x$.

5. Solve the following problems by any method of your choice.

   (a) $(D^2 - 8D + 9)y = 8\sin 5x$.

   (b) $y'' - 4y' + 3y = \sin 3x \sin 2x$.

   (c) $(D^3 - D^2 - D + 1)y = x^2 + 1$.

   (d) Solve the initial value problem: $y'' + 16y = e^{-3x} + \cos 4x$, $y(0) = 0, y'(0) = -\frac{1}{25}$.

(e) $(D^2 - 2D - 8)y = 4\cos 2x$.

6. In the following problems $y_p = \dfrac{1}{p(D)}g(x)$. Find the original equation in derivative form for which y_p is the particular solution and solve the equation.

(a) $y_p = \dfrac{1}{(D-1)^2 + 1}xe^x$.

(b) $y_p = \dfrac{1}{(D^2 + 4)}e^x \cos x$.

(c) $y_p = \dfrac{1}{(D^2 + 16)}\{e^{-3x} + \cos 4x\}$.

Chapter 5

Linear Equations with Variable Coefficients

5.1 Introduction

In Chapters 3 and 4 we considered linear equations where the coefficients of y and its derivatives were constants. We now consider three methods, *Reduction of order*, *Variation of parameters* and *Cauchy-Euler* that are useful when dealing with equations with variable coefficients. The first two deal with equations of second degree, i.e.,

$$(D^2 + p(x)D + q(x))y = Q(x), \qquad (5.1)$$

where the coefficients $p(x), q(x)$ need not necessarily be constants but are continuous functions of x, usually for all real x.

The methods we have studied so far are inapplicable in this situation. Of the first two methods considered here, the *Reduction of order* deals with the homogeneous case. The second, *Variation of parameters* deals with the nonhomogeneous case. This method is particularly useful when the coefficients are constants but the right hand side of (5.1) has functions such as $\ln x, \sec x$, etc. Recall that in the latter case, the methods of Chapter 4 are not applicable.

Finally we consider a class of equations where the coefficients have a special form, often called *Cauchy–Euler equations*:

$$a_0 x^n \frac{d^n y}{dx^n} + a_1 x^{n-1} \frac{d^{n-1} y}{dx^{n-1}} + a_2 x^{n-2} \frac{d^{n-2} y}{dx^{n-2}} + \cdots + a_{n-1} x \frac{dy}{dx} + a_n y = F(x),$$

where $a_0, a_1, \cdots, a_n$ are all constants. Note that each term is of the form $x^k \dfrac{d^k y}{dx^k}$. Here the order of equation can be higher than two. Although the coefficients do not *appear* to be constants, they can be made so by a simple change of the independent variable. The resulting equation is usually solved by an interesting variation of the operator method and sometimes by the first two methods to be discussed here.

Although the methods of this chapter may be applied to the types of equations we have considered in Chapters 3 and 4 (constant coefficients and the right side of (5.1) a combination of exponentials, polynomials, sines and cosines), the methods considered in those chapters may be simpler. A word of caution: The formulas developed here are not particularly simple and need to be committed to memory!

Note that Theorem 3.1 is applicable to (5.1). In particular, any two arbitrary constants uniquely define a solution of (5.1). When (5.1) is homogeneous, that is $Q(x) = 0$, all we need is two linearly independent solutions of (5.1), say y_1, y_2 and the general solution of (5.1) can be written as $y = c_1 y_1 + y_2$.

How do the first two methods work? In the *reduction of order* (which applies to homogeneous equations with variable coefficients), given one solution y_1 of (5.1), the method produces another solution y_2 linearly independent from y_1. The solution of (5.1) can then be written down as $y = c_1 y_1 + c_2 y_2$ where c_1, c_2 are arbitrary constants.

On the other hand, *variation of parameters*, applies to those types of (5.1), where the solution of the homogeneous part of (5.1) is known (e.g., when the coefficients are constants), and $Q(x)$ contains functions with possibly *infinitely many* linearly independent derivatives. The UC method and the method of operators are often useless in such cases. In this case, one first computes the complementary part of the solution of (5.1) somehow (we denoted this in Chapter 4 by y_c) and uses this to find y_p for (5.1).

5.2 Homogeneous equations – Method of Reduction of Order

This method derives its name from the fact that a second order equation is replaced by a first order equation for its solution. But one needs to know at least one solution of (5.1) somehow. Luckily, in most cases this can often be guessed! Essentially, given one solution of equation (5.1), the reduction of order method manufactures another solution linearly independent from the first. When it works, the method is quite powerful.

Suppose that we are given the following homogeneous second order linear differ-

Chapter 5. Linear Equations with Variable Coefficients

ential equation
$$y'' + p(x)y' + q(x)y = 0, \tag{5.2}$$

where $p(x)$ and $q(x)$ are functions of x. Suppose also that we are given a solution $y = y_1$ of (5.2) and let us assume that

$$y_2 = v(x)y_1$$

is another solution of (5.2). Our aim is to find $v(x)$. Since, by assumption, $y = y_1$ is a solution of (5.2), we have
$$y_1'' + py_1' + qy_1 = 0. \tag{5.3}$$

Also since $y_2 = vy_1$ we have

$$y_2' = v'y_1 + vy_1' \tag{5.4}$$
$$y_2'' = v''y_1 + v'y_1' + v'y_1' + vy_1''$$
$$= v''y_1 + 2v'y_1' + vy_1''. \tag{5.5}$$

Substituting (5.4), (5.5) in (5.2) we get

$$v''y_1 + v'(2y_1' + py_1) + v(y_1'' + py_1' + qy_1) = 0, \tag{5.6}$$

and because of (5.3), the last term in (5.6) is zero. Hence, equation (5.6) now becomes

$$v''y_1 + v'(2y_1' + py_1) = 0,$$

which we rewrite as
$$\frac{v''}{v'} = -\frac{2y_1' + py_1}{y_1} = \frac{-2y_1'}{y_1} - p. \tag{5.7}$$

Integrating with respect to x throughout we get

$$\ln v' = -\ln y_1^2 - \int p\, dx$$

which can be rewritten as
$$v'y_1^2 = \exp\left(-\int p\, dx\right) \tag{5.8}$$

and from which it is immediate that

$$v = \int \frac{\exp\left(-\int p\, dx\right)}{y_1^2} dx. \tag{5.9}$$

The new solution then is
$$y_2 = y_1 \cdot v,$$
where v is given by (5.9). Notice the appearance of $\exp(-\int p\,dx)$ as in the case of linear equations of first order.

Linear independence of y_1 and y_2

How do we know that the given solution y_1 is linearly independent from the new computed solution y_2? We compute their Wronskian (Theorem 3.2):

$$W(y_1, y_2) = \begin{vmatrix} y_1 & y_2 \\ y_1' & y_2' \end{vmatrix} = \begin{vmatrix} y_1 & y_1 v \\ y_1' & y_1' v + y_1 v' \end{vmatrix} = y_1^2 v' = \exp\left(-\int p\,dx\right) \neq 0$$

from equation (5.8) and the fact that an exponential function is never zero.

Example 5.1. *Given that x is a solution of*
$$(x^2 + 1)y'' - 2xy' + 2y = 0$$
find a linearly independent solution by reducing the order.

Solution: Note that the coefficient of y'' in equation (5.2) is 1. Hence, we first divide throughout by $(x^2 + 1)$ to get
$$y'' - \frac{2x}{x^2 + 1} y' + \frac{2}{x^2 + 1} y = 0.$$

Here $y_1 = x$, $p(x) = -2x/(x^2 + 1)$, so
$$\exp\left(-\int p\,dx\right) = \exp(\ln(x^2 + 1)) = x^2 + 1.$$

Hence,
$$v = \int \frac{x^2 + 1}{x^2} dx = \int 1 + \frac{1}{x^2} dx = x - \frac{1}{x}$$

and the required solution is $y = v \cdot y_1 = x(x - 1/x) = x^2 - 1$. Thus the complete solution to the given equation is $y = c_1 x + c_2(x^2 - 1)$.

Example 5.2. *Solve the equation*
$$y'' - 4y' + 4y = 0.$$

Solution: We have already seen this and similar equations earlier. The auxiliary equation has two equal roots 2, 2 and therefore one solution is e^{2x}. Here $p(x) = -4$ and to find the other solution, use (5.9) to get

$$v = \int \frac{\left(e^{-\int -4dx}\right)}{(e^{2x})^2} dx = \int \frac{e^{4x}}{e^{4x}} dx = x$$

so that the second solution is $y_2 = xe^{2x}$ as we have seen before.

Remark 21. The method derives its name from the fact that the solution of a second order equation such as (5.2) is reduced to the solution of a first order (linear) differential equation (5.6) (with the substitution $w = v', w' = v''$ and all functions involved are functions of x).

Remark 22. The method requires *one solution be known*! Sometimes $y = x$ is an obvious choice. But the cases where one solution is known a priori are not common. In cases where no solution is known the method is useless.

Remark 23. Notice that equation (5.9) involves only the function $p(x)$ (the coefficient of y') only!

5.3 Nonhomogeneous equations – Method of Variation of Parameters

This method is very much similar to the last method except that it especially applies to nonhomogeneous equations. Given a second order equation

$$y'' + p(x)y' + q(x)y = Q(x), \qquad (5.10)$$

we assume we know two linearly independent solutions of the homogeneous part, that is y_c. The method is mostly used when $p(x)$ and $q(x)$ are constants which we have seen before. Once this is known, one replaces the arbitrary constants in y_c by *functions* to manufacture y_p! The method of variation of parameters, due to Lagrange, is quite powerful especially when $Q(x)$ is a complicated function. We assume that we can solve the homogeneous part of equation (5.10)

$$y'' + p(x)y' + q(x)y = 0. \qquad (5.11)$$

Let y_1 and y_2 be two linearly independent solutions of (5.11) so that the general solution of (5.11) is

$$y_c = c_1 y_1 + c_2 y_2. \tag{5.12}$$

Since y_1, y_2 are linearly independent, their Wronskian is nonzero, i.e.,

$$W(y_1, y_2) = \begin{vmatrix} y_1 & y_2 \\ y_1' & y_2' \end{vmatrix} = y_1 y_2' - y_1' y_2 \neq 0. \tag{5.13}$$

We replace the constants c_1 and c_2 in (5.12) by the functions $v_1(x)$ and $v_2(x)$, and wish to determine v_1, v_2 so that a particular solution y_p exists,

$$y_p = v_1 y_1 + v_2 y_2$$

which is a solution of (5.10). Since we have to determine two functions, we have the freedom to impose two conditions. We have already used one in replacing the costants c_1, c_2 by two functions. The second condition would appear shortly. It is easy to verify that

$$y_p' = \{v_1 y_1' + v_2 y_2'\} + \{v_1' y_1 + v_2' y_2\}. \tag{5.14}$$

As our second condition we impose that the quantity inside the second braces be zero, i.e.,

$$v_1' y_1 + v_2' y_2 = 0. \tag{5.15}$$

With this simplification, equation (5.14) becomes

$$y_p' = v_1 y_1' + v_2 y_2'. \tag{5.16}$$

We differentiate this to get

$$y_p'' = v_1' y_1' + v_1 y_1'' + v_2' y_2' + v_2 y_2''. \tag{5.17}$$

Since y_p is assumed to be a solution of (5.10), we substitute for y_p'', y_p', y_p from equations (5.16) and (5.17) in (5.10):

$$\begin{aligned} y_p'' + p y_p' + q y_p &= v_1' y_1' + v_1 y_1'' + v_2' y_2' + v_2 y_2'' \\ &\quad + p v_1 y_1' + p v_2 y_2' + q v_1 y_1 + q v_2 y_2 \\ &= v_1 (y_1'' + p y_1' + q y_1) + v_2 (y_2'' + p y_2' + q y_2) + v_1' y_1' + v_2' y_2' \quad (5.18) \\ &= Q(x). \end{aligned}$$

Chapter 5. Linear Equations with Variable Coefficients

In equation (5.18), the expressions inside parentheses are zero since y_1, y_2 are assumed to be solutions of (5.11). The last equality follows since y_p is a solution of (5.10). We have from equations (5.15) and (5.18) that

$$v_1'y_1 + v_2'y_2 = 0$$
$$v_1'y_1' + v_2'y_2' = Q. \tag{5.19}$$

Solving equations (5.19) it is easy to see that we get

$$v_1' = \frac{-y_2 Q}{W(y_1, y_2)}, \quad v_2' = \frac{y_1 Q}{W(y_1, y_2)}$$

and it follows that

$$v_1 = \int \frac{-y_2 Q}{W(y_1, y_2)} dx, \quad v_2 = \int \frac{y_1 Q}{W(y_1, y_2)} dx, \tag{5.20}$$

and of course

$$y_p = v_1 y_1 + v_2 y_2.$$

Example 5.3. *Solve the equation*

$$y'' + y = \tan x.$$

Solution: This cannot be done by any of the methods we have studied in Chapter 4. The complementary solution to this equation is $y_c = c_1 \cos x + c_2 \sin x$ giving $y_1 = \cos x$ and $y_2 = \sin x$. Also $W(y_1, y_2) = \cos^2 x + \sin^2 x = 1$. By the formulas in (5.20)

$$v_1 = \int \{-\sin x \tan x\} dx, \quad v_2 = \int \{\cos x \tan x\} dx.$$

It is easy to see that $v_2 = \int \sin x \, dx = -\cos x$ and

$$v_1 = \int (-\sin^2 x / \cos x) dx$$
$$= \int (\cos^2 x - 1)/\cos x \, dx$$
$$= \int (\cos x - \sec x) dx = \sin x - \ln|\sec x + \tan x|.$$

Hence,

$$y_p = \cos x(\sin x - \ln|\sec x + \tan x|) - \sin x \cos x$$
$$= -\cos x \ln|\sec x + \tan x|,$$

and the complete solution is

$$y = c_1 \cos x + c_2 \sin x - \cos x \ln|\sec x + \tan x|.$$

Remark 24. As is obvious from the last problem, although the formulas (5.20) may seem simple, the integrals may not be particularly easy!

5.4 Cauchy–Euler equations

A typical such equation is of the form

$$a_0 x^n \frac{d^n y}{dx^n} + a_1 x^{n-1} \frac{d^{n-1} y}{dx^{n-1}} + a_2 x^{n-2} \frac{d^{n-2} y}{dx^{n-2}} + \ldots + a_{n-1} x \frac{dy}{dx} + a_n y = F(x), \quad (5.21)$$

where $a_0, a_1, \ldots, a_n$ are all constants. Note that each term is of the form $x^k \frac{d^k y}{dx^k}$.

Equation (5.21) may not seem like a linear equation with constant coefficients, but a simple change of independent variable can make it so. We define a new independent variable t by

$$x = e^t, \ x > 0,$$

so that

$$t = \ln x \text{ and } \frac{dx}{dt} = x.$$

Thus, y is a functions of x which is now a function of t. We now compute the derivatives of y with respect to the new independent variable t. By chain rule

$$\frac{dy}{dt} = \frac{dy}{dx}\frac{dx}{dt} = x\frac{dy}{dx}. \quad (5.22)$$

Since we use D to denote derivatives with respect to x, we will use the symbol θ to denote derivatives with respect to t. Observe that θ has all the properties of D and can be used freely when we use operator methods. We can therefore write

$$\frac{dy}{dt} = \theta y, \ \frac{d^2 y}{dt^2} = \theta^2 y, \ldots, \text{ etc.}$$

Thus, (5.22) can be written as
$$\theta y = xDy,$$
and more generally,
$$\theta f(x) = x \cdot Df(x). \tag{5.23}$$

From equation (5.23) we now have
$$\begin{aligned}\theta^2 y &= \theta(\theta y) \\ &= \theta(xDy) \\ &= \frac{d}{dx}(xDy) \cdot \frac{dx}{dt} \\ &= (xD^2y + Dy) \cdot x \\ &= x^2 D^2 y + xDy\end{aligned}$$

from which
$$x^2 D^2 y = \theta^2 y - xDy = \theta^2 y - \theta y = \theta(\theta - 1)y. \tag{5.24}$$

Likewise,
$$\begin{aligned}\theta^3 y &= \theta(\theta^2 y) \\ &= \frac{d}{dx}(x^2 D^2 y + xDy) \cdot \frac{dx}{dt} \\ &= x \cdot (2xD^2y + x^2 D^3 y + Dy + xD^2 y) \\ &= x^3 D^3 y + 3x^2 D^2 y + xDy\end{aligned}$$

from which we get
$$\begin{aligned}x^3 D^3 y &= \theta^3 y - 3x^2 D^2 y - xDy \\ &= \theta^3 y - 3(\theta^2 y - \theta y) - \theta y \\ &= \theta^3 y - 3\theta^2 y + 2\theta y \\ &= \theta(\theta - 1)(\theta - 2)y, \end{aligned} \tag{5.25}$$

and likewise one can easily show that
$$x^n D^n y = \theta(\theta - 1)(\theta - 2)\ldots(\theta - (n-1))y. \tag{5.26}$$

To solve equation (5.21) then, all one needs to do is to replace $x\dfrac{dy}{dx}$, $x^2\dfrac{d^2y}{dx^2}$, etc., as per equation (5.26). The resulting equation is in terms of the operator θ with independent variable t and coefficients that are constants. We solve this by methods we have studied so far (including operator methods!) and in the final result replace t by $\ln x$.

Example 5.4. *Solve*

$$x^2 \frac{d^2y}{dx^2} - 2x\frac{dy}{dx} + 2y = x^3, \quad x > 0.$$

Solution: With our usual notation the given equation is

$$x^2 D^2 y - 2x Dy + 2y = x^3.$$

We substitute $x = e^t$ and replace $x^2 D^2 y, x Dy$, etc., as per equation (5.26) to get

$$(\theta)(\theta - 1)y - 2\theta y + 2y = e^{3t}.$$

Simplifying,

$$\theta^2 y - 3\theta y + 2y = e^{3t}.$$

The auxiliary equation is $m^2 - 3m + 2 = 0$ whose roots are $m = 1, 2$. Hence, the complementary solution is

$$y_c = c_1 e^t + c_2 e^{2t}.$$

To find the particular solution y_p,

$$y_p = \frac{1}{\theta^2 - 3\theta + 2} e^{3t} = \frac{e^{3t}}{3^2 - 3(3) + 2} = \frac{e^{3t}}{2},$$

so the complete solution is

$$y = c_1 e^t + c_2 e^{2t} + \frac{e^{3t}}{2}.$$

We substitute for $t = \ln x$ to finally get

$$y = c_1 x + c_2 x^2 + \frac{x^3}{2}.$$

Example 5.5. *Solve*

$$x^2 y'' + xy' + y = 4\sin(\ln x).$$

Solution: Writing the equation in terms of operator D we have

$$(x^2 D^2 + xD + 1)y = 4\sin(\ln x).$$

Using equation (5.26) we rewrite the last equation in terms of t using the operator θ to get

$$(\theta(\theta-1) + \theta + 1)y = 4\sin t,$$

or

$$(\theta^2 + 1)y = 4\sin t. \tag{5.27}$$

The auxiliary equation here is $m^2 + 1 = 0$ and the complementary solution is

$$y_c = c_1 \cos t + c_2 \sin t.$$

Note that $\sin t$ is part of the complementary solution. From Remark 20, the particular solution is given by

$$y_p = 4\left\{\frac{t}{2}\right\} \int \sin t \, dt,$$

that is,

$$y_p = -2t\cos t.$$

The complete solution is thus

$$y = c_1 \cos t + c_2 \sin t - 2t \cos t,$$

which after substituting back $t = \ln x$ gives us

$$y = c_1 \cos(\ln x) + c_2 \sin(\ln x) - 2\ln x \cos(\ln x), \quad x > 0.$$

Remark 25. It should be noted that some equations that appear to be of the Cauchy-Euler type can be solved by previously learned methods. For example, in Example 5.4, it is easy to verify that $y = x$ is an obvious solution of the homogeneous equation $x^2 \frac{d^2y}{dx^2} - 2x\frac{dy}{dx} + 2y = 0$ and we can use reduction of order to find another linearly independent solution and hence y_c. One can then use variation of parameters to find a particular solution. However, the methods discussed here are usually much simpler to use!

5.5 Exercises

1. Use the reduction of order method to solve the following problems given one of the solutions y_1.

    (a) $(D-3)^2 y = 0$, $y_1 = e^{3x}$.

    (b) $x^2 y'' + 2xy' = 0$, $y_1 = 1$.

    (c) $x^2 y'' - xy' + y = 0$, $y_1 = x$.

    (d) $x^2 y'' + 2xy' - 2y = 0$, $y_1 = x$.

    (e) $x^2 y'' - 4xy' + 4y = 0$, $y_1 = x$.

    (f) $(x^2 - 1)y'' - 2xy' + 2y = 0$, $y_1 = x$.

    (g) $2x^2 y'' + 3xy' - y = 0$, $y_1 = \sqrt{x}$.

    (h) $(2x+1)y'' - 4(x+1)y' + 4y = 0$, $y_1 = e^{2x}$.

    (i) $(x^2 - 2x + 2)y'' - x^2 y' + x^2 y = 0$, $y_1 = x$.

    (j) $x^2 y'' + xy' + (x^2 - 1/4)y = 0$, $y_1 = x^{-1/2} \sin x$.

    (k) Prove that if $1+p+q = 0$ than $y = e^x$ is a solution of $y'' + p(x)y' + q(x)y = 0$. Use this fact to solve $(x-1)y'' - xy' + y = 0$.

2. Use the method of variation of parameters to solve the following problems.

    (a) $y'' - 4y = e^{3x}$.

    (b) $y'' - 3y' + 2y = e^x$.

    (c) $(x^2 + 1)y'' - 2xy' + 2y = 6(x^2 + 1)^2$.

    (d) $y'' + y = \sec x$.

    (e) $x^2 y'' - 6xy' + 10y = 3x^4 + 6x^3$, given that x^2 and x^5 are linearly independent solutions.

    (f) $y'' - 2y' = 8xe^{2x}$, and by two other methods.

    (g) $y'' - 2y' + y = 2x$.

    (h) $y'' + 2y' + y = e^{-x} \ln x$.

    (i) $y'' - 3y' + 2y = (1 + e^{-x})^{-1}$.

    (j) $y'' + y = \sec x \tan x$.

    (k) $y''(x^2 - 1) - 2xy' + 2y = (x^2 - 1)^2$.

3. Solve the following problems using the Cauchy–Euler method.

(a) $x^2 y'' - xy' + y = 0$.

(b) $2x^2 y'' - 5xy' + 3y = 0$.

(c) $x^2 y'' - 3xy' + 6y = 0$.

(d) $9 x^2 y'' + 3xy' + y = 0$.

(e) $x^3 y''' + 2x^2 y'' - 10xy' - 8y = 0$.

(f) $x^2 y'' + xy' + y = 4 \cos \ln x$.

(g) $x^2 y'' - 3xy' + 5y = 5x^2$.

4. Solve by any method.

(a) $(x^2 D^2 + xD - 1)y = 0$ given that one solution of the equation is $y = x + \dfrac{1}{x}$.

(b) $(x \sin x + \cos x) y'' - x \cos x y' + y \cos x = 0$, $x \neq 0$ given that $y = x$ is a solution.

(c) Solve the IVP: $(x^2 D^2 + 4xD + 2)y = x \ln x$ given that $y(1) = y'(1) = 0$.

(d) Solve the IVP: $x^2 y'' - xy' + y = x^2$, $x > 0$, $y(1) = 1, y'(1) = 0$.

Chapter 6

Power Series Solutions

6.1 Introduction

The linear differential equations we have studied so far all had *closed form solutions*, that is, their solutions could be expressed in terms of *elementary functions*, viz. exponential, trigonometric (including inverse trigonometric), polynomial, and logarithmic functions. As we know from calculus courses, most such elementary functions have expansions in terms of power series. Some famous functions with their corresponding power series are:

$$e^x = 1 + x + \frac{x^2}{2!} + \ldots = \sum_{n=0}^{\infty} \frac{x^n}{n!},$$

$$\sin x = x - \frac{x^3}{3!} + \frac{x^5}{5!} - \ldots = \sum_{n=0}^{\infty} (-1)^n \frac{x^{2n+1}}{(2n+1)!},$$

$$\cos x = 1 - \frac{x^2}{2!} + \frac{x^4}{4!} - \ldots = \sum_{n=0}^{\infty} (-1)^n \frac{x^{2n}}{(2n)!}.$$

But there are a whole class of functions, called *special functions*, which are not elementary functions and which occur frequently in mathematical physics. They usually satisfy second order homogeneous linear differential equations. These equations can sometimes be solved by discovering a power series that satisfies the differential equation but the solution series may not be summable to an elementary function. In this chapter we study the methods of solution to such equations.

Example 6.1. *Solve the equation*

$$y'' + y = 0 \qquad (6.1)$$

by using the power series method.

Solution: This equation, as we know, has the solution $y = c_1 \cos x + c_2 \sin x$. Let us see how to solve this using power series method. We assume that the solution has a power series of the form

$$y = \sum_{n=0}^{\infty} a_n x^n. \tag{6.2}$$

To solve the equation means to find the coefficients a_n. And in most cases what we really find is a *recurrence relation* between the a_n's, that is, an equation that defines a_n in terms of finitely many previous coefficients a_{n-1}, a_{n-2}, etc.

It is easy to see that

$$y = a_0 + a_1 x + a_2 x^2 + a_3 x^3 + \ldots = \sum_{n=0}^{\infty} a_n x^n,$$

$$y' = a_1 + 2a_2 x + 3a_3 x^2 + 4a_4 x^3 + \ldots = \sum_{n=1}^{\infty} n a_n x^{n-1},$$

$$y'' = 2 \cdot a_2 + 3 \cdot 2 \cdot a_3 x + 4 \cdot 3 \cdot a_4 x^2 + \ldots = \sum_{n=2}^{\infty} n \cdot (n-1) \cdot a_n x^{n-2}.$$

We now substitute this to equation (6.1) to get

$$\sum_{n=2}^{\infty} n \cdot (n-1) \cdot a_n x^{n-2} + \sum_{n=0}^{\infty} a_n x^n = 0. \tag{6.3}$$

The idea is to combine the two summation symbols but that seems difficult since the first series starts from $n = 2$ while the second starts from $n = 0$, and the powers of x are different. *Our aim is to rewrite the summations so that the exponent of x is the same in both.* Since the power of x is n in the second series, we need to modify the first series.

Consider the first series in equation (6.3). We define a new summation index k and set $k = n - 2$. Then $n = k + 2$. Also $n = 2 \Rightarrow k = 0$, so that k now ranges from 0 to ∞. We also change the subscripts of the coefficients (most important step). We then get

$$\sum_{n=2}^{\infty} n \cdot (n-1) \cdot a_n x^{n-2} = \sum_{k=0}^{\infty} (k+2) \cdot (k+1) \cdot a_{k+2}\, x^k$$

$$= 2 \cdot a_2 + 3 \cdot 2 \cdot a_3 x + 4 \cdot 3 \cdot a_4 x^2 + \ldots,$$

Chapter 6. Power Series Solutions 147

and the equality shows that the series still is the same although its summation representation has changed.

We change k back to n since the second series has summation index n and substitute this in (6.3):

$$\sum_{n=0}^{\infty}(n+2)\cdot(n+1)\cdot a_{n+2}\,x^n + \sum_{n=0}^{\infty} a_n x^n$$
$$= \sum_{n=0}^{\infty}\Big\{(n+2)\cdot(n+1)\cdot a_{n+2} + a_n\Big\}x^n = 0. \tag{6.4}$$

Remark 26. When we changed the summation index in the first summation so that the power of x is the same in both summations, the first series started from $k = 0$ as it is in the second. This is purely a coincidence and we will see examples where this is generally not the case.

Since the right hand side of (6.4) is zero, we equate the coefficient of x^n to zero in (6.4) and obtain

$$(n+2)\cdot(n+1)\cdot a_{n+2} + a_n = 0,$$

from which it is immediate that

$$a_{n+2} = -\frac{a_n}{(n+2)(n+1)}, \quad n \geq 0. \tag{6.5}$$

Equation (6.5) is a **recurrence relation** between the coefficients and to "solve" an equation such as (6.5) is to get such a relation. A *recurrence relation* among the values of a sequence (like $\{a_n\}$ here) does not explicitly provide the values of the terms of the sequence. In equation (6.5), a_{n+2} is given in terms of a_n and to compute the latter, one has to know a_{n-2} and so on.

Remark 27. Generally, an explicit formula for a_n in terms of n, is cumbersome and often difficult. For this reason, one often computes the first few terms using the recurrence relation. This is all that is required in most applications.

From (6.5), given a_0 we can find $a_2, a_4, a_6, \ldots$ and given a_1 we can compute $a_3, a_5, a_7, \ldots$ etc., but equation (6.5) does not define a_0 or a_1! These are arbitrary constants (since we have a second order equation). Thus, we quickly get

$$a_2 = (-1)\frac{a_0}{2\cdot 1}$$
$$a_4 = (-1)\frac{a_2}{4\cdot 3} = (-1)^2\frac{a_0}{4\cdot 3\cdot 2\cdot 1}, \quad \text{etc.}$$

and likewise

$$a_3 = (-1)\frac{a_1}{3 \cdot 2}$$
$$a_5 = (-1)\frac{a_3}{5 \cdot 4} = (-1)^2 \frac{a_1}{5 \cdot 4 \cdot 3 \cdot 2}, \quad \text{etc.}$$

In this example it is easy to see that

$$a_{2n} = (-1)^n \frac{a_0}{(2n)!}, \quad a_{2n+1} = (-1)^n \frac{a_1}{(2n+1)!}.$$

Substituting this in (6.2) we finally get

$$y = a_0 \Big\{ \sum_{n=0}^{\infty} (-1)^n \frac{x^{2n}}{(2n)!} \Big\} + a_1 \Big\{ \sum_{n=0}^{\infty} (-1)^n \frac{x^{2n+1}}{(2n+1)!} \Big\}$$

which we recognize as

$$y = a_0 \cos x + a_1 \sin x.$$

This is the essence of the power series method. It essentially consists of assuming a power series expansion for y, computing corresponding series for y', y'', etc., and substituting all these in the given equation. The process of manipulating and shifting the indices is, one must admit, rather tedious work and mistakes are likely. Later in this chapter we consider a more elegant method that dispenses with this drudgery work!

Note: *For the rest of this and the next chapter, we will be concerned with second order homogeneous equations only.*

6.2 Some theory - Analytic functions and ordinary points

Given a function $f(x)$ which is differentiable n times at a point $x = a$, its Taylor polynomial is

$$f(x) = f(a) + (x-a)f'(a) + \frac{(x-a)^2}{2!}f''(a) + \ldots + \frac{(x-a)^n}{n!}f^{(n)}(a) + R(x),$$

where $R(x)$ is called the "error term". If $f(x)$ has derivatives of all orders at $x = a$, and if the error term goes to zero as $n \to \infty$, we get the *Taylor series* of $f(x)$ around $x = a$:

$$f(x) = \sum_{n=0}^{\infty} f^{(n)}(a) \frac{(x-a)^n}{n!}.$$

Chapter 6. Power Series Solutions

A function $f(x)$ that has a Taylor series at $x = a$ is said to be *analytic at $x = a$*. Associated with the Taylor series for f at $x = a$ is a real number $r > 0$ with the following property: The Taylor series for f converges absolutely within the interval $(a - r, a + r)$ and diverges outside. We call r the *radius of convergence*.

In the special case $a = 0$, the Taylor series is often called the *Maclaurin series* which is

$$f(x) = f(0) + xf'(0) + \frac{x^2}{2!}f''(0) + \frac{x^3}{3!}f'''(0) + \ldots = \sum_{n=0}^{\infty} \frac{x^n}{n!} f^{(n)}(0).$$

For many important functions (e.g., $e^x, \sin x, \cos x$), their Maclaurin series converges for all real x. We will mostly be concerned with Maclaurin series only in this chapter.

Given a second order homogeneous linear differential equation,

$$a_0(x)y'' + a_1(x)y' + a_2(x)y = 0, \qquad (6.6)$$

a point $x = a$ is called an *ordinary point* if the two functions

$$P(x) = \frac{a_1(x)}{a_0(x)} \quad \text{and} \quad Q(x) = \frac{a_2(x)}{a_0(x)}$$

are *both* analytic at $x = a$. If $P(x), Q(x)$ are not both analytic at $x = a$, then $x = a$ is called a *singular point*. However, we will only be concerned with ordinary points in this chapter.

Theorem 6.1. *The solution space of (6.6) is a vector space of dimension two. Assume that $x = a$ is an ordinary point of (6.6). Then there are two nontrivial linearly independent solutions f_1 and f_2 of (6.6) of the form*

$$\sum_{n=0}^{\infty} a_n (x - a)^n$$

which converge in some interval $|x - a| < r$, $r > 0$. Any solution of (6.6) is of the form

$$f(x) = c_1 f_1(x) + c_2 f_2(x),$$

where c_1, c_2 are arbitrary constants.

We note that the statement about the dimension of the solution space is from Theorem 3.1. We consider another example.

Example 6.2. *Solve the equation*

$$y'' + xy' + y = 0 \tag{6.7}$$

using the power series method.

Solution: Here $P(x) = x, Q(x) = 1$ and both are analytic everywhere, in particular at the origin. Hence, equation (6.7) has two linearly independent Maclaurin series for its solution. We assume a power series expansion for y as in equation (6.2), and get

$$y = \sum_{n=0}^{\infty} a_n x^n, \quad y' = \sum_{n=1}^{\infty} n a_n x^{n-1}, \quad y'' = \sum_{n=2}^{\infty} n(n-1) a_n x^{n-2}. \tag{6.8}$$

Substituting this in (6.7) one gets

$$\sum_{n=2}^{\infty} n(n-1) a_n x^{n-2} + \sum_{n=1}^{\infty} n a_n x^n + \sum_{n=0}^{\infty} a_n x^n = 0, \tag{6.9}$$

where the power of x in the second series is now n because of the coefficient x for y' in (6.7). Our aim is to combine all this into one sum. As a first step, we want to make sure the power of x is n in all of them. This is the case for the second and third sums, but not in the first.

By making the substitution $k = n - 2$, we get $n = k + 2$. Since n goes from 2 to ∞ it follows that k goes from 0 to ∞. The first sum now becomes

$$\sum_{k=0}^{\infty} (k+2)(k+1) a_{k+2} x^k.$$

For uniformity we change k back to n and substitute back in (6.9) to get

$$\sum_{n=0}^{\infty} (n+2)(n+1) a_{n+2} x^n + \sum_{n=1}^{\infty} n a_n x^n + \sum_{n=0}^{\infty} a_n x^n = 0.$$

Although the power of x is n in all sums now, the second starts from $n = 1$ while the others start from $n = 0$. We take care of this by removing the first term in the first and third sums from the summation symbols. This effectively makes all of them start from $n = 1$. We thus get

$$2 a_2 + a_0 + \sum_{n=1}^{\infty} \left\{ (n+2)(n+1) a_{n+2} + n a_n + a_n \right\} x^n = 0, \tag{6.10}$$

Chapter 6. Power Series Solutions

where the first two terms are terms corresponding to $n = 0$ in the first and third summations.

Since the right hand side of (6.10) is zero, we equate the constant terms and coefficients of x^n, $n \geq 1$ in (6.10) to zero to finally get

$$a_2 = -\frac{1}{2}a_0 \tag{6.11}$$

$$a_{n+2} = -\frac{a_n}{n+2}, \quad n \geq 1. \tag{6.12}$$

Purely by chance, for $n = 0$, the expression (6.12) for a_{n+2} already contains the equation (6.11), so that we might as well write

$$a_{n+2} = -\frac{a_n}{n+2}, \quad n \geq 0. \tag{6.13}$$

Equation (6.13) is the recurrence relation for the coefficients and the main result we are after! From it, by setting $n = 1, 3, 5, \ldots$, we immediately get

$$n = 1, \quad a_3 = -\frac{a_1}{3} = (-1)\frac{a_1}{1 \cdot 3}$$

$$n = 3, \quad a_5 = -\frac{a_3}{5} = (-1)^2\frac{a_1}{5 \cdot 3 \cdot 1}$$

$$n = 5, \quad a_7 = -\frac{a_5}{7} = (-1)^3\frac{a_1}{7 \cdot 5 \cdot 3 \cdot 1}$$

$$\vdots \qquad \vdots$$

$$a_{2n+1} = (-1)^n\frac{a_1}{1 \cdot 3 \cdot 5 \cdots (2n+1)}, \quad n \geq 1. \tag{6.14}$$

Similarly, by taking $n = 2, 4, 6, \ldots$, etc., we get

$$a_2 = (-1)\frac{a_0}{2}$$

$$a_4 = (-1)\frac{a_2}{4} = (-1)^2\frac{a_0}{2 \cdot 4}$$

$$a_6 = (-1)\frac{a_4}{6} = (-1)^3\frac{a_0}{2 \cdot 4 \cdot 6}$$

$$\vdots \qquad \vdots$$

$$a_{2n} = (-1)^n\frac{a_0}{2 \cdot 4 \cdot 6 \cdot 8 \cdots 2n}, \quad n \geq 1. \tag{6.15}$$

Since a_0 and a_1 are not defined, they are arbitrary and independent. By substituting (6.14), (6.15) to (6.2), the final solution is

$$y = a_0 + a_1 x + a_1 \sum_{n=1}^{\infty}(-1)^n \frac{x^{2n+1}}{1 \cdot 3 \cdot 5 \cdot \ldots (2n+1)} + a_0 \sum_{n=1}^{\infty}(-1)^n \frac{x^{2n}}{2 \cdot 4 \cdot 6 \cdot \ldots (2n)},$$

which we can rewrite as

$$y = a_0 \left\{ \sum_{n=0}^{\infty}(-1)^n \frac{x^{2n}}{2 \cdot 4 \cdot 6 \cdot \ldots (2n)} \right\} + a_1 \left\{ \sum_{n=0}^{\infty}(-1)^n \frac{x^{2n+1}}{1 \cdot 3 \cdot 5 \cdot \ldots (2n+1)} \right\}.$$

Remark 28. Notice that the two series inside the braces are the two guaranteed by Theorem 6.1. Most problems are pretty similar to equation (6.7). And the series for y, y', y'' are as in (6.8). Often, y, y', y'' have coefficients which are simple polynomials in x. With such coefficients, the power of x often changes and we adjust this so that they all have the same power of x by manipulating the start value of the summation index. Eventually, we remove the first few terms in one or all so that all the summations start from the same value and have the same power of x.

Example 6.3. *Given the differential equation*

$$(x^2 + 1)y'' + y' = 0,$$

and that y admits a Maclaurin series of the form $y = \sum_{n=0}^{\infty} a_n x^n$, obtain a recurrence relation for the coefficients a_n.

Solution: Here $P(x) = 1/(x^2 + 1), Q(x) = 0$. The origin $x = 0$ is an ordinary point of the given equation. As in the previous examples,

$$y = \sum_{n=0}^{\infty} a_n x^n, \quad y' = \sum_{n=1}^{\infty} n a_n x^{n-1}, \quad y'' = \sum_{n=2}^{\infty} n(n-1) a_n x^{n-2}.$$

Rewriting the given equation as $x^2 y'' + y'' + y' = 0$ and substituting for y', y'' we get

$$\sum_{n=2}^{\infty} n(n-1) a_n x^n + \sum_{n=2}^{\infty} n(n-1) a_n x^{n-2} + \sum_{n=1}^{\infty} n a_n x^{n-1} = 0.$$

We adjust the power of x in second and third summations to be n,

$$\sum_{n=2}^{\infty} n(n-1) a_n x^n + \sum_{n=0}^{\infty} (n+2)(n+1) a_{n+2} x^n + \sum_{n=0}^{\infty} (n+1) a_{n+1} x^n = 0.$$

We make the second and third summations start from $n = 2$ by removing terms corresponding to $n = 0, 1$:

$$\underbrace{(2a_2 + a_1)}_{n=0} + \underbrace{(6a_3 + 2a_2)x}_{n=1} + \sum_{n=2}^{\infty} \left\{ n(n-1)a_n + (n+2)(n+1)a_{n+2} + (n+1)a_{n+1} \right\} x^n = 0.$$

Equating the various powers of x to zero we get

$$2a_2 + a_1 = 0$$
$$3a_3 + a_2 = 0$$
$$n(n-1)a_n + (n+2)(n+1)a_{n+2} + (n+1)a_{n+1} = 0$$

Hence, the recurrence relation sought is

$$a_2 = -\frac{1}{2} a_1$$
$$a_3 = -\frac{1}{3} a_2 = \frac{1}{6} a_1$$
$$a_{n+2} = -\frac{1}{(n+2)} a_{n+1} - \frac{n(n-1)}{(n+2)(n+1)} a_n, \quad n \geq 2 \qquad (6.16)$$

a_0 and a_1 arbitrary .

In (6.16), $n \geq 2$ since this is the lower limit of the summation. You would notice that the relation $3a_3 + a_2 = 0$ is already contained in (6.16). Hence, the limit for n in (6.16) can be changed to $n \geq 1$. But this is coincidental!

Remark 29. The power series method to find the crucial recurrence relation between the various a_n's that is presented here is admittedly cumbersome and laborious. In the next section we look at this from a different point of view and consider a method that avoids manipulations of summation indices, etc. It is very elegant and fast, just like the operator method. In the process we will learn a theorem that has very many uses.

6.3 Relationship between $\{a_n\}$ and $\{f^{(n)}(0)\}$[1]

Given the second order differential equation (6.6), and assuming origin is an ordinary point, it is clear from the previous sections and examples, that the aim of the

---

[1]Much of the material in this section appears in P. K. Subramanian, *Successive Differentiation and Leibniz's Theorem*, The College Mathematical Journal, Vol 35, No. 4, pp 274–282.

power series method is to find a series of the form $y = \sum_{n=0}^{\infty} a_n x^n$ that satisfies the differential equation. We noted that one really finds a recurrence relation satisfied by the coefficients $\{a_n\}$. The series $\sum_{n=0}^{\infty} a_n x^n$ contains only powers of x and hence is the Maclaurin series for $y = f(x)$. In particular, it is assumed that the origin is an ordinary point of (6.6).

We saw in the last section that the Maclaurin series for $y = f(x)$ is of the form $\sum_{n=0}^{\infty} f^{(n)}(0) \frac{x^n}{n!}$. Hence,

$$y = f(x) = \sum_{n=0}^{\infty} a_n x^n \equiv \sum_{n=0}^{\infty} f^{(n)}(0) \frac{x^n}{n!},$$

and comparing the coefficients of x^n in both series, we see that

$$\boxed{a_n = \frac{f^{(n)}(0)}{n!}, \quad f^{(n)}(0) = n!\, a_n} \tag{6.17}$$

Remark 30. A word about notations. The nth derivative of f at the origin, $f^{(n)}(0)$, has many notations in the literature. Some denote this by $y_n(0)$, some others by $y^n(0)$, and many others by $(y_n)_0$. We will dispense with these cumbersome notations, allow ourselves to be sloppy and simply write y_n for $f^{(n)}(x)$, the nth derivative of $y = f(x)$ at any point x, *as well as at the origin*, $f^{(n)}(0)$. This should cause no confusion; the meaning would be quite clear from the context. If an equation containing y_n also involves x, clearly $y_n(x)$ is meant. Otherwise $y_n(0)$.

Using our notation it follows from (6.17) that,

$$\boxed{a_n\, n! = y_n} \tag{6.18}$$

Remark 31. From equation (6.18) it is clear that *to find a recurrence relation between the coefficients* $\{a_n\}$, *it suffices to find a recurrence relation amongst the derivatives at the origin, that is between* $\{y_n\}$.

Example 6.4. *Consider the equation*

$$y'' + y = 0 \tag{6.19}$$

from Example 6.1. Obtain a recurrence relation for the coefficients $\{a_n\}$ *of the solution to* (6.19).
Solution: Using our new notation, we rewrite this as $y_2 + y = 0$. By differentiating

this repeatedly, one gets $y_3 + y_1 = 0$, $y_4 + y_2 = 0, \ldots$ and in general

$$y_{n+2} + y_n = 0. \tag{6.20}$$

Equation (6.20) is the recurrence relation between the y_n's. Using (6.18) we immediately get

$$a_{n+2}(n+2)! + a_n n! = 0.$$

Since $(n+2)! = (n+2)(n+1)n!$, simplification of the last equation yields

$$a_{n+2} = -\frac{a_n}{(n+2)(n+1)}, \tag{6.21}$$

which is the same as (6.5), and we did not have to substitute power series or manipulate coefficients! What are the limits on n? The limit for n is $n \geq 0$ since equation (6.21) for a_{n+2} is valid for all $n \geq 0$. However, (6.21) does not define a_0 or a_1. They are arbitrary.

But not all equations are as simple as (6.1). Consider the equation of Example 6.3,

$$(x^2 + 1)y'' + y' = 0.$$

First of all observe that the given equation itself is a relation between y'' and y'. To get similar relations among higher order derivatives we differentiate the given equation:

$$(x^2 + 1)y_2 + y_1 = 0$$
$$(x^2 + 1)y_3 + (2x + 1)y_2 = 0$$
$$(x^2 + 1)y_4 + (4x + 1)y_3 + 2y_2 = 0.$$

Letting $x = 0$ (remember we need derivatives at the origin), these equations become

$$y_2 + y_1 = 0, \quad y_3 + y_2 = 0, \quad y_4 + y_3 + 2y_2 = 0,$$

etc., but there is no way we can discern any pattern here. The process of differentiating the equations becomes cumbersome as we continue *because of the product term $(x^2 + 1)y''$ in the original equation. What we need is a method for differentiating the product of two functions n-times without having to proceed step by step!* Enter Gottfried Wilhelm Leibniz, the co-inventor of the calculus! With his theorem, we can differentiate the given differential equation n–times. Leibniz's theorem has many applications besides those to differential equations.

6.4 Successive differentiation and Leibniz's Theorem

An unusually powerful theorem, due to Leibniz, shows how to compute derivatives of *any* order n for products of functions! In other words, it is not necessary to compute derivatives of products of functions, one step at a time. For convenience, we use the differential operator D to denote derivatives. In particular D^n denotes the nth derivative.

Theorem 6.2. *(Leibniz) Higher order derivatives of the product of two functions*[2]: *If f and g are functions of x that are differentiable n times, then*

$$D^n(fg) = \binom{n}{0}\{D^n(f)\}\{g\} + \binom{n}{1}\{D^{n-1}(f)\}\{D(g)\} + \binom{n}{2}\{D^{n-2}(f)\}\{D^2(g)\}$$
$$+ \ldots + \binom{n}{n}\{f\}\{D^n(g)\}$$
$$= \sum_{r=0}^{n} \binom{n}{r} (D^{n-r}(f))(D^r(g)).$$

Notice that the theorem resembles the Binomial Theorem for the nth power of the sum of two terms, where the binomial coefficient $\binom{n}{r} = \dfrac{n!}{r!(n-r)!}$. The following observations are important in applying this theorem:

1. In every term, the sum of the orders of the derivatives of f and g is always n.

2. We start with the nth derivative of f and reduce it by one in each successive term. In the last term there is no derivative of f.

3. The formula is symmetrical with respect to f and g, that is, they can be interchanged if we remember that $\binom{n}{r} = \binom{n}{n-r}$.

To appreciate the power of the theorem, let us consider $h(x) = e^x/x$. Although the computation of $h'(x) = e^x(x-1)/x^2$ is straightforward, finding $h''(x)$ and $h'''(x)$ gets laborious. On the other hand we can use Leibniz's theorem. We choose $f(x) =$

---

[2]This theorem is easily proved using mathematical induction.

e^x, $g(x) = 1/x$. This gives

$$h''(x) = \binom{2}{0}(e^x)(1/x) + \binom{2}{1}(e^x)(-1/x^2) + \binom{2}{2}(e^x)(2/x^3)$$
$$= \frac{e^x}{x} - \frac{2e^x}{x^2} + \frac{2e^x}{x^3},$$

where we have used e^x as the first function and $1/x$ as the second function. (The choice of the first function is often dictated by the ease with which its higher derivatives can be computed, and in this case $D^n e^x = e^x$.) Simplified, this yields $h''(x) = e^x(x^2 - 2x + 2)/x^3$.

Likewise,

$$h'''(x) = \binom{3}{0}(e^x)(1/x) + \binom{3}{1}(e^x)(-1/x^2) + \binom{3}{2}(e^x)(2/x^3) + \binom{3}{3}(e^x)(-6/x^4)$$
$$= \frac{e^x}{x} - \frac{3e^x}{x^2} + \frac{6e^x}{x^3} - \frac{6e^x}{x^4}$$

which simplifies to $e^x(x^3 - 3x^2 + 6x - 6)/x^4$.

6.5 Leibniz's Theorem and differential equations

How is Leibniz's Theorem useful in differential equations, in particular finding n^{th} derivative? To understand this, let us see how to find the nth *derivative of the product of two functions*.

Example 6.5. *If*
$$f(x) = x^4 + 1, \quad g(x) = e^x,$$

find the nth derivative of fg.

Solution: By Leibniz's Theorem and noting that

$$g^{(n)} = e^x, \quad f' = 4x^3$$
$$f'' = 12x^2$$
$$f''' = 24x$$
$$f^{(4)} = 24$$
$$f^{(5)} = f^{(6)} = \ldots = f^{(n)} = 0,$$

we have

$$D^n(fg) = \binom{n}{0}(e^x)(x^4+1) + \binom{n}{1}(e^x)(4x^3) + \binom{n}{2}(e^x)(12x^2)$$
$$+ \binom{n}{3}(e^x)(24x) + \binom{n}{4}(e^x)(24)$$
$$= e^x\{(x^4+1) + 4nx^3 + 6n(n-1)x^2$$
$$+ 4n(n-1)(n-2)x + n(n-1)(n-2)(n-3)\}.$$

We consider the equation of Example 6.3 again.

Example 6.6. *Find a power series solution around the origin for the equation*

$$(x^2+1)y'' + y' = 0 \qquad (6.22)$$

using the Leibniz's theorem.

Solution: We rewrite the equation as $(x^2+1)y_2 + y_1 = 0$ and differentiate it n-times term by term.

$$D^n\{(x^2+1)y_2\} = \binom{n}{0}(x^2+1)y_{n+2} + \binom{n}{1}(2x)y_{n+1} + \binom{n}{2}(2)y_n$$
$$D^n\{y_1\} = y_{n+1}.$$

We now have the n-th derivative of the given equation:

$$\binom{n}{0}(x^2+1)y_{n+2} + \binom{n}{1}(2x)y_{n+1} + \binom{n}{2}(2)y_n + y_{n+1} = 0$$

and since we need derivatives at the origin, put $x=0$ in the last equation to get

$$y_{n+2} + y_{n+1} + n(n-1)y_n = 0, \quad n \geq 1.$$

This is the recurrence relation satisfied by y_n's. To get the corresponding relation for a_n, we use (6.18):

$$a_{n+2}(n+2)! + a_{n+1}(n+1)! + n(n-1)a_n n! = 0 \qquad (6.23)$$

from which

$$a_{n+2} = -\frac{1}{(n+2)}a_{n+1} - \frac{n(n-1)}{(n+2)(n+1)}a_n, \quad n \geq 1.$$

and this is the same as (6.16). Again, no infinite series to substitute or coefficients to manipulate! The limits for n are determined by those values for which a_{n+2} is well defined in the last equation; in this case, $n \geq 1$. But then the formula for a_{n+2} above does not define a_2. Remember the given equation itself defines relations between derivatives. We let $x = 0$ in the equation (6.22)! This gives $y_2 = -y_1$ and by (6.18) we get $a_2 = -\frac{1}{2}a_1$. The coefficients a_0 and a_1 are arbitrary.

Example 6.7. *Find the power series solution around the origin for the initial value problem*

$$y'' + xy' + (x^2 + 2)y = 0, \tag{6.24}$$

given that $y(0) = y'(0) = 1$. Find the first six coefficients of the series.

Solution: Rewrite the equation as $y_2 + xy_1 + (x^2 + 2)y = 0$ and differentiate it term by term n–times by Leibniz's theorem to get

$$\{y_{n+2}\} + \left\{\binom{n}{0}y_{n+1}x + \binom{n}{1}y_n(1)\right\}$$
$$+ \left\{\binom{n}{0}(x^2+2)y_n + \binom{n}{1}(2x)y_{n-1} + \binom{n}{2}2y_{n-2}\right\} = 0$$
$$\{y_{n+2}\} + \{xy_{n+1} + ny_n\} + \{(x^2+2)y_n + (n)2xy_{n-1} + n(n-1)y_{n-2}\} = 0.$$

At $x = 0$ this reduces to the recurrence relation

$$y_{n+2} + (n+2)y_n + n(n-1)y_{n-2} = 0.$$

From (6.18) we can translate the last equation to

$$a_{n+2}(n+2)! = -(n+2)n!a_n - n(n-1)(n-2)!a_{n-2},$$

which simplifies to

$$a_{n+2} = -\frac{1}{n+1}a_n - \frac{1}{(n+2)(n+1)}a_{n-2}, \quad n \geq 2. \tag{6.25}$$

The last equation contains a_{n-2} which is meaningful only for $n \geq 2$; hence the limits on n.

We cannot use (6.25) to find a_2 or a_3, but we can use equation (6.24)! First of all, note that the initial conditions $y(0) = y'(0) = 1$ simply mean that $a_0 = a_1 = 1$. Putting $x = 0$ in (6.24),

$$y_2 = -2y \iff 2!a_2 = -2a_0 \iff a_2 = -a_0 = -1.$$

To find a_3, we differentiate (6.24) once to obtain

$$y_3 + xy_2 + y_1 + (x^2+2)y_1 + 2xy = 0$$

and we get immediately (by letting $x = 0$ and use (6.18)) that

$$y_3 = -3\,y_1 \iff 3!\,a_3 = -3\,a_1 \iff a_3 = -\frac{1}{2}a_1 = -\frac{1}{2}.$$

Plugging $n = 2, n = 3$ in (6.25) it is easy to compute $a_4 = \frac{1}{4}$, $a_5 = \frac{3}{40}$, giving the value of the first six coefficients of the series for y. Thus, the solution is given by

$$y = 1 + x - x^2 - \tfrac{1}{2}x^3 + \tfrac{1}{4}x^4 + \tfrac{3}{40}x^5 + \ldots.$$

That is all there is to solving second order linear equations by power series. Leibniz has taken the drudgery out of the computations and even made it fun. Now try doing this problem the long way!

6.6 Exercises

1. Express the series $\sum_{n=2}^{\infty} n(n-1)c_n x^{n-2}$ as a series where the generic term is x^k instead of x^{n-2}.

2. Rewrite $\sum_{n=3}^{\infty} n(n-1)(n-2)x^{n-3}$ so that the power of x is n instead of $n-3$.

3. Are the two series $x^2 \sum_{n=0}^{\infty} n^2(n-2)c_n x^n$ and $\sum_{n=2}^{\infty} (n-2)^2(n-4)c_{n-2}x^n$ the same or different?

4. Consider the equation $y' + y = 0$.

    (a) Solve this equation directly.

    (b) Show that the origin is an ordinary point of this equation.

    (c) Let $y = \sum_{n=0}^{\infty} c_n x^n = c_0 + c_1 x + c_2 x^2 + \ldots + c_n x^n + \ldots$ be a power series solution for the given equation. Write down the power series for y' using sigma notation.

    (d) Rewrite the given equation as the sum of two power series using your answer in part (c).

    (e) Rewrite your answer to part (d) as a single power series. Write down the first several terms.

(f) Using your answer to (e), equate coefficients of x^n on both sides of the equation to zero and express $c_n, n \geq 1$ in terms of c_0. Derive the recurrence relation for the c_n's.

(g) Write down the power series for y. Are your answers to parts (a) and (g) the same?

5. In the following problems prove that the origin is an ordinary point and find a power series solution for y by finding a recurrence relations among the coefficients.

   (a) $y'' + xy' + (2x^2 - 1)y = 0$.

   (b) $y'' + xy' + (3x - 2)y = 0$.

   (c) $y' + 2xy = 0$.

   (d) $2y'' + xy' + y = 0$.

6. Differentiate the function $f(x) = (x+1)^3 \ln(1+x)$ five times using Leibniz's theorem. ($f^5(x) = -6!/(1+x)^2$)

7. Differentiate the equation $(1+x^2)y'' - xy' + xy = 0$ n-times by Leibniz's theorem.

8. Consider the equation $y' + y = 0$ once again and let $y = \sum_{n=0}^{\infty} c_n x^n$. Derive the recurrence relation for the c_n's using Leibnitz's theorem as follows:

   (a) Differentiate the given equation n times.

   (b) Use the formula $c_n n! = y_n$ (equation (6.18)) to rewrite your answer to part (a) in terms of c_n.

   (c) Derive the recurrence relation for the c_n-s from your answer to part (b). Is it the same as the one you obtained in problem 4(f)?

9. Consider $y = \arcsin x$.

   (a) Prove that it satisfies the second order differential equation $(1 - x^2)y'' - xy' = 0$.

   (b) Use part (a) to differentiate the equation n times using Leibniz's rule.

   (c) Use your answer to part (b) to find the recurrence relation satisfied by the coefficients a_n in the power series expansion for $y = \arcsin x$.

   (d) Compute the first three nonzero coefficients in the power series expansion for $y = \arcsin x$.

10. Use Leibniz theorem to find a power series solution for the following equations by finding a recurrence relation between the coefficients.

    (a) $(x^2 + 2)y'' + 2xy' + 3y = 0$ given that $y(0) = 1, y'(0) = 1$.
    (b) $y'' + xy' + (2x^2 - 1)y = 0$.
    (c) $y'' + xy' + (3x - 2)y = 0$.
    (d) $y'' - y' + 2xy = 0$.
    (e) $y' + 2xy = 0$.
    (f) $2y'' + xy' + y = 0$.
    (g) $y'' - xy = 0$. This is called Airy's equation and is important in mathematical physics.

11. Find the recurrence relation and the first four coefficients in the power series solution for $y'' = (x+1)y$.

12. Find the recurrence relation satisfied by the coefficients a_n in the power series solution for $y'' + xy' + y = 0$.

Chapter 7

Systems of Linear Equations

7.1 Introduction

Thus far we have considered solutions of one differential equation at a time. In this chapter we consider a system of two differential equations, with constant coefficients, in which we have an independent variable t and *two* dependent variables $x(t)$ and $y(t)$. A typical example is:

$$\begin{aligned} 2x' - 2y' - 3x &= e^t \\ 2x' + 2y' + 3x + 8y &= e^t, \end{aligned} \quad (7.1)$$

where, for convenience, primes denote derivatives with respect to t. Similarly one could consider a system of three equations in three unknown functions. Such systems occur frequently in mathematical models of biological systems.

7.2 A mathematical model

In Section 2.5, we considered mixture problems involving a storage tank containing a solvent (usually water) with some chemical (usually salt) dissolved in it. The tank had an inlet pipe through which additional solvent (with or without the chemical in it) and an outlet pipe to drain the contents of the tank. An examination of the rate at which additional solvent entered the tank (through the inlet pipe), and the rate at which it drained out of the tank (through the outlet pipe) led us to a first order differential equation.

In this section, we consider a more complicated situation where we have two tanks each with its own inlet and outlet pipes, and additional pipes interconnecting the tanks. Here a consideration of the rate at which solvent enters and leaves a tank gives rise to a linear differential equation. With two tanks, one thus gets two linear differential equations. The two equations taken together form what is called a system of equations.

Two storage tanks A and B, with equal capacity of C liters, are full with brine and are connected to each other. See Figure 7.1. Fluid can be pumped to each other as well as out of the tanks. Initially tank A contains 5 kg of salt (in C liters), whereas tank B contains 2 kg of salt. At time $t = 0$, pure water flows into A (from outside) at 6 li/m (liters per minute), brine flows from A to B at 8 li/m, brine is pumped *back from B into A* at 2 li/m, and finally brine is pumped out of B at 6 li/m. The problem is to determine the amount of salt in each tank at any given time t.

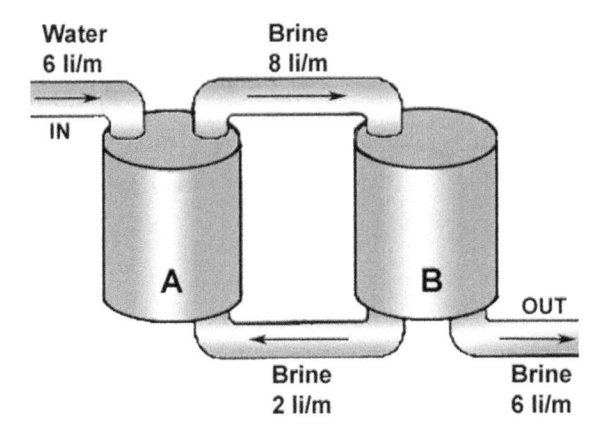

Figure 7.1: Two-tanks model

At any given time t, tank A gets 6 li/m water from outside, 2 li/m brine from B and pumps out 8 li/m to tank B. Hence, it still has C liters of solution at all time. On the other hand, tank B gets 8 li/m brine from A and pumps out 2 li/m to tank A and 6 li/m outside. Thus, tank B also maintains C liters of fluid at all time in it. Let x and y be the amount of salt at time t in tanks A and B, respectively. The concentration of salt in A is x/C kg/li at time t (since A has C liters of fluid at any time t) and the concentration in B is y/C kg/li.

Consider tank A. The only brine coming is from B, *at the rate* of 2 li/m with concentration y/C kg/li, so that salt enters A *at the rate* of $2y/C$ kg/m. Similarly, the amount of salt leaving A to be pumped to B is $8x/C$ kg/m. Thus, the *rate* at which the amount of salt changes in A ($dx/dt = x'$) is its *input rate – output rate* and is therefore given by the equation,

$$x' = \frac{2y}{C} - \frac{8x}{C}$$

and similarly for tank B,

$$y' = \frac{8x}{C} - \frac{8y}{C}.$$

This is a system of two linear equations with constant coefficients and the solution of this system provides $x(t)$ and $y(t)$.

7.3 How do we solve such a system?

Different authors use different notations, the method of undetermined coefficients, and high powered linear algebra (matrices, eigenvalues, etc.,), but we will consistently use our friend the operator D and where possible use the operator method to find particular solutions. Let us consider the simultaneous system (7.1) again.

Example 7.1. *Solve the system of equations* (7.1).
Solution: Using the operator D we can rewrite this system as

$$\begin{aligned}(2D-3)x - 2Dy &= e^t \\ (2D+3)x + (2D+8)y &= e^t,\end{aligned} \qquad (7.2)$$

which is of the form

$$\begin{aligned}p_1(D)x + p_2(D)y &= g_1 \\ p_3(D)x + p_4(D)y &= g_2,\end{aligned} \qquad (7.3)$$

where $p_i(D)$ are first degree polynomials in D with constant coefficients, and g_i are functions of t. We can eliminate y (or x, whichever is convenient) by operating on the first equation in (7.3) by p_4, the second by p_2 (remember these operators are polynomials in D and commute) and subtract to get

$$(p_1(D)p_4(D) - p_2(D)p_3(D))x = p_4(D)g_1 - p_2(D)g_2. \qquad (7.4)$$

Using matrix determinant, this is easier to remember as:

$$\begin{vmatrix} p_1(D) & p_2(D) \\ p_3(D) & p_4(D) \end{vmatrix} x = - \begin{vmatrix} p_2(D) & g_1 \\ p_4(D) & g_2 \end{vmatrix}. \qquad (7.5)$$

Had we eliminated x instead of y we would have obtained

$$\begin{vmatrix} p_1(D) & p_2(D) \\ p_3(D) & p_4(D) \end{vmatrix} y = \begin{vmatrix} p_1(D) & g_1 \\ p_3(D) & g_2 \end{vmatrix}. \tag{7.6}$$

In equations (7.5) and (7.6) the determinant on the left hand side is the same. On the right, the first column of the determinant is simply the coefficients of y (the variable that is being eliminated) for equation (7.5), and that of x in equation (7.6). These would be very useful later. *Note that there is no negative sign on the right hand side in equation (7.6) when we eliminate x.*

Theorem 7.1. *The number of arbitrary constants in the solution of the system of equations (7.3) equals the order of*

$$\begin{vmatrix} p_1(D) & p_2(D) \\ p_3(D) & p_4(D) \end{vmatrix} = p_1(D)p_4(D) - p_2(D)p_3(D)$$

provided this is not zero. If this is zero but the right hand side of (7.4) is non-zero, there is no solution. If the right side of (7.4) is also zero, there are infinitely many solutions with $x(t)$ arbitrary and $y(t)$ is determined by one of the system equations.

Since p_i are all first degree polynomials, the order of the determinant is usually two, and there are two constants in the solution of equation (7.3). But this is not always the case! The order can be one sometimes. We will see examples later.

Let us solve equation (7.2) by eliminating y. Substituting in equation (7.5) we get

$$\begin{vmatrix} 2D-3 & -2D \\ 2D+3 & 2D+8 \end{vmatrix} x = -\begin{vmatrix} -2D & e^t \\ 2D+8 & e^t \end{vmatrix}, \tag{7.7}$$

which gives us

$$\{(2D-3)(2D+8) - (-2D)(2D+3)\} x = -\{(-2D)e^t - (2D+8)e^t\}$$
$$(8D^2 + 16D - 24)x = 4De^t + 8e^t$$
$$(D^2 + 2D - 3)x = \tfrac{3}{2}e^t. \tag{7.8}$$

Equation (7.8) is linear of second degree and there should be two constants in its solution. Using our usual methods we obtain

$$x = \underbrace{c_1 e^{-3t} + c_2 e^t}_{x_c} + \underbrace{\tfrac{3}{8} t e^t}_{x_p}, \tag{7.9}$$

Chapter 7. Systems of Linear Equations

where x_c and x_p are the complementary and particular solutions, respectively, and c_1, c_2 are the only arbitrary constants.

We could find y the same way to first obtain the determinant equation

$$\begin{vmatrix} 2D-3 & -2D \\ 2D+3 & 2D+8 \end{vmatrix} y = \begin{vmatrix} 2D-3 & e^t \\ 2D+3 & e^t \end{vmatrix}, \qquad (7.10)$$

and after simplification get the equation

$$(D^2 + 2D - 3)y = -\tfrac{3}{4}e^t, \qquad (7.11)$$

etc. But we would be duplicating our efforts and furthermore, since there are only two constants for this system (Theorem 7.1) and they already appear in the solution of x, *there can be no other arbitrary constants in the solution of y*. We should exploit the fact we have a system of equations and determine y from the system just as we do in basic algebra. Indeed, if we add the two equations in (7.1),

$$4x' + 8y = 2e^t,$$

that is,

$$\begin{aligned} y &= \tfrac{1}{4}e^t - \tfrac{1}{2}x' \\ &= \tfrac{1}{4}e^t - \tfrac{1}{2}\bigl\{ -3c_1 e^{-3t} + c_2 e^t + \tfrac{3}{8}te^t + \tfrac{3}{8}e^t \bigr\} \\ &= \tfrac{3}{2}c_1 e^{-3t} - \tfrac{1}{2}c_2 e^t - \tfrac{3}{16}te^t + \tfrac{1}{16}e^t. \end{aligned}$$

7.4 Pathologies - When things don't go according to plan

One needs to be careful in using the determinant notation (equations (7.5) or (7.6)). It is possible that entries in one of the columns may be *identical*! This has several implications.

1. *An attempt to eliminate y often eliminates y' and the resulting equation is of first order, not of order 2. Similarly for x.*
2. *x and y are independent.*
3. *x (as well as y) is the solution of a linear first order equation with a single constant.*

So what do we do? Consider the following example.

Example 7.2. *Solve*
$$2x' + y' - x - y = -2t,$$
$$x' + y' + x - y = t^2. \tag{7.12}$$

Solution: We rewrite the given equations using the operator D:

$$(2D - 1)x + (D - 1)y = -2t$$
$$(D + 1)x + (D - 1)y = t^2.$$

In determinant form this is

$$\begin{vmatrix} 2D - 1 & D - 1 \\ D + 1 & D - 1 \end{vmatrix} x = - \begin{vmatrix} D - 1 & -2t \\ D - 1 & t^2 \end{vmatrix}, \tag{7.13}$$

which we can write as

$$\{(2D - 1)(D - 1) - (D + 1)(D - 1)\} x = -\{(D - 1)t^2 - (D - 1)(-2t)\}, \tag{7.14}$$

or

$$(D - 1)\{(2D - 1) - (D + 1)\} x = (D - 1)\{-t^2 - 2t\}. \tag{7.15}$$

First of all note that the factor $(D-1)$ on both sides of (7.15). This occurs because the entries in the second column on the left (and the first column on the right) in equation (7.13) both containing coefficients of y, *are identical*. This is usually a tell-tale sign that warns us not to use determinants to eliminate y (or x).

If we now proceed blindly to find the complementary solution x_c we would be dealing with the equation

$$(D - 1)\{(2D - 1) - (D + 1)\} x = 0.$$

However, $(D-1)$ is an extraneous factor and this introduces an additional extraneous solution $c_1 e^t$ corresponding to $(D-1)x = 0$ in x_c. Instead of using (7.15) then, we simply use elementary methods to eliminate y (and y')! In (7.12), we subtract the second equation from the first to get

$$x' - 2x = -2t - t^2,$$

that is,

$$(D - 2)x = -2t - t^2,$$

Chapter 7. Systems of Linear Equations   169

which is a first order equation in x as we suspected earlier (one could also get to this equation by canceling the extraneous factor $(D-1)$ in (7.15) provided one looks for the common factor on both sides). Hence,

$$\begin{aligned} x &= c_1 e^{2t} + \frac{1}{D-2}(-2t - t^2) \\ &= c_1 e^{2t} + \frac{1}{2}\frac{1}{1-\frac{D}{2}}(2t + t^2) \\ &= c_1 e^{2t} + \frac{1}{2}\left(1 + \frac{D}{2} + \frac{D^2}{4}\right)(2t + t^2) \\ &= \underbrace{c_1 e^{2t}}_{x_c} + \underbrace{\frac{1}{2}(t^2 + 3t + \frac{3}{2})}_{x_p}. \end{aligned}$$

We have used the operator method to find the particular solution, but the method of undetermined coefficients would have been quicker.

Remark 32. Note that x has only one arbitrary constant.

Remark 33. The factor $(D-1)$ in equation (7.15) affects only x_c, but not x_p. This is because from (7.15),

$$\begin{aligned} x_p &= \frac{1}{(D-1)\{(2D-1)-(D+1)\}}\{(D-1)(-t^2 - 2t)\} \\ &= \frac{1}{(2D-1)-(D+1)}\{-t^2 - 2t\} \end{aligned}$$

and the additional factor $(D-1)$ cancels out!

We continue to find y by eliminating x' in (7.12) to get

$$y' + 3x - y = 2t^2 + 2t.$$

Hence,

$$\begin{aligned} (D-1)y &= 2t^2 + 2t' - 3x \\ &= -3c_1 e^{2t} + \frac{1}{2}t^2 - \frac{5}{2}t - \frac{9}{4} \end{aligned}$$

after simplification. Hence

$$\begin{aligned} y &= c_2 e^t + \frac{1}{D-1}\left\{-3c_1 e^{2t} + \frac{1}{4}(2t^2 - 10t - 9)\right\} \\ &= c_2 e^t - 3c_1 e^{2t} - (1 + D + D^2)\{\tfrac{1}{4}(2t^2 - 10t - 9)\} \\ &= c_2 e^t - 3c_1 e^{2t} - \tfrac{1}{4}(2t^2 - 6t - 15). \end{aligned}$$

Remark 34. Although there are two constants in the solution of y, only c_2 is arbitrary.

In dealing with system of equations then, it is wise to check if the variables x and y are independent before proceeding with evaluating the determinant in (7.5) when we attempt to solve for x. But this would be self evident in when one examines this determinant. The entries in the second column on the left hand side (and the first column on the right) are identical. In that case one could do what we did in the last example. Alternately, one could eliminate x and solve for y (equation (7.6)). Indeed, in the last problem, there are no extraneous factors:

$$\begin{vmatrix} 2D-1 & D-1 \\ D+1 & D-1 \end{vmatrix} y = - \begin{vmatrix} 2D-1 & -2t \\ D+1 & t^2 \end{vmatrix}. \tag{7.16}$$

Although $(D-1)$ is a common factor on the left hand side, just like in (7.15), it does not occur on the right, and we do get a second order differential equation for y. We could proceed as we did in the Example 7.1 but obviously this involves much more labor!

Example 7.3. *Solve the system of equations*

$$2x' - x + y' - y = t,$$
$$2x' + 2x + y' + 2y = t^2.$$

Solution: Using the operator D and writing the equations in determinant form,

$$\begin{vmatrix} 2D-1 & D-1 \\ 2(D+1) & D+2 \end{vmatrix} x = - \begin{vmatrix} D-1 & t \\ D+2 & t^2 \end{vmatrix},$$

that is,

$$3Dx = t^2 + 1. \tag{7.17}$$

It follows that the left hand side of (7.17) is of degree 1, hence there is only one arbitrary constant. Solving the last equation we get

$$x = \tfrac{1}{9}t^3 + \tfrac{1}{3}t + c_1.$$

If we subtract the top equation from the bottom in the given system we get

$$3x + 3y = t^2 - t,$$

from which
$$3y = t^2 - t - \tfrac{1}{3}t^3 - t - 3c_1,$$
that is,
$$y = -\tfrac{1}{9}t^3 + \tfrac{1}{3}t^2 - \tfrac{2}{3}t - c_1.$$
Thus,
$$x = \tfrac{1}{9}t^3 + \tfrac{1}{3}t + c_1, \quad y = -\tfrac{1}{9}t^3 + \tfrac{1}{3}t^2 - \tfrac{2}{3}t - c_1.$$

7.5 Exercises

1. Assume that primes denote derivatives with respect to t and $D \equiv \tfrac{d}{dt}$. Rewrite the system of equations
$$2x' - 3x + y' + 4y = 1$$
$$x' - y' = t + 1$$
using D.

2. Write the system of equations
$$2Dx + 3x - 2Dy = e^t$$
$$2Dx - 3x + 2Dy + 8y = e^t$$
in the form
$$p_1(D)x + p_2(D)y = e^t$$
$$p_3(D)x + p_4(D)y = e^t,$$
where p_1, p_2, p_3, p_4 are polynomials in D.

3. Compute the order of the system of equations
$$(D - 1)x + (2D - 3)y = \sin t$$
$$(D + 1)x - Dy = \cos t$$

4. Find the number of arbitrary constants in the solution of the system of equa-

tions

$$x' - x + y' - y = t$$
$$2x' + 2x + 2y' - y = 0$$

5. Solve the following systems of equations:

   (a) $x' = y$
   $y' = -x + 2y$

   (b) $x' + y' - 2x - 4y = e^{4t}$
   $x' + y' - y = e^{4t}$

   (c) $5x' + y' - 3x + y = 0$
   $4x' + y' - 3x = -t$

   (d) $x' + y' - x - 4y = e^t$
   $x' + y' + x = e^{3t}$

   (e) $x' + y' + y = \sin t$
   $x' + y' - x - y = 0$

   (f) $5x' + y' - 5x - y = 0$
   $4x' + y' - 3x = t$

   (g) $x' + y' - x - 6y = e^{2t}$
   $x' + 2y' - 2x - 6y = t$

   (h) $3x' + 2y' - x + y = t - 3$
   $x' + y' - x = t + 1$

   (i) $2x' + y' + x + 5y = 4t$
   $x' + y' + 2x + 2y = 2t$

   (j) $2x' + y' - x - y = 2e^t$
   $x' + y' + x - y = e^t$

   (k) $2x' + y' - x - y = 0$
   $x' + y' + 2x - y = t$

   (l) $x' = x + 3y$
   $y' = 3x + y$

   (m) $x'' + y' - x + y = \sin t$
   $y'' + x' - x + y = \cos t$

   (n) $x' + 2x - 3y = t$
   $y' - 3x + 2y = e^{2t}$

(o) $x'' - 3x - 4y = 0$
$y'' + y + x = 0$

(p) $3x - 3x' + 4y = 3t + 1$
$3y' + 3y + 2x = e^t$

(q) $x' + 8x + 2y' + y = 0$
$6x' - 2x - 3y' + 11y = 0$

Chapter 8

The Laplace Transform

8.1 Introduction

In this chapter we will discuss another technique, called the *Laplace transform*, that is especially useful in solving initial value problems. The Laplace transform, as the name suggests, takes a function f and turns it into another function F. In engineering-related areas, such as signal processing and control system, one can see $f(t)$ as a function in "time" domain, and $F(s)$ as the equivalent function in "frequency" domain. For our purposes in relation to differential equation, the Laplace transform converts a linear differential equation into an algebraic equation, which in general is easier to solve. Applying the inverse mapping (*inverse transform*) to the solution of the algebraic equation then gives us the solution to the differential equation.

Definition 8.1. *Let f be a real-valued function in real variable t defined for $t > 0$. The **Laplace transform** F of f is the function*

$$F(s) = \mathcal{L}\{f(t)\} := \int_0^\infty e^{-st} f(t) dt, \tag{8.1}$$

provided that the limit exists.

Notice that (8.1) is an improper integral and it is computed as the limit

$$\int_0^\infty e^{-st} f(t) dt = \lim_{R \to \infty} \int_0^R e^{-st} f(t) dt.$$

Let us consider the following examples.

Example 8.1. *Find the Laplace transform of $f(t) = t$, $t \geq 0$.*

Solution: Using Definition 8.1 and integration by parts,

$$\mathcal{L}\{f(t)\} = \int_0^\infty te^{-st}dt$$

$$= \lim_{R\to\infty} \int_0^R te^{-st}dt$$

$$= \lim_{R\to\infty} \left. -\frac{t}{s}e^{-st} - \frac{1}{s^2}e^{-st}\right|_0^R$$

$$= \lim_{R\to\infty} \left(-\frac{R}{s}e^{-sR} - \frac{1}{s^2}e^{-sR}\right) - \left(0 - \frac{1}{s^2}\right)$$

$$= \frac{1}{s^2}, \quad \text{for } s > 0.$$

Note that when $s \leq 0$, the integral diverges.

Example 8.2. *Let $f(t) = e^{at}$, where a is a constant and $t > 0$. Find $\mathcal{L}\{f(t)\}$.*

Solution: Again by Definition 8.1, we have

$$\mathcal{L}\{f(t)\} = \int_0^\infty e^{-st}e^{at}dt$$

$$= \lim_{R\to\infty} \int_0^R e^{(a-s)t}dt$$

$$= \lim_{R\to\infty} \left. \frac{e^{(a-s)t}}{a-s}\right|_0^R$$

$$= \lim_{R\to\infty} \frac{e^{(a-s)R}}{a-s} - \frac{1}{a-s}$$

$$= \frac{1}{s-a}, \quad \text{for } s > a.$$

Notice that if $s \leq a$, then the integral diverges.

From the above example, it follows easily that

$$\mathcal{L}(1) = \mathcal{L}(e^{0t}) = \frac{1}{s}, \ s > 0. \tag{8.2}$$

Example 8.3. *Compute the Laplace transform of the function*

$$u_a(t) = \begin{cases} 0, & t < a \\ 1, & t \geq a, \end{cases}$$

where $a \geq 0$ is a constant. This function is called a unit step function (often also called the Heaviside function). We reserve the notation $u_a(t)$ to denote the unit step function with jump discontinuity at $t = a$.

Solution: Using the same definition, it easily follows that

$$\mathcal{L}\{u_a(t)\} = \int_0^\infty e^{-st} u_a(t) dt$$
$$= \int_a^\infty e^{-st} dt$$
$$= \lim_{R\to\infty} \frac{-e^{-st}}{s}\Big|_a^R$$
$$= \frac{e^{-as}}{s}, \quad s > 0.$$

$f(t)$	$\mathcal{L}\{f(t)\}$
c	$\dfrac{c}{s}$
e^{at}	$\dfrac{1}{s-a}$
t^n, $n = 1, 2, \ldots$	$\dfrac{n!}{s^{n+1}}$
u_a	$\dfrac{e^{-as}}{s}$
$\sin at$	$\dfrac{a}{s^2 + a^2}$
$\cos at$	$\dfrac{s}{s^2 + a^2}$
$\sinh at$	$\dfrac{a}{s^2 - a^2}$
$\cosh at$	$\dfrac{s}{s^2 - a^2}$

Table 8.1: Brief list of Laplace transform of some elementary functions

8.2 Properties of Laplace transform

Not every function has a Laplace transform. The existence of transform is determined by whether or not the improper integral (8.1) converges. The following theorem states the criteria that a function must have to ensure the existence of the Laplace transform.

Theorem 8.1. *(Existence and Uniqueness) Let $f(t)$ be a function that is **piecewise continuous** on the interval $[0, \infty)$ and of **exponential order** c. Then its*

Laplace transform $\mathcal{L}\{f\}(s)$ exists for $s > c$. Moreover, suppose $g(t)$ is another function satisfying the same condition and that there exists another constant C for which $\mathcal{L}\{f\}(s) = \mathcal{L}\{g\}(s)$ for all $s > C$. Then $f(t) = g(t)$ for all $t \in [0, \infty)$.

Recall that a piecewise continuous function is one that is continuous at every point in the interval, except possibly at a finite number of points where it has a jump discontinuity. A function is of exponential order c if it does not grow faster than the exponential function e^{ct}, that is,

$$|f(t)| \leq Ke^{ct}, \quad \text{for all } t \geq T,$$

where K and T are constants. It follows that an easy way to check whether a function is of exponential order is by computing the limit

$$\lim_{t\to\infty} \frac{f(t)}{e^{ct}}.$$

If the limit exists and is finite, then $f(t)$ is of exponential order.

The function $f(t) = 3e^{2t}\cos t$ is continuous and of exponential order 2 with $K = 3$ since $|3e^{2t}\cos t| = 3|e^{2t}| \cdot |\cos t| \leq 3e^{2t}$. Hence, it has a Laplace transform. On the other hand, the Laplace transform for the function $f(t) = e^{t^2}$ does not exist since for any c,

$$\lim_{t\to\infty} \frac{e^{t^2}}{e^{ct}} = \lim_{t\to\infty} e^{t(t-c)} = \infty,$$

which shows that e^{t^2} is not of exponential order.

Fortunately, most functions that occur in applications involving linear differential equations with constant coefficients are usually (piecewise) continuous and of exponential order.

There are several important properties of Laplace transform that are crucial for our work from now on. The first one is **linearity**, which is given by the following theorem:

Theorem 8.2. *Let f_1, f_2 be functions for which $\mathcal{L}\{f_1\}, \mathcal{L}\{f_2\}$ exist, and c_1, c_2 be arbitrary constants. Then*

$$\boxed{\mathcal{L}\{c_1 f_1(t) + c_2 f_2(t)\} = c_1 \mathcal{L}\{f_1(t)\} + c_2 \mathcal{L}\{f_2(t)\}}. \tag{8.3}$$

Proof: The proof is quite straightforward. By linearity properties of the integral, we get

$$\mathcal{L}\{c_1 f_1(t) + c_2 f_2(t)\} = \int_0^\infty e^{-st}[c_1 f_1(t) + c_2 f_2(t)]dt$$
$$= c_1 \int_0^\infty e^{-st} f_1(t)dt + c_2 \int_0^\infty e^{-st} f_2(t)dt$$
$$= c_1 \mathcal{L}\{f_1(t)\} + c_2 \mathcal{L}\{f_2(t)\}. \quad \square$$

Example 8.4. *Compute the Laplace transform* $\mathcal{L}\{\sin^2 at\}$.
Solution: Using the half-angle identity $\sin^2 at = \frac{1}{2} - \frac{1}{2}\cos 2at$ and the linearity property, we have

$$\mathcal{L}\{\sin^2 at\} = \mathcal{L}\left\{\frac{1}{2}\right\} - \mathcal{L}\left\{\frac{1}{2}\cos 2at\right\}$$
$$= \frac{1}{2}\mathcal{L}\{1\} - \frac{1}{2}\mathcal{L}\{\cos 2at\}$$
$$= \left(\frac{1}{2} \cdot \frac{1}{s}\right) - \left(\frac{1}{2} \cdot \frac{s}{s^2 + (2a)^2}\right)$$
$$= \frac{2a^2}{s(s^2 + 4a^2)}.$$

The second property comes from a quick observation that

$$\int_0^\infty e^{-st} e^{at} f(t)dt = \int_0^\infty e^{-(s-a)} f(t)dt,$$

which tells us

$$\boxed{\mathcal{L}\{e^{at} f(t)\} = F(s-a)}. \tag{8.4}$$

This property is often called the **translation** property.

The next property deals with Laplace transform of the derivative $\mathcal{L}\{f'\}$, which exists if f' satisfies the existence condition given in Theorem 8.1 (with f replaced with f' in the statement of the theorem). If that is the case, then by Definition 8.1

$$\mathcal{L}\{f'\} = \int_0^\infty e^{-st} f'(t)dt = \lim_{R \to \infty} \int_0^R e^{-st} f'(t)dt.$$

Using integration by parts with $u = e^{-st}$ and $dv = f'(t)dt$, we have

$$\lim_{R\to\infty} \left[e^{-st}f(t)\Big|_0^R + \int_0^R sf(t)e^{-st}dt\right]$$
$$= \lim_{R\to\infty} \left[\frac{f(R)}{e^{sR}} - f(0) + s\int_0^R f(t)e^{-st}dt\right].$$

Note that the first term goes to 0 since $f(t)$ is of exponential order, giving us the formula

$$\boxed{\mathcal{L}\{f'\} = s\mathcal{L}\{f\} - f(0)}. \tag{8.5}$$

From the above formula, one can recursively obtain the formula for the second order derivatives, of course assuming that f, f' are continuous and f'' is piecewise continuous, and all of them are of exponential order.

$$\mathcal{L}\{f''\} = s\mathcal{L}\{f'\} - f'(0)$$
$$= s[s\mathcal{L}\{f\} - f(0)] - f'(0)$$
$$= s^2\mathcal{L}\{f\} - sf(0) - f'(0).$$

The Laplace transform for higher order derivatives can be derived in a similar fashion.

Example 8.5. *Find the Laplace transform of the equation*

$$f''(t) - 6f'(t) + 5f(t) = 0 \tag{8.6}$$

with initial conditions $f(0) = 3$ and $f'(0) = 7$.

Solution: Applying Laplace transform on both sides of the equation and its linearity property, we have

$$\mathcal{L}\{f''\} - 6\mathcal{L}\{f'\} + 5\mathcal{L}\{f\} = 0$$
$$[s^2\mathcal{L}\{f\} - sf(0) - f'(0)] - 6[s\mathcal{L}\{f\} - f(0)] + 5\mathcal{L}\{f\} = 0 \tag{8.7}$$
$$(s^2 - 6s + 5)\mathcal{L}\{f\} - (s - 6)f(0) - f'(0) = 0.$$

Substituting the initial values $f(0) = 3, f'(0) = 7$ gives us

$$\mathcal{L}\{f\} = \frac{3s - 11}{s^2 - 6s + 5}. \tag{8.8}$$

8.3 The inverse transform

The last example in the previous section shows us how Laplace transform converts a differential equation (8.6) into an algebraic equation (8.7), which can be easily solved to get (8.8). The next question is, given $\mathcal{L}\{f\}$, how can we obtain the solution to the original differential equation, which is f? Obviously, we seek an *inverse mapping* for the Laplace transform. From Theorem 8.1, it follows that such inverse, denoted by $\mathcal{L}^{-1}$, exists and is unique, and

$$\mathcal{L}^{-1}\{F(s)\} = \mathcal{L}^{-1}\{\mathcal{L}\{f(t)\}\} = f(t)$$

as is expected.

The inverse Laplace transform is formally defined in terms of complex integral (also known as *Fourier-Mellin integral*). However, it is beyond the scope of this book and for problems involving inverse transform in this chapter, we will use Table 8.1, together with algebraic techniques, such as partial fractions. The linearity property of the inverse transform follows naturally from the linearity of the Laplace transform itself, and is often very useful.

Example 8.6. *Find the inverse Laplace transform of* $F(s) = \dfrac{1}{s+3}$.

Solution: From Table 8.1, it is clear that

$$\mathcal{L}^{-1}\left\{\frac{1}{s+3}\right\} = \mathcal{L}^{-1}\left\{\frac{1}{s-(-3)}\right\} = e^{-3t}.$$

Example 8.7. *Compute the inverse Laplace transform*

$$\mathcal{L}^{-1}\left\{\frac{s+1}{s^2-9}\right\}.$$

Solution: Note that

$$\begin{aligned}\mathcal{L}^{-1}\left\{\frac{s+1}{s^2-9}\right\} &= \mathcal{L}^{-1}\left\{\frac{s}{s^2-9}\right\} + \mathcal{L}^{-1}\left\{\frac{1}{s^2-9}\right\} \\ &= \cosh 3t + \mathcal{L}^{-1}\left\{\frac{1}{3}\frac{3}{s^2-9}\right\} \\ &= \cosh 3t + \frac{1}{3}\sinh 3t.\end{aligned}$$

Example 8.8. *Find the inverse Laplace transform of*

$$F(s) = \frac{1}{s^2 + 6s + 13}.$$

Solution: We approach this problem by first completing the square.

$$\frac{1}{s^2 + 6s + 13} = \frac{1}{(s^2 + 6s + 9) + 4}$$
$$= \frac{1}{(s+3)^2 + 2^2}$$
$$= \frac{1}{2} \frac{2}{(s-(-3))^2 + 2^2}.$$

From Table 8.1 and by translation property (8.4),

$$\frac{1}{2} \frac{2}{(s-(-3))^2 + 2^2} = \frac{1}{2} F(s-(-3)) = \frac{1}{2} \mathcal{L}\left\{e^{-3t} \sin 2t\right\},$$

which follows that

$$\mathcal{L}^{-1}\left\{\frac{1}{2} \frac{2}{(s-(-3))^2 + 2^2}\right\} = \frac{1}{2} e^{-3t} \sin 2t.$$

8.4 Solving initial value problems

Our goal now is to use the Laplace transform and inverse transform to solve initial value problems for linear differential equations with constant coefficients. We have learned several techniques for this in Chapters 3 and 4. Those methods require us to first find the general solution to the equation, and then by using the given initial conditions, we find the desired solution. However, with Laplace transform, finding a general solution is not needed. We return to Example 8.5 to illustrate this method.

Example 8.9. *In Example 8.5, we found the Laplace transform*

$$F(s) = \mathcal{L}\{f\} = \frac{3s - 11}{s^2 - 6s + 5}$$

to the equation $f''(t) - 6f'(t) + 5f(t) = 0$. Compute the inverse transform and verify that it is the solution to the given equation.

Chapter 8. The Laplace Transform

Solution: We first rewrite $F(s)$ as partial fractions

$$\frac{3s-11}{s^2-6s+5} = \frac{A}{s-5} + \frac{B}{s-1},$$

which gives us the equation

$$3s - 11 = A(s-1) + B(s-5).$$

By substituting appropriate values for s, we find $A = 1$ and $B = 2$. Thus by linearity,

$$\mathcal{L}^{-1}\left\{\frac{3s-11}{s^2-6s+5}\right\} = \mathcal{L}^{-1}\left\{\frac{1}{s-5}\right\} + \mathcal{L}^{-1}\left\{\frac{2}{s-1}\right\}$$
$$= e^{5t} + 2e^t.$$

Verifying that $f(t) = e^{5t} + 2e^t$ is indeed the solution to the differential equation is easy. Since

$$f'(t) = 5e^{5t} + 2e^t \text{ and } f''(t) = 25e^{5t} + 2e^t,$$

clearly

$$f''(t) - 6f'(t) + 5f(t) = 25e^{5t} + 2e^t - 6(5e^{5t} + 2e^t) + 5(e^{5t} + 2e^t) = 0$$
$$f(0) = 3 \text{ and } f'(0) = 7.$$

In the next example, we will show how we solve a linear differential equation that involves discontinuous function using Laplace transform. Many physical problems is often modeled using discontinuous applications. Some examples are the on/off switching of electrical circuit, signaling pulse, or the sudden invasion of a species to an existing population. It may not be so convenient to solve a differential equation with discontinuity using methods in Chapters 3 and 4. Laplace transform provides a tool to deal with it.

Example 8.10. *Solve the initial value problem*

$$\frac{dy}{dt} = -3y + u_2(t), \ y(0) = -2,$$

where

$$u_2(t) = \begin{cases} 0 & t < 2 \\ 1 & t \geq 2 \end{cases}$$

is the unit step function with jump discontinuity at $t = 2$.

Solution: Taking Laplace transform on both sides of the equation we get

$$\mathcal{L}\left\{\frac{dy}{dt}\right\} = -3\mathcal{L}\{y\} + \mathcal{L}\{u_2\}$$

$$s\mathcal{L}\{y\} - y(0) = -3\mathcal{L}\{y\} + \frac{e^{-2s}}{s}$$

$$(s+3)\mathcal{L}\{y\} = -2 + \frac{e^{-2s}}{s}$$

$$\mathcal{L}\{y\} = \frac{-2}{s+3} + \frac{e^{-2s}}{s(s+3)}.$$

Now we take the inverse transform to get

$$y = \mathcal{L}^{-1}\left\{\frac{-2}{s+3}\right\} + \mathcal{L}^{-1}\left\{\frac{e^{-2s}}{s(s+3)}\right\}. \tag{8.9}$$

The first term of (8.9) is easy as from the table we obtain

$$\mathcal{L}^{-1}\left\{\frac{-2}{s+3}\right\} = -2e^{-3t}. \tag{8.10}$$

To compute the second term, we use partial fraction to rewrite

$$\frac{1}{s(s+3)} = \frac{1/3}{s} - \frac{1/3}{s+3}.$$

Hence,

$$\mathcal{L}^{-1}\left\{\frac{e^{-2s}}{s(s+3)}\right\} = \frac{1}{3}\mathcal{L}^{-1}\left\{\frac{e^{-2s}}{s}\right\} - \frac{1}{3}\mathcal{L}^{-1}\left\{\frac{e^{-2s}}{s+3}\right\}$$

$$= \frac{1}{3}u_2(t) - \frac{1}{3}\mathcal{L}^{-1}\left\{\frac{e^6 e^{-2(s+3)}}{s+3}\right\}$$

$$= \frac{1}{3}u_2(t) - \frac{1}{3}e^6 e^{-3t}u_2(t)$$

$$= \frac{1}{3}u_2(t) - \frac{1}{3}e^{(-3t+6)}u_2(t). \tag{8.11}$$

Combining (8.10) and (8.11), the solution is given by

$$y(t) = -2e^{-3t} + \frac{1}{3}u_2(t) - \frac{1}{3}e^{-3t+6}u_2(t).$$

With Laplace transform, the first-order equation in the above example can be solved simultaneously even though there is discontinuity at $t = 2$. The problem can also be solved using the method from Chapter 2. However, one needs to solve two

Chapter 8.   The Laplace Transform   185

different initial-value problems for different time period, namely

$$\frac{dy}{dt} = -3y \quad \text{for } 0 < t < 2 \tag{8.12}$$

$$\frac{dy}{dt} = -3y + 1 \quad \text{for } t \geq 2. \tag{8.13}$$

The first equation uses initial value $y(0) = -2$. Having found the solution to this problem on the time interval $(0, 2)$, we compute $y(2)$ and use it as the initial value for the second equation.

Example 8.11. *A storage tank with capacity 100 liters, shown in Figure 8.1, is full with brine. Connected to it are two input valves A and B, each of which delivers brine solution with different concentration. Initially, the tank contains 5 kg of salt (in 100 liters). At time $t = 0$, brine solution containing 0.3 kg of salt per liter flows into the tank from valve A at the rate 6 liters/min. At time $t = 5$ min., valve A is closed and valve B is opened, delivering brine solution, whose salt concentration is 0.6 kg/liter, at the rate 6 liters/min. The brine is pumped out of the tank also at 6 liters/min and thus maintaining the constant volume of the tank at all times. Determine the amount of salt in the tank at any given time t.*

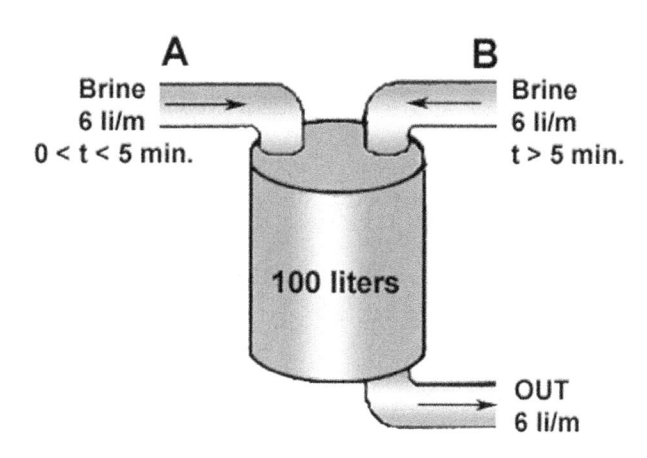

Figure 8.1: Mixing tank

Solution: Let $x(t)$ denote the amount of salt (in kg) in the tank at time t. Then the concentration of salt in the tank at time t is $x(t)/100$ kg/liter. The salt is added into the tank through the input valves at the rate $g(t)$, where

$$g(t) = \begin{cases} 0.3 \text{ kg/liter} \times 6 \text{ liters/min} = 1.8 \text{ kg/min}, & 0 < t < 5 \quad (\text{valve } A) \\ 0.6 \text{ kg/liter} \times 6 \text{ liters/min} = 3.6 \text{ kg/min}, & t \geq 5 \quad (\text{valve } B). \end{cases}$$

On the other hand, the amount of salt leaving the tank is $6x(t)/100$ kg/min. Hence, the rate of change of the amount of salt in the tank is given by

$$\frac{dx}{dt} = \text{input rate} - \text{output rate},$$

that is,

$$\frac{dx}{dt} = g(t) - \frac{6x}{100} \qquad (8.14)$$

with the initial condition

$$x(0) = 5. \qquad (8.15)$$

Before we proceed with Laplace transform, we notice that $g(t)$ is a step function with jump discontinuity at $t = 5$. Thus, we need to rewrite $g(t)$ in terms of $u_5(t)$, a *unit* step function whose Laplace transform is simply e^{-5s}/s. A quick observation tells us

$$g(t) = 1.8 + 1.8 u_5(t)$$

and equation (8.14) now becomes

$$\frac{dx}{dt} = 1.8 + 1.8 u_5 - 0.06 x. \qquad (8.16)$$

We take the Laplace transform of (8.16) and substitute the initial value (8.15) to get

$$\mathcal{L}\{x'\} = 1.8\mathcal{L}\{1\} + 1.8\mathcal{L}\{u_5\} - 0.06\mathcal{L}\{x\}$$
$$s\mathcal{L}\{x\} - x(0) = \frac{1.8}{s} + 1.8\frac{e^{-5s}}{s} - 0.06\mathcal{L}\{x\}$$
$$(s + 0.06)\mathcal{L}\{x\} = 5 + \frac{1.8}{s} + 1.8\frac{e^{-5s}}{s}$$
$$\mathcal{L}\{x\} = \frac{5}{s + 0.06} + \frac{1.8}{s(s + 0.06)} + \frac{1.8 e^{-5s}}{s(s + 0.06)}.$$

Chapter 8. The Laplace Transform

The solution is then given by

$$x = \mathcal{L}^{-1}\left\{\frac{5}{s+0.06}\right\} + \mathcal{L}^{-1}\left\{\frac{1.8}{s(s+0.06)}\right\} + \mathcal{L}^{-1}\left\{\frac{1.8e^{-5s}}{s(s+0.06)}\right\},$$

where the first term is

$$\mathcal{L}^{-1}\left\{\frac{5}{s+0.06}\right\} = 5e^{-0.06t} \qquad (8.17)$$

and for the last two terms we again consider partial fraction

$$\frac{1}{s(s+0.06)} = \frac{1/0.06}{s} - \frac{1/0.06}{s+0.06},$$

from which it follows that

$$\mathcal{L}^{-1}\left\{\frac{1.8}{s(s+0.06)}\right\} = \mathcal{L}^{-1}\left\{1.8\frac{1/0.06}{s}\right\} - \mathcal{L}^{-1}\left\{1.8\frac{1/0.06}{s+0.06}\right\}$$
$$= 30 - 30e^{-0.06t} \qquad (8.18)$$

and

$$\mathcal{L}^{-1}\left\{\frac{1.8e^{-5s}}{s(s+0.06)}\right\} = \mathcal{L}^{-1}\left\{1.8(1/0.06)\frac{e^{-5s}}{s}\right\} - \mathcal{L}^{-1}\left\{1.8(1/0.06)\frac{e^{-5s}}{s+0.06}\right\}$$
$$= 30u_5(t) - 30\mathcal{L}^{-1}\left\{\frac{e^{-5(s+0.06)}e^{0.3}}{s+0.06}\right\}$$
$$= 30u_5(t) - 30e^{0.3}e^{-0.06t}u_5(t)$$
$$= 30u_5(t) - 30e^{-0.06(t-5)}u_5(t). \qquad (8.19)$$

From (8.17), (8.18) and (8.19), we have the solution

$$x(t) = -25e^{-0.06t} + 30 + 30u_5(t) - 30e^{-0.06(t-5)}u_5(t),$$

or equivalently,

$$x(t) = -25e^{-0.06t} + 30 + 30 \cdot \begin{cases} 0, & 0 < t < 5 \\ 1 - e^{-0.06(t-5)}, & t \geq 5 \end{cases}.$$

8.5 Exercises

1. Determine whether the following improper integrals converge or diverge:

(a) $\displaystyle\int_2^\infty \frac{1}{2x}dx$

(b) $\displaystyle\int_1^\infty \frac{1}{x^2}dx$

(c) $\displaystyle\int_0^\infty e^{ax}dx,\ a<0$

2. Use Definition 8.1 to determine the Laplace transform of the following functions:

   (a) $f(t) = 3t^2$

   (b) $f(t) = \sin t$

   (c) $f(t) = te^{-t}$

   (d) $f(t) = e^{-3t}\cos 2t$

   (e) $f(t) = \begin{cases} 0, & 0 < t < 4 \\ 2, & t > 4 \end{cases}$

   (f) $f(t) = \begin{cases} e^t, & 0 < t < 4 \\ 1, & t > 4 \end{cases}$

3. Find the Laplace transform $\mathcal{L}\{f(t)\}$ of the following functions:

   (a) $f(t) = 1 - 2t^3$

   (b) $f(t) = \sin 3t + 2\cos t$

   (c) $f(t) = t^2 + \sin 2t$

   (d) $f(t) = \cos^2 3t$

   (e) $f(t) = e^t \sin 3t - t^3 + 2$

   (f) $f(t) = \cos\sqrt{2}t - te^{2t} + e^{-t}$

4. Find the inverse Laplace transform $\mathcal{L}^{-1}\{F(s)\}$ of the following functions:

   (a) $F(s) = \dfrac{1}{s^3}$

   (b) $F(s) = \dfrac{24}{(s-2)^5}$

   (c) $F(s) = \dfrac{s}{s^2-2}$

   (d) $F(s) = \dfrac{3s}{s^2+2}$

   (e) $F(s) = \dfrac{2s-8}{(s+2)(s-1)}$

(f) $F(s) = \dfrac{2s-1}{2s^2 - 5s - 3}$

5. Solve the following initial value problems using Laplace transform:

   (a) $y' - y = e^{-t}$, $y(0) = 1$

   (b) $y' + 7y = -1$, $y(0) = -2$

   (c) $y'' - 5y' + 6y = e^{2t}$, $y(0) = 0, y'(0) = -1$

   (d) $y'' - 3y' + 2y = \sin t$, $y(0) = 0, y'(0) = -1$

   (e) $y'' - y = g(t)$, $y(0) = 2, y'(0) = 1$, where

   $$g(t) = \begin{cases} 1, & t < 3 \\ 0, & t > 3 \end{cases}$$

   (f) Consider the tank problem in Example 8.11. Suppose at initial time $t = 0$ valve B is opened for 10 minutes and then switched off and valve A is opened. Find the amount of salt in the tank at any given time t.

Chapter 9

Numerical Methods

9.1 Euler's Method

The equations we have considered so far in this book have been *nice* in the sense that their solutions were expressible as combinations of well known functions such as polynomials, trigonometric or exponential functions, etc. Such solutions are often called *closed form solutions*. Unfortunately, in most cases, differential equations which model real-life situations are too complicated and their exact solutions are hard or even impossible to obtain. In such cases, one uses *numerical methods*, in which one approximates the value of the actual solution at various points in an interval of interest. In this chapter we will discuss the numerical approach to solve initial value problem (IVP) of the form:

$$y' = f(t,y), \quad y(t_0) = y_0. \tag{9.1}$$

As we mentioned earlier, numerical methods attempt to find an approximation to the solution of the IVP at specified points on some interval $[a,b]$ which contains t_0. Generally, a numerical method starts with the initial value y_0 and uses an appropriate equation to compute the changes in y values at various points over the interval $[a,b]$. These y values generated by numerical method give an approximation to the solution of the IVP. A word of caution: As with all approximation methods used to compute the value of a function, errors are introduced and the efficacy of a method depends upon the nature and magnitude of the error. We will have more to say about errors later.

The simplest numerical method for solving (9.1) is the *Euler's method*. The main idea of Euler's method is linearization, that is, the use of tangent line to approximate the solution curve $y(t)$. We recall from Chapter 1 that the graph of a solution to a differential equation is always tangent to the vectors on the slope field, and hence the slope field gives us a good idea of the qualitative behavior of the solution.

To find an approximate solution to (9.1) over the interval $[a, b]$, we first divide $[a, b]$ into equally spaced (for convenience) subintervals with nodes $t_0, t_1, \ldots, t_n$ with

$$a = t_0 < t_1 < \ldots < t_{n-1} < t_n = b$$

and $h = t_i - t_{i-1}, i = 1, 2, \ldots, n$. This common distance h between two consecutive nodes is called the *step size* and can be computed as

$$h = \frac{b-a}{n},$$

where n is the number of subintervals.

We start with the first subinterval $[t_0, t_1]$. Recall that the equation of the tangent line to the curve $y(t)$ at the point $(t_0, y(t_0))$ is given by

$$y = y(t_0) + y'(t_0)(t - t_0) \qquad (9.2)$$

and therefore the tangent line approximation to $y(t)$ at the point $t_1 = t_0 + h$ is

$$y(t_1) \approx y(t_0) + y'(t_0)(t_1 - t_0)$$

which is valid whenever h is sufficiently small. Since $t_1 - t_0 = h$ and $y'(t_0) = f(t_0, y_0)$, we can write

$$y(t_1) \approx y(t_0) + h f(t_0, y_0). \qquad (9.3)$$

If w_1 is an approximation to the exact value $y(t_1)$, then the above equation can be written as

$$w_1 = w_0 + h f(t_0, w_0), \qquad (9.4)$$

with $w_0 = y(t_0) = y_0$ being the initial value.

Repeating the above process for the next subinterval $[t_1, t_2]$, we arrive at the equation

$$y(t_2) \approx y(t_1) + h f(t_1, y(t_1)). \qquad (9.5)$$

Letting w_i be an approximation to $y(t_i)$ as before, we have

$$w_2 = w_1 + h f(t_1, w_1). \qquad (9.6)$$

Chapter 9. Numerical Methods

In general, **Euler's method** can be written as a *recursive formula*:

$$w_{i+1} = w_i + hf(t_i, w_i), \quad i = 0, 1, \ldots, n-1. \\ w_0 = y(t_0) = y_0 \tag{9.7}$$

Example 9.1. *Use Euler's method with $h = 0.1$ to find the approximate solution to the initial value problem:*

$$y' = -2y^2 + ty + t^2, \ y(0) = 1$$

on $[0, 0.3]$.

Solution: The given ODE has no closed-form solution and hence using a numerical method is our only possible option. Here $f(t,y) = -2y^2 + ty + t^2$ with $t_0 = 0, y_0 = 1$. Since $h = 0.1$, we have $t_1 = 0.1, t_2 = 0.2$, and $t_3 = 0.3$. Applying Euler's formula (9.7) recursively with $w_0 = y_0 = 1$ gives us

$$\begin{aligned} w_1 &= w_0 + hf(t_0, w_0) \\ &= 1 + 0.1 f(0, 1) = 1 + (0.1)(-2) = 0.8. \\ w_2 &= w_1 + hf(t_1, w_1) \\ &= 0.8 + 0.1 f(0.1, 0.8) = 0.8 + (0.1)(-2(0.8^2) + (0.1)(0.8) + 0.1^2) = 0.681. \\ w_3 &= w_2 + hf(t_2, w_2) \\ &= 0.681 + 0.1 f(0.2, 0.681) = 0.681 + (0.1)(-2(0.681^2) + (0.2)(0.681) + 0.2^2) \\ &= 0.6059. \end{aligned}$$

and therefore $y(0.1) \approx 0.8, y(0.2) \approx 0.681$ and $y(0.3) \approx 0.6059$.

We mentioned earlier that numerical methods generally introduce errors in our computation. How good is Euler's method? In general the accuracy in Euler's method is dependent on the step size. Smaller step sizes generally give better approximation. We illustrate this by means of the following example (which has a closed form solution!).

Example 9.2. *Use Euler's method to find the approximate solution to the initial value problem:*

$$y^2 y' + 2t = 0, \ y(0) = 3$$

on the interval $[0, 1]$ taking step sizes $h = 1/4, 1/8, 1/16$.

Solution: We rewrite the given ODE as $y' = -2t/y^2$ which is of the form (9.1) with $f(t, y) = -2t/y^2$ with $t_0 = 0$ and $w_0 = 3$. Applying Euler's method (9.7) with $h = 1/4$ we obtain these approximations:

$$w_1 = w_0 + hf(t_0, w_0)$$
$$= 3 + 0.25f(0, 3) = 3 + (0.25)(0) = 3.$$
$$w_2 = w_1 + hf(t_1, w_1)$$
$$= 3 + 0.25f(0.25, 3) = 3 + (0.25)(-2(0.25)/3^2) = 2.9861.$$
$$w_3 = w_2 + hf(t_2, w_2)$$
$$= 2.9861 + 0.25f(0.5, 2.9861) = 2.9861 + (0.25)(-2(0.5)/2.9861^2) = 2.9581.$$
$$w_4 = w_3 + hf(t_3, w_3)$$
$$= 2.9581 + 0.25f(0.75, 2.9581) = 2.9581 + (0.25)(-2(0.75)/2.9581^2) = 2.9152.$$

t	$w_i(h=0.25)$	$w_i(h=0.125)$	$w_i(h=0.0625)$	Exact
0	3	3	3	3
0.25	3	2.9965	2.9948	2.9930
0.5	2.9861	2.9791	2.9755	2.9720
0.75	2.9581	2.9472	2.9417	2.9362
1	2.9152	2.9001	2.8923	2.8845

Table 9.1: Numerical and exact solutions of $y^2 y' + 2t = 0$, $y(0) = 3$. The numerical approximations are obtained by using Euler's method.

Note that the values w_1, w_2, w_3, w_4 generated by Euler's method above are approximations to the exact solutions at the points $t = 0.25, 0.5, 0.75, 1$, respectively. Similarly, taking $h = 1/8$ one can compute the approximations to the exact solutions at $t = 0.125, 0.25, 0.375, \ldots, 0.875, 1$ ($t = ih$, $i = 1, 2, \ldots, 8$), and with $h = 1/16$ we obtain approximations at the points $t = ih, i = 1, 2, \ldots, 16$.

The exact solution to this ODE is $\frac{1}{3}y^3 + t^2 = c$ (see Example 2.1) and with the given initial value the particular solution is $\frac{1}{3}y^3 + t^2 = 9$. Table 9.1 shows the exact and numerical solutions at $t = 0, 0.25, 0.5, 0.75, 1$ generated by Euler's method with different step sizes. You will observe that taking smaller stepsizes, such as $h = 1/8$, requires us to compute formula (9.7) eight times to obtain the approximate value of $y(1)$, and with $h = 1/16$, the computation needs to be performed sixteen times. Table 9.1 only shows the approximations at $t = 0.25, 0.5, 0.75, 1$ and omits those at intermediate t values.

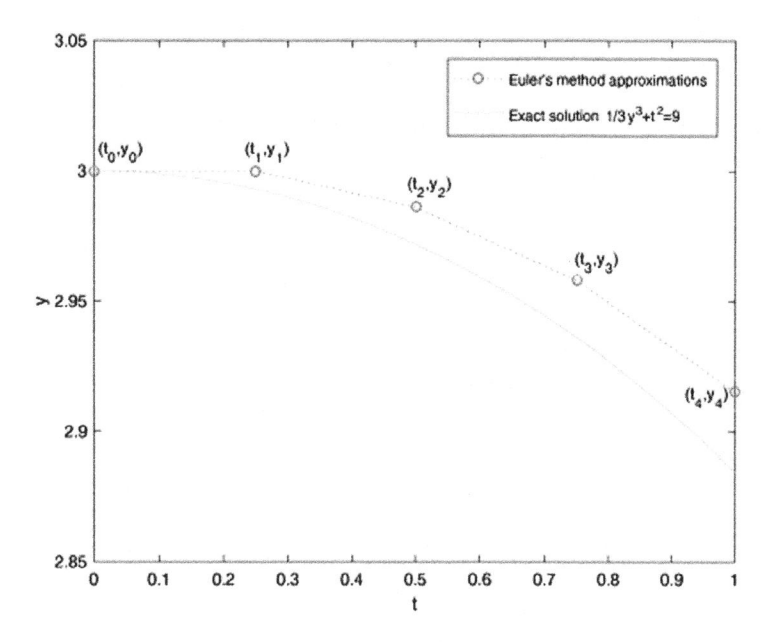

Figure 9.1: Euler's method approximations with $h = 0.25$ vs. exact solution for $y^2 y' + 2t = 0$ with $y(0) = 3$

9.2 Truncation error of Euler's Method

Since the aim of a numerical method is to produce reasonably accurate approximations, we need to look closely at how much these approximations differ from the exact solutions. In numerical analysis, the difference between the exact solution and the approximate (numerical) solution is called the *error*. That is, if $y(t_i)$ and w_i denote the exact and approximate solutions, respectively, then the error $= |y(t_i) - w_i|$. From Table 9.1 we can see that the difference between the approximations w_i and the exact solutions is smaller when h is smaller. For instance,

$$|y(0.5) - w_i(0.5)| \approx \begin{cases} 0.0141, & \text{when } h = 0.25 \\ 0.0071, & \text{when } h = 0.125 \\ 0.0035, & \text{when } h = 0.0625 \end{cases} \qquad (9.8)$$

This suggests that more accurate approximations can be obtained when h is sufficiently small.

Furthermore, we notice that as stepsize h is halved, the error is also halved. To better analyze the relationship between the error and the stepsize, we will look at the analytic derivation of the Euler's method that is based on the following Taylor's theorem.

Theorem 9.1. *Suppose f is n times differentiable on $[a, b]$ and $f^{(n)}(t)$ is continuous on $[a, b]$. Let $t_0 \in [a, b]$. Then for every $t \in [a, b]$, there exists a number ξ between t_0 and t with $f(t) = P_n(t) + R_n(t)$, where*

$$P_n(t) = f(t_0) + f'(t_0)(t - t_0) + \frac{f''(t_0)}{2!}(t - t_0)^2 + \ldots + \frac{f^{(n)}(t_0)}{n!}(t - t_0)^n \qquad (9.9)$$

$$= \sum_{k=0}^{n} \frac{f^{(k)}(t_0)}{k!}(t - t_0)^k \qquad (9.10)$$

and

$$R_n(t) = \frac{f^{(n+1)}(\xi)}{(n + 1)!}(t - t_0)^{n+1}. \qquad (9.11)$$

Here $P_n(t)$ is called the nth Taylor polynomial for f about t_0 and $R_n(t)$ is the remainder term.

Applying Taylor's theorem to $y(t)$ about the point t_i we have

$$y(t_{i+1}) = y(t_i + h) = y(t_i) + hy'(t_i) + \frac{h^2}{2!}y''(\xi) \qquad (9.12)$$

for some $\xi \in [t_i, t_{i+1}]$. Since $y'(t_i) = f(t_i, y(t_i))$, we now have

$$y(t_{i+1}) = y(t_i) + hf(t_i, y(t_i)) + \frac{h^2}{2!}y''(\xi). \qquad (9.13)$$

Letting w_i be the approximate value of $y(t_i)$ and dropping the remainder term give us the Euler's method

$$w_{i+1} = w_i + hf(t_i, w_i) \qquad (9.14)$$

as before. The remainder term $R(t, h) = \frac{1}{2}h^2 y''(\xi)$ is called the residual of the Euler's method and the quantity $\tau(t, h) = \frac{1}{h} R(t, h)$ is called the *local truncation error*. Since the local truncation error of the Euler's method here is $\frac{1}{2}hy''(\xi)$, Euler's method is often called a *first order method*, which is commonly written as $O(h)$. The meaning of $O(h)$ is that the local truncation error roughly behaves as h, and in particular we can expect the error to reduce by half when we halve the step size h. This is indeed what we see in (9.8).

It is reasonable to guess that reducing the step size improves the accuracy of the Euler's method. Although this may be true in many cases, it is also worth mentioning that another type of error called the *roundoff error* may grow and deteriorate the

Chapter 9. Numerical Methods 197

accuracy as step size decreases to a very small number. The roundoff (rounding) error is the error that arises due to computers' inability to represent numbers or perform arithmetic exactly, but instead use only a fixed number of digits. Consequently, they produce errors which can get carried on to the subsequent computations. Moreover, with small h, more iterations are needed to approximate the solution over the same interval. In the next few sections we will learn several ways to improve the Euler's method so that the approximations can be sufficiently accurate with fewest number of iterations and without having to reduce h to a very small number.

9.3 Modified Euler's Method

Recall that Euler's method is based on approximating the solution curve $y(t)$ on the interval $[t_i, t_{i+1}]$ with the line through (t_i, w_i) with slope $f(t_i, w_i)$:

$$w_{i+1} = w_i + h \underbrace{f(t_i, w_i)}_{\text{slope}} \tag{9.15}$$

One can improve Euler's method by taking the *average* of the slopes at the two endpoints of the interval $[t_i, t_{i+1}]$, that is,

$$\text{slope} = m_i = \frac{1}{2}\Big[f(t_i, w_i) + f(t_{i+1}, w_{i+1})\Big]. \tag{9.16}$$

Hence, Euler's method (9.7) can be modified as

$$w_{i+1} = w_i + h m_i. \tag{9.17}$$

Note that the second term of the slope m_i requires us to compute $f(t_{i+1}, w_{i+1})$, however, w_{i+1} is not yet available at this time. We replace t_{i+1} with $t_i + h$ and w_{i+1} with $w_i + hf(t_i, w_i)$, the value obtained by Euler's method. Substituting (9.16) into (9.17) we obtain the *Modified Euler's method*

$$w_{i+1} = w_i + \frac{h}{2}\Big[\underbrace{f(t_i, w_i)}_{k_{1i}} + \underbrace{f(t_i + h, w_i + hf(t_i, w_i))}_{k_{2i}}\Big], \tag{9.18}$$

which has a local truncation error of $O(h^2)$, which is better than $O(h)$ since when h is small, h^2 is even smaller leading to increased number of significant digits in the result. The formula above can be written as follows:

For $i = 0, 1, \ldots, n-1$,
$$\begin{aligned} t_{i+1} &= t_i + h \\ k_{1i} &= f(t_i, w_i) \\ k_{2i} &= f(t_{i+1}, w_i + hk_{1i}) \\ w_{i+1} &= w_i + \frac{h}{2}(k_{1i} + k_{2i}) \end{aligned} \qquad (9.19)$$

We now apply the Modified Euler's method to the same example and compare the results with those given by the Euler's method.

Example 9.3. *Use the Modified Euler's method to approximate the solution to the initial value problem:*
$$y^2 y' + 2t = 0, \ y(0) = 3$$
on the interval $[0,1]$ taking the step size $h = 1/4$.

Solution: Again here $f(t,y) = -2t/y^2$ with $t_0 = 0$ and $y_0 = w_0 = 3$. Applying the Modified Euler's method formula (9.19) with $h = 1/4$ we obtain these approximations:

$t_1 = t_0 + h = 0.25$
$k_{10} = f(t_0, w_0) = -2(0)/3^2 = 0$
$k_{20} = f(t_1, w_0 + hk_{10}) = f(0.25, 3 + 0.25(0)) = f(0.25, 3) = -2(0.25)/3^2 = -0.0556$
$w_1 = w_0 + \frac{h}{2}(k_{10} + k_{20}) = 3 + \frac{0.25}{2}(0 - 0.0556) = 2.9931$

$t_2 = t_1 + h = 0.5$
$k_{11} = f(t_1, w_1) = -2(0.25)/2.9931^2 = -0.0558$
$k_{21} = f(t_2, w_1 + hk_{11}) = f(0.5, 2.9931 + 0.25(-0.0558)) = f(0.5, 2.9792) = -0.1127$
$w_2 = w_1 + \frac{h}{2}(k_{11} + k_{21}) = 2.9931 + \frac{0.25}{2}(-0.0558 - 0.1127) = 2.9720$

$t_3 = t_2 + h = 0.75$
$k_{12} = f(t_2, w_2) = -2(0.5)/2.9720^2 = -0.1132$
$k_{22} = f(t_3, w_2 + hk_{12}) = f(0.75, 2.9720 + 0.25(-0.1132)) = f(0.75, 2.9437) = -0.1731$
$w_3 = w_2 + \frac{h}{2}(k_{12} + k_{22}) = 2.9720 + \frac{0.25}{2}(-0.1132 - 0.1731) = 2.9362$

Chapter 9. Numerical Methods

t	E ($h=0.0625$)	ME ($h=0.25$)	ME ($h=0.125$)	Exact
0	3	3	3	3
0.25	2.9948	2.9931	2.9930	2.9930
0.5	2.9755	2.9720	2.9720	2.9720
0.75	2.9417	2.9362	2.9362	2.9362
1	2.8923	2.8846	2.8845	2.8845

Table 9.2: Numerical and exact solutions of $y^2 y' + 2t = 0$, $y(0) = 3$. The numerical approximations are obtained by using Euler's method (E) with $h = 0.0625$ and the Modified Euler's method (ME) with $h = 0.25$ and $h = 0.125$.

$$t_4 = t_3 + h = 1$$
$$k_{13} = f(t_3, w_3) = -2(0.75)/2.9362^2 = -0.1740$$
$$k_{23} = f(t_4, w_3 + hk_{13}) = f(1, 2.9362 + 0.25(-0.1740)) = f(1, 2.8927) = -0.2390$$
$$w_4 = w_3 + \frac{h}{2}(k_{13} + k_{23}) = 2.9362 + \frac{0.25}{2}(-0.1740 - 0.2390) = 2.8846$$

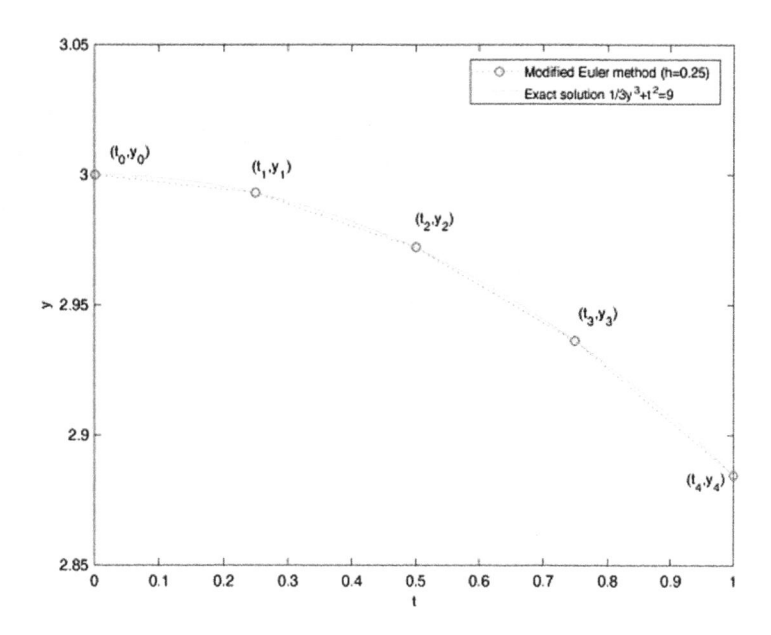

Figure 9.2: Modified Euler's method approximations vs. exact solution

Table 9.2 shows the result of Modified Euler's method with $h = 1/4$ and $h = 1/8$. Note that even with $h = 1/4$, the Modified Euler's method can give better approximations compare to Euler's method with $h = 1/16$. See Table 9.2 and Figure 9.2.

9.4 Higher order Taylor Methods

Another way to improve the accuracy without having to make the step size h too small is to come up with a method whose local truncation error is of order $O(h^p)$ with p as large as possible. Since the Euler's method is derived via Taylor's theorem by including only the first derivative term, our first attempt is to include higher order derivative terms in the derivation.

Suppose the solution $y(t)$ to the IVP (9.1) on $[a,b]$ has $(n+1)$ continuous derivatives. Then by Taylor's theorem, we can write

$$y(t_{i+1}) = y(t_i + h) = y(t_i) + hy'(t_i) + \frac{h^2}{2!}y''(t_i) + \ldots + \frac{h^n}{n!}y^{(n)}(t_i) + \frac{h^{n+1}}{(n+1)!}y^{(n+1)}(\xi_i), \tag{9.20}$$

for some $\xi_i \in (t_i, t_{i+1})$. Furthermore, since $y'(t) = f(t, y(t))$, it follows that

$$\begin{aligned} y''(t) &= f'(t, y(t)) \\ y'''(t) &= f''(t, y(t)) \\ &\vdots \\ y^{(n)}(t) &= f^{(n-1)}(t, y(t)). \end{aligned} \tag{9.21}$$

Substituting (9.21) into (9.20) we obtain

$$\begin{aligned} y(t_{i+1}) = y(t_i) &+ hf(t_i, y(t_i)) + \frac{h^2}{2!}f'(t_i, y(t_i)) + \ldots + \frac{h^n}{n!}f^{(n-1)}(t_i, y(t_i)) \\ &+ \frac{h^{n+1}}{(n+1)!}f^{(n)}(\xi_i, y(\xi_i)). \end{aligned} \tag{9.22}$$

We let w_i be an approximation to the exact solution $y(t_i)$ as before and omit the remainder term in (9.22) to obtain

$$w_{i+1} = w_i + \underbrace{hf(t_i, w_i) + \frac{h^2}{2!}f'(t_i, w_i) + \ldots + \frac{h^n}{n!}f^{(n-1)}(t_i, w_i)}_{hT^{(n)}(t_i, w_i)}.$$

Hence, the higher order Taylor method can be written as

Chapter 9.   Numerical Methods

$$w_0 = y(t_0) = y_0$$
$$w_{i+1} = w_i + hT^{(n)}(t_i, w_i), \quad i = 0, 1, \ldots, n-1, \tag{9.23}$$

where

$$T^{(n)}(t_i, w_i) = f(t_i, w_i) + \frac{h}{2}f'(t_i, w_i) + \ldots + \frac{h^{n-1}}{n!}f^{(n-1)}(t_i, w_i).$$

We call this Taylor method of order n. Note that the Euler's method is a special case of Taylor method where $n = 1$. The remainder term in the expansion (9.22) is $O(h^{n+1})$ which implies that Taylor method of order n has $O(h^n)$ local truncation error.

Example 9.4. *Use Taylor method with $n = 4$ to find the approximate solution to the initial value problem:*

$$y' + y = 2\cos t, \ y(0) = 2$$

on the interval $[0, 1]$ with step size $h = 1/2$.

Solution: We first write the differential equation in the form of (9.1):

$$y' = 2\cos t - y,$$

that is, $f(t, y) = 2\cos t - y$. Hence,

$$f'(t, y) = -2\sin t - y' = -2\sin t - 2\cos t + y.$$
$$f''(t, y) = -2\cos t + 2\sin t + y' = -2\cos t + 2\sin t + (2\cos t - y) = 2\sin t - y$$
$$f'''(t, y) = 2\cos t - y' = 2\cos t - (2\cos t - y) = y.$$

Substituting the above derivatives to Taylor's method of order 4 gives us:

$$w_{i+1} = w_i + hT^{(4)}(t_i, w_i)$$
$$= w_i + h\left[f(t_i, w_i) + \frac{h}{2!}f'(t_i, w_i) + \frac{h^2}{3!}f''(t_i, w_i) + \frac{h^3}{4!}f'''(t_i, w_i)\right]$$
$$= w_i + h\left[(2\cos t_i - w_i) + \frac{h}{2}(-2\sin t_i - 2\cos t_i + w_i) + \frac{h^2}{6}(2\sin t_i - w_i) + \frac{h^3}{24}w_i\right].$$

Since $h = 0.5$, $t_0 = 0, t_1 = 0.5$ and $t_2 = 1$. Using $w_0 = y(t_0) = 2$, we have

$$w_1 = w_0 + h\left[(2\cos t_0 - w_0) + \frac{h}{2}(-2\sin t_0 - 2\cos t_0 + w_0) + \frac{h^2}{6}(2\sin t_0 - w_0) + \frac{h^3}{24}w_0\right]$$
$$= 2 + (0.5)\left[(2-2) + \frac{0.5}{2}(0 - 2 + 2) + \frac{0.5^2}{6}(0-2) + \frac{0.5^3}{24}(2)\right]$$
$$= 1.9635.$$

$$w_2 = w_1 + h\left[(2\cos t_1 - w_1) + \frac{h}{2}(-2\sin t_1 - 2\cos t_1 + w_1) + \frac{h^2}{6}(2\sin t_1 - w_1) + \frac{h^3}{24}w_1\right]$$
$$= 1.9635 + (0.5)\left[(2\cos(0.5) - 1.9635) + \frac{0.5}{2}(-2\sin(0.5) - 2\cos(0.5) + 1.9635)\right.$$
$$\left. + \frac{0.5^2}{6}(2\sin(0.5) - 1.9635) + \frac{0.5^3}{24}(1.9635)\right]$$
$$= 1.7497.$$

The exact solution to the above IVP is $y = e^{-t} + \cos t + \sin t$. Note that $y(0.5) = 1.9635$ and $y(1) = 1.7497$ indicating the accuracy of the approximations w_1 and w_2.

We now apply the Taylor method to the previous example and compare the accuracy with those given by the Euler's method.

Example 9.5. *Use the Taylor method with $n = 2$ to find the approximate solution to the initial value problem:*

$$y^2 y' + 2t = 0, \ y(0) = 3$$

on the interval $[0,1]$ taking step size $h = 1/4$.

Solution: We write the differential equation as $y' = -2t/y^2$ as before giving us $f(t,y) = -2t/y^2$. By Chain Rule, the derivative of $f(t,y)$ with respect to t is

$$f'(t,y) = -2y^{-2} + 4ty^{-3}y',$$

which upon substitution of $y' = f(t,y) = -2t/y^2$, we obtain

$$f'(t,y) = -2y^{-2} - 8t^2 y^{-5}. \tag{9.24}$$

By (9.23), the formula for Taylor method with $n = 2$ is given by

$$w_{i+1} = w_i + h\left[f(t_i, w_i) + \frac{h}{2}f'(t_i, w_i)\right]$$
$$= w_i + h\left[(-2t_i/w_i^2) + \frac{h}{2}(-2w_i^{-2} - 8t_i^2 w_i^{-5})\right], \quad i = 0, 1, 2, 3. \quad (9.25)$$

Here $t_0 = 0, t_1 = 0.25, t_2 = 0.5, t_3 = 0.75$ and $w_0 = y(t_0) = 3$. We compute w_i using (9.25) to get

$$w_1 = w_0 + h\left[(-2t_0/w_0^2) + \frac{h}{2}(-2w_0^{-2} - 8t_0^2 w_0^{-5})\right]$$
$$= 3 + (0.25)\left[(-2(0)/3^2) + \frac{0.25}{2}(-2(3)^{-2} - 8(0)^2(3^{-5}))\right]$$
$$= 2.9931.$$

$$w_2 = w_1 + h\left[(-2t_1/w_1^2) + \frac{h}{2}(-2w_1^{-2} - 8t_1^2 w_1^{-5})\right]$$
$$= 2.9931 + (0.25)\left[(-2(0.25)/2.9931^2) + \frac{0.25}{2}(-2(2.9931)^{-2} - 8(0.25)^2(2.9931^{-5}))\right]$$
$$= 2.9721.$$

$$w_3 = w_2 + h\left[(-2t_2/w_2^2) + \frac{h}{2}(-2w_2^{-2} - 8t_2^2 w_2^{-5})\right]$$
$$= 2.9721 + (0.25)\left[(-2(0.5)/2.9721^2) + \frac{0.25}{2}(-2(2.9721)^{-2} - 8(0.5)^2(2.9721^{-5}))\right]$$
$$= 2.9364.$$

$$w_4 = w_3 + h\left[(-2t_3/w_3^2) + \frac{h}{2}(-2w_3^{-2} - 8t_3^2 w_3^{-5})\right]$$
$$= 2.9364 + (0.25)\left[(-2(0.75)/2.9364^2) + \frac{0.25}{2}(-2(2.9364)^{-2} - 8(0.75)^2(2.9364^{-5}))\right]$$
$$= 2.8850.$$

t	Euler ($h = 0.25$)	Taylor order 2 ($h = 0.25$)	Exact
0	3	3	3
0.25	3	2.9931	2.9930
0.5	2.9861	2.9721	2.9720
0.75	2.9581	2.9364	2.9362
1	2.9152	2.8850	2.8845

Table 9.3: Numerical solutions of $y^2 y' + 2t = 0, y(0) = 3$ obtained by using the Euler's method and Taylor method of order 2 with $h = 0.25$.

Comparing these values with the exact solution and also with the approximations obtained by using Euler's method with the same step size, we can see that Taylor method of order 2 gives us a much better approximations for the same step size.

9.5 Runge-Kutta Methods

The Taylor methods we learned in the previous section have an advantage of high-order local truncation error. However, one obvious drawback is that it requires the computation and evaluation of derivatives of f, which may be complicated and computationally expensive. This is in fact one of the main reasons that Taylor methods are rarely used in practice.

In this section, we study another way to achieve high order of local truncation method *while avoiding the computation of the derivatives*. The family of numerical methods that are derived using this technique is called the Runge-Kutta methods (named after the German mathematicians C.Runge and M.W. Kutta, who first discovered them). In fact, both Euler's and Modified Euler methods are specific cases of Runge-Kutta methods.

Recall that the Modified Euler's method is derived by taking the average of the slopes or the first derivative of y at the two endpoints of the interval of interest $[t_i, t_{i+1}]$. Runge-Kutta methods are a family of algorithms that take into account the information of the slopes at several points on $[t_i, t_{i+1}]$ to extrapolate the solution to the future time step.

The Modified Euler's method we see in section 9.3 is also known as the second order Runge-Kutta method (RK2). One of the most widely used Runge-Kutta methods is the following fourth order Runge-Kutta method (RK4):
For $i = 0, 1, \ldots, n$,

$$
\begin{aligned}
t_{i+1} &= t_i + h \\
k_{1i} &= f(t_i, w_i) \\
k_{2i} &= f\left(t_i + \frac{h}{2}, w_i + \frac{h}{2} k_{1i}\right) \\
k_{3i} &= f\left(t_i + \frac{h}{2}, w_i + \frac{h}{2} k_{2i}\right) \\
k_{4i} &= f(t_{i+1}, w_i + h k_{3i}) \\
w_{i+1} &= w_i + \frac{h}{6}(k_{1i} + 2k_{2i} + 2k_{3i} + k_{4i}),
\end{aligned}
\qquad (9.26)
$$

where $w_0 = y_0 = y(t_0)$.

Assuming the solution $y(t)$ has up to fifth order continuous derivatives, RK4 has local truncation error of $O(h^4)$, which is the same as Taylor method of order 4. However, in RK4 we are not required to compute these derivatives explicitly.

The following examples illustrate the computational procedure of RK4.

Example 9.6. *Use RK4 method with $h = 0.1$ to find the approximate solution to the initial value problem:*

$$y' = -2y^2 + ty + t^2, \; y(0) = 1$$

on $[0, 0.3]$.

Solution: Letting $f(t, w) = -2w^2 + tw + t^2$, $t_0 = 0$, and $w_0 = y(0) = 1$, we compute the approximations as follows:

$t_1 = 0.1$

$k_{10} = f(t_0, w_0) = f(0, 1) = -2$

$k_{20} = f(t_0 + (h/2), w_0 + (h/2)k_{10}) = f(0.05, 1 + 0.05(-2)) = -1.5725$

$k_{30} = f(t_0 + (h/2), w_0 + (h/2)k_{20}) = f(0.05, 1 + 0.05(-1.5725)) = -1.6493$

$k_{40} = f(t_1, w_0 + hk_{30}) = f(0.1, 1 + 0.1(-1.6493)) = -1.3012$

$w_1 = w_0 + (h/6)(k_{10} + 2k_{20} + 2k_{30} + k_{40})$

$\quad = 1 + (0.1/6)(-2 + 2(-1.5725) + 2(-1.6493) + (-1.3012)) = 0.8376.$

$t_2 = 0.2$

$k_{11} = f(t_1, w_1) = f(0.1, 0.8376) = -1.3093$

$k_{21} = f(t_1 + (h/2), w_1 + (h/2)k_{11}) = f(0.1 + 0.05, 0.8376 + 0.05(-1.3093)) = -1.0540$

$k_{31} = f(t_1 + (h/2), w_1 + (h/2)k_{21}) = f(0.1 + 0.05, 0.8376 + 0.05(-1.0540)) = -1.0919$

$k_{41} = f(t_2, w_1 + hk_{31}) = f(0.2, 0.8376 + 0.1(-1.0919)) = -0.8755$

$w_2 = w_1 + (h/6)(k_{11} + 2k_{21} + 2k_{31} + k_{41})$

$\quad = 0.8376 + (0.1/6)(-1.3093 + 2(-1.0540) + 2(-1.0919) + (-0.8755)) = 0.7296.$

$t_3 = 0.3$

$k_{12} = f(t_2, w_2) = f(0.2, 0.7296) = -0.8788$

$k_{22} = f(t_2 + (h/2), w_2 + (h/2)k_{12}) = f(0.2 + 0.05, 0.7296 + 0.05(-0.8788)) = -0.7065$

$$k_{32} = f(t_2 + \frac{h}{2}, w_2 + (h/2)k_{22}) = f(0.2 + 0.05, 0.7296 + 0.05(-0.7065)) = -0.7281$$

$$k_{42} = f(t_3, w_2 + hk_{32}) = f(0.3, 0.7296 + 0.1(-0.7281)) = -0.5758$$

$$w_3 = w_2 + (h/6)(k_{12} + 2k_{22} + 2k_{32} + k_{42})$$

$$= 0.7296 + (0.1/6)(-0.8788 + 2(-0.7065) + 2(-0.7281) + (-0.5758)) = 0.6576.$$

Thus, RK4 gives the approximations

$$y(0.1) \approx 0.8376, y(0.2) \approx 0.7296, y(0.3) \approx 0.6576.$$

Example 9.7. *Use RK4 method to find approximate solution to the initial value problem:*

$$y^2 y' + 2t = 0, \ y(0) = 3$$

on the interval $[0, 1]$ taking step sizes $h = 0.25$.

Solution: With $f(t, w) = -2t/w^2$, $h = 0.25$, $t_0 = 0$ and $w_0 = 3$, we compute the approximations as follows:

$$t_1 = 0.25$$

$$k_{10} = f(t_0, w_0) = f(0, 3) = 0$$

$$k_{20} = f(t_0 + (h/2), w_0 + (h/2)k_{10}) = f(0.125, 3 + 0.125(0)) = -0.0278$$

$$k_{30} = f(t_0 + (h/2), w_0 + (h/2)k_{20}) = f(0.125, 3 + (0.125)(-0.0278)) = -0.0278$$

$$k_{40} = f(t_1, w_0 + hk_{30}) = f(0.25, 3 + 0.25(-0.0278)) = -0.0558$$

$$w_1 = w_0 + (h/6)(k_{10} + 2k_{20} + 2k_{30} + k_{40})$$

$$= 3 + (0.25/6)(0 + 2(-0.0278) + 2(-0.0278) + (-0.0558)) = 2.9930$$

$$t_2 = 0.5$$

$$k_{11} = f(t_1, w_1) = f(0.25, 2.9930) = -0.0558$$

$$k_{21} = f(t_1 + (h/2), w_1 + (h/2)k_{11}) = f(0.25 + 0.125, 2.9930 + 0.125(-0.0558)) = -0.0841$$

$$k_{31} = f(t_1 + (h/2), w_1 + (h/2)k_{21}) = f(0.25 + 0.125, 2.9930 + 0.125(-0.0841)) = -0.0843$$

$$k_{41} = f(t_2, w_1 + hk_{31}) = f(0.5, 2.9930 + 0.25(-0.0843)) = -0.1132$$

$$w_2 = w_1 + (h/6)(k_{11} + 2k_{21} + 2k_{31} + k_{41})$$

$$= 2.9930 + (0.25/6)((-0.0558) + 2(-0.0841) + 2(-0.0843) + (-0.1132)) = 2.9720$$

Similarly, we can obtain w_3 and w_4:

$t_3 = 0.75, k_{12} = -0.1132, k_{22} = -0.1429, k_{32} = -0.1432, k_{42} = -0.1740, w_3 = 2.9362$

$t_4 = 1, k_{13} = -0.1740, k_{23} = -0.2060, k_{33} = -0.2066, k_{43} = -0.2404, w_4 = 2.8845.$

t	Euler $h = 0.0625$	Modified Euler $h = 0.125$	Taylor order 2 $h = 0.25$	RK4 $h = 0.25$	Exact
0	3	3	3	3	3
0.25	2.9948	2.9930	2.9931	2.9930	2.9930
0.5	2.9755	2.9720	2.9721	2.9720	2.9720
0.75	2.9417	2.9362	2.9364	2.9362	2.9362
1	2.8923	2.8845	2.8850	2.8845	2.8845

Table 9.4: Numerical and exact solutions of $y^2 y' + 2t = 0$, $y(0) = 3$. The numerical approximations are obtained by using Euler's method ($h = 0.0625$), Modified Euler's method ($h = 0.125$), Taylor method of order 2 ($h = 0.25$) and RK4 ($h = 0.25$).

For comparison, Table 9.4 shows the numerical approximations to the solution of the IVP in Example 9.7 generated by Euler's method ($h = 0.0625$), Modified Euler's method ($h = 0.125$), Taylor's method of order 2 ($h = 0.25$), and RK4 ($h = 0.25$). It is clear that RK4 gives approximations that are accurate up to four decimal digits and it is better than those obtained by the other methods.

Note: The astute student would have noticed the remarkable resemblance formula (9.26) for Runga-Kutta method (RK4) bears to *Simpson's rule* used in numerical integration,
$$\int_a^b f(x)dx \approx \frac{b-a}{6}\left[f(a) + 4f\left(\frac{a+b}{2}\right) + f(b)\right].$$
This is no coincidence! In fact the inspiration for RK4 came initially from Simpson's rule!

9.6 Applications

9.6.1 Systems of first order equations

Let $x(t)$ and $y(t)$ be functions of an independent variable t, and x', y' their derivatives. In Chapter 7 we considered systems of equations such as

$$x' = x + 3y$$
$$y' = 3x + y$$

and discussed methods of solving them. The operator methods we used work only if the system has a closed form solution. When this is not the case, we have to resort to numerical methods. In this section we investigate how to use Runge-Kutta type methods to accomplish this.

We will find it advantageous to use vector notation. In the example above, we write
$$\mathbf{y}' = \begin{pmatrix} x' \\ y' \end{pmatrix} \text{ and } \mathbf{f}(t, \mathbf{y}) = \begin{pmatrix} x + 3y \\ 3x + y \end{pmatrix},$$

where boldface letters denote vectors. Using this notation we can rewrite the given equations in a compact form

$$\mathbf{y}' = \mathbf{f}(t, \mathbf{y}), \quad \mathbf{y}(0) = \mathbf{y}_0. \tag{9.27}$$

In this notation, $\mathbf{y}$ is a vector with components x and y, both of which are functions of independent variable t. The vector $\mathbf{y}'$ is the vector of the first order derivatives $x'(t)$ and $y'(t)$, and $\mathbf{y}_0$ is the vector containing the initial values.

As before, to apply the numerical methods we first discretize the interval of interest $[a, b]$ such that
$$a = t_0 < t_1 < \ldots < t_{n-1} < t_n = b.$$

Euler's method (9.7) to approximate the solution to the system (9.27) on $[a, b]$ can then be written as

$$\begin{aligned} \mathbf{w}_{i+1} &= \mathbf{w}_i + h\mathbf{f}(t_i, \mathbf{w}_i), \quad i = 0, 1, \ldots, n-1. \\ \mathbf{w}_0 &= \mathbf{y}(t_0) = \mathbf{y}_0. \end{aligned} \tag{9.28}$$

Here $\mathbf{w} = [w_1, w_2]^T$, where w_1 and w_2 approximate the exact solutions $x(t)$ and $y(t)$, respectively.

Likewise, the fourth order Runge-Kutta method for system of first order equations is given by

Chapter 9. Numerical Methods

For $i = 0, 1, \ldots, n-1$,

$$\begin{aligned}
t_{i+1} &= t_i + h \\
\mathbf{k}_{1i} &= \mathbf{f}(t_i, \mathbf{w}_i) \\
\mathbf{k}_{2i} &= \mathbf{f}\!\left(t_i + \frac{h}{2}, \mathbf{w}_i + \frac{h}{2}\mathbf{k}_{1i}\right) \\
\mathbf{k}_{3i} &= \mathbf{f}\!\left(t_i + \frac{h}{2}, \mathbf{w}_i + \frac{h}{2}\mathbf{k}_{2i}\right) \\
\mathbf{k}_{4i} &= \mathbf{f}(t_{i+1}, \mathbf{w}_i + h\mathbf{k}_{3i}) \\
\mathbf{w}_{i+1} &= \mathbf{w}_i + \frac{h}{6}(\mathbf{k}_{1i} + 2\mathbf{k}_{2i} + 2\mathbf{k}_{3i} + \mathbf{k}_{4i}),
\end{aligned} \quad (9.29)$$

where $\mathbf{w}_0 = \mathbf{y}_0 = \mathbf{y}(t_0)$.

We illustrate the methods using the example given in the beginning of this section.

Example 9.8. *Consider the system of first order linear equations*

$$\begin{aligned} x' &= x + 3y \\ y' &= 3x + y, \end{aligned} \quad (9.30)$$

with initial conditions $x(0) = 3, y(0) = 1$. Approximate the solution to the system at $t = 0.1, 0.2, 0.3$ by using Euler's method and RK4 with $h = 0.1$.

Solution: As discussed previously, the given system can be written in vector notation as $\mathbf{y}' = \mathbf{f}(t, \mathbf{y})$ with

$$\mathbf{y}' = \begin{pmatrix} x' \\ y' \end{pmatrix}, \ \mathbf{f}(t, \mathbf{y}) = \begin{pmatrix} x + 3y \\ 3x + y \end{pmatrix}, \ \text{and} \ \mathbf{w}_0 = \begin{pmatrix} x(0) \\ y(0) \end{pmatrix} = \begin{pmatrix} 3 \\ 1 \end{pmatrix}.$$

Letting $t_0 = 0, t_i = t_{i-1} + h, i = 1, 2, 3$ and applying the Euler's method with $h = 0.1$, we have

$$\begin{aligned}
t_1 &= 0.1 \\
\mathbf{w}_1 &= \mathbf{w}_0 + h\mathbf{f}(t_0, \mathbf{w}_0) \\
&= \begin{pmatrix} 3 \\ 1 \end{pmatrix} + 0.1 \begin{pmatrix} 3 + 3(1) \\ 3(3) + 1 \end{pmatrix} = \begin{pmatrix} 3.6 \\ 2 \end{pmatrix}
\end{aligned}$$

$$t_2 = 0.2$$
$$\mathbf{w}_2 = \mathbf{w}_1 + h\mathbf{f}(t_1, \mathbf{w}_1)$$
$$= \begin{pmatrix} 3.6 \\ 2 \end{pmatrix} + 0.1 \begin{pmatrix} 3.6 + 3(2) \\ 3(3.6) + 2 \end{pmatrix} = \begin{pmatrix} 4.56 \\ 3.28 \end{pmatrix}$$
$$t_3 = 0.3$$
$$\mathbf{w}_3 = \mathbf{w}_2 + h\mathbf{f}(t_2, \mathbf{w}_2)$$
$$= \begin{pmatrix} 4.56 \\ 3.28 \end{pmatrix} + 0.1 \begin{pmatrix} 4.56 + 3(3.28) \\ 3(4.56) + 3.28 \end{pmatrix} = \begin{pmatrix} 6 \\ 4.976 \end{pmatrix}.$$

Now using RK4 with $h = 0.1$ we obtain

$$\mathbf{k}_{10} = \mathbf{f}(t_0, \mathbf{w}_0) = \begin{pmatrix} 3 + 3(1) \\ 3(3) + 1 \end{pmatrix} = \begin{pmatrix} 6 \\ 10 \end{pmatrix}.$$
$$\mathbf{w}_0 + (h/2)\mathbf{k}_{10} = \begin{pmatrix} 3 \\ 1 \end{pmatrix} + (0.1/2) \begin{pmatrix} 6 \\ 10 \end{pmatrix} = \begin{pmatrix} 3.3 \\ 1.5 \end{pmatrix}.$$
$$\mathbf{k}_{20} = \mathbf{f}(t_0 + (h/2), \mathbf{w}_0 + (h/2)\mathbf{k}_{10}) = \begin{pmatrix} 3.3 + 3(1.5) \\ 3(3.3) + 1.5 \end{pmatrix} = \begin{pmatrix} 7.8 \\ 11.4 \end{pmatrix}$$
$$\mathbf{w}_0 + (h/2)\mathbf{k}_{20} = \begin{pmatrix} 3 \\ 1 \end{pmatrix} + (0.1/2) \begin{pmatrix} 7.8 \\ 11.4 \end{pmatrix} = \begin{pmatrix} 3.39 \\ 1.57 \end{pmatrix}.$$
$$\mathbf{k}_{30} = \mathbf{f}(t_0 + (h/2), \mathbf{w}_0 + (h/2)\mathbf{k}_{20}) = \begin{pmatrix} 3.39 + 3(1.57) \\ 3(3.39) + 1.57 \end{pmatrix} = \begin{pmatrix} 8.1 \\ 11.74 \end{pmatrix}$$
$$\mathbf{w}_0 + h\mathbf{k}_{30} = \begin{pmatrix} 3 \\ 1 \end{pmatrix} + (0.1) \begin{pmatrix} 8.1 \\ 11.74 \end{pmatrix} = \begin{pmatrix} 3.81 \\ 2.174 \end{pmatrix}.$$
$$\mathbf{k}_{40} = \mathbf{f}(t_1, \mathbf{w}_0 + h\mathbf{k}_{30}) = \begin{pmatrix} 3.81 + 3(2.174) \\ 3(3.81) + 2.174 \end{pmatrix} = \begin{pmatrix} 10.332 \\ 13.604 \end{pmatrix}$$
$$\mathbf{w}_1 = \mathbf{w}_0 + (h/6)(\mathbf{k}_{10} + 2\mathbf{k}_{20} + 2\mathbf{k}_{30} + \mathbf{k}_{40})$$
$$= \begin{pmatrix} 3 \\ 1 \end{pmatrix} + (0.1/6) \left[\begin{pmatrix} 6 \\ 10 \end{pmatrix} + 2 \begin{pmatrix} 7.8 \\ 11.4 \end{pmatrix} + 2 \begin{pmatrix} 8.1 \\ 11.74 \end{pmatrix} + \begin{pmatrix} 10.332 \\ 13.604 \end{pmatrix} \right]$$
$$= \begin{pmatrix} 3.8022 \\ 2.1647 \end{pmatrix}$$

Chapter 9. Numerical Methods

We continue the procedure to obtain

$$\mathbf{k}_{11} = \begin{pmatrix} 10.2964 \\ 13.5713 \end{pmatrix}, \mathbf{k}_{21} = \begin{pmatrix} 12.8469 \\ 15.7944 \end{pmatrix}, \mathbf{k}_{31} = \begin{pmatrix} 13.3079 \\ 16.2881 \end{pmatrix}, \mathbf{k}_{41} = \begin{pmatrix} 16.5136 \\ 19.1925 \end{pmatrix},$$

$$\mathbf{w}_2 = \begin{pmatrix} 5.1209 \\ 3.7802 \end{pmatrix}$$

$$\mathbf{k}_{12} = \begin{pmatrix} 16.4615 \\ 19.1428 \end{pmatrix}, \mathbf{k}_{22} = \begin{pmatrix} 20.1560 \\ 22.5692 \end{pmatrix}, \mathbf{k}_{32} = \begin{pmatrix} 20.8547 \\ 23.2947 \end{pmatrix}, \mathbf{k}_{42} = \begin{pmatrix} 25.5354 \\ 27.7287 \end{pmatrix},$$

$$\mathbf{w}_3 = \begin{pmatrix} 7.1878 \\ 6.0902 \end{pmatrix}$$

The exact solution to the system (9.30) with the given initial condition is $x(t) = 2e^{4t} + e^{-2t}, y(t) = 2e^{4t} - e^{-2t}$ (verify!). Hence at $t = 0.1, 0.2, 0.3$, the exact solutions are

$$\mathbf{y}(0.1) = (x(0.1), y(0.1)) = (3.8024, 2.1649)$$
$$\mathbf{y}(0.2) = (x(0.2), y(0.2)) = (5.1214, 3.7808)$$
$$\mathbf{y}(0.3) = (x(0.3), y(0.3)) = (7.1890, 6.0914)$$

The table below shows the approximations given by Euler and RK4 and their errors.

t	Exact	Euler	Error	RK4	Error
0	(3,1)	(3,1)	0	(3,1)	0
0.1	(3.8024,2.1649)	(3.6,2)	0.2611	(3.8022,2.1647)	0.0003
0.2	(5.1214,3.7808)	(4.56,3.28)	0.7523	(5.1209,3.7802)	0.0008
0.3	(7.1890,6.0914)	(6,4.976)	1.6303	(7.1878,6.0902)	0.0017

Table 9.5: Exact and numerical solutions to the system (9.30) obtained by Euler and RK4 methods, and their respective errors.

Since $\mathbf{y}$ is a two-dimensional vector, the error is computed as $\|\mathbf{y} - \mathbf{w}\|$, the norm of the difference between the exact solution $\mathbf{y}$ and the approximation $\mathbf{w}$. We note that the errors generated by RK4 approximations are much smaller compare to those generated by Euler method.

The plot of the solutions also confirms this observations and shows that the approximations given by RK4 are indeed very close to the exact solution.

From the above examples, we can see that the computations involved in implementing numerical methods, especially RK4, can be very tedious. For this reason,

(a) $x(t)$ (b) $y(t)$

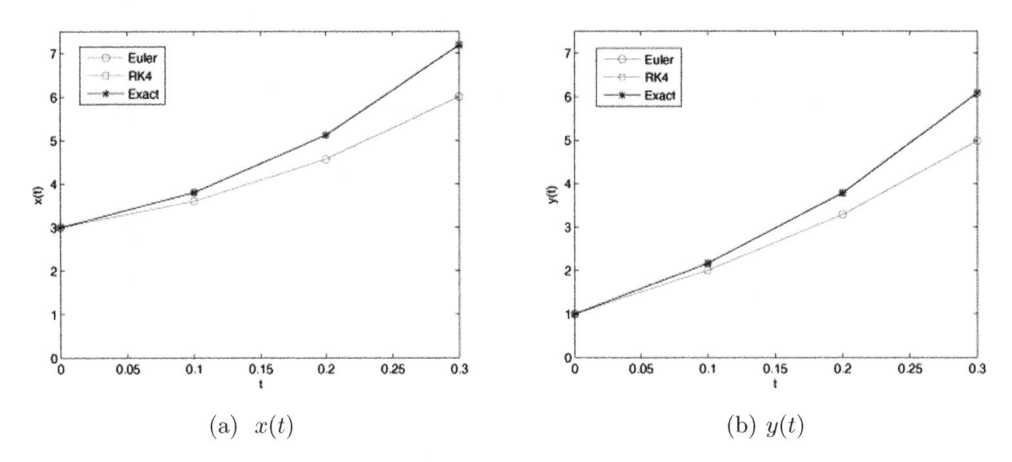

Figure 9.3: Exact vs. numerical solutions for the system (9.30)

numerical methods are usually implemented using computer software. The pseudocode for RK4 is shown below:

```
INPUT endpoints a,b; step size h; initial condition y(a)
OUTPUT approximation w_i to y(t_i) for i = 1,2,...N
Step 1 Set N = (b-a)/h
           t_0 = a
           w_0 = y(a)
Step 2 Printout (t_0, w_0)
Step 3 For i = 0,1,...,N-1, do Steps 4-7
    Step 4 Set k_{1i} = f(t_i, w_i);
               k_{2i} = f(t_i + h/2, w_i + hk_{1i}/2);
               k_{3i} = f(t_i + h/2, w_i + hk_{2i}/2);
               k_{4i} = f(t_i + h, w_i + hk_{3i});
    Step 5 Set w_{i+1} = w_i + h(k_{1i} + 2k_{2i} + 2k_{3i} + k_{4i})/6;
    Step 6 Printout (t_i, w_i);
    Step 7 Set t_{i+1} = t_i + h;
Step 8 Stop.
```

9.6.2 Predator-prey model

A predator-prey model consists of a pair of nonlinear differential equations that describe the dynamics of competing predator and prey species in an ecosystem. It was initially developed by Alfred Lotka and Vito Volterra separately in 1920s, and therefore the predator-prey model is also known as Lotka-Volterra equations.

Suppose $x(t)$ and $y(t)$ represent the prey and predator populations over time. The classical Lotka-Volterra equations are given by

$$\begin{aligned} \frac{dx}{dt} &= ax - bxy \\ \frac{dy}{dt} &= -cy + dxy, \end{aligned} \tag{9.31}$$

where a, b, c, d are positive constants. Note that in the absence of predator ($y = 0$), we have $dx/dt = ax$ indicating that the prey population will grow exponentially. Similarly, when the prey is absent ($x = 0$) the predator will die off exponentially. Hence, the constants a and c represent the natural growth rate of prey and the natural death rate of predator, respectively, in isolation from each other. The terms bxy and dxy are called the *interaction terms*. The constant b is the rate at which prey is eaten by a single predator and d/b gives the fraction of a predator surviving by eating one prey. Note that this first order system is a nonlinear system due to interaction terms involving xy and in fact, it is not possible to solve the system explicitly. Numerical method is an approach that must be taken to approximate the solution.

The plot of the solution $x(t)$ and $y(t)$ versus t is often called the *time series graph*. Although such plot gives us information of the population size of each species over time, it does not describe the interaction between the two species and how they affect one another. Recall that the system such as (9.31) can be written in vector form as $\mathbf{y}' = \mathbf{f}(\mathbf{y})$, where

$$\mathbf{y} = \begin{pmatrix} x \\ y \end{pmatrix}, \ \mathbf{y}' = \begin{pmatrix} \frac{dx}{dt} \\ \frac{dy}{dt} \end{pmatrix}, \text{ and } \mathbf{f}(\mathbf{y}) = \begin{pmatrix} ax - bxy \\ -cy + dxy \end{pmatrix}.$$

By evaluating $\mathbf{f}(\mathbf{y})$ at various points $\mathbf{y} = (x, y)$ and plotting the resulting vectors in the xy-plane, we obtain a direction field of tangent vectors to the solutions of the system. This xy-plane is called the *phase plane* and a plot that shows a representative sample of trajectories is called a *phase portrait*. One can also think of a phase portrait as the path traversed by a particle that moves with velocity $\mathbf{y}'$ given by the system. A qualitative understanding of the behavior of the solutions can be visualized from its direction field and more precise information of a particular solution can be obtained from its phase portrait. The following example illustrates this idea.

Example 9.9. *Snowshoe hare is the primary food of Canadian lynx. Their interaction can be modeled by the following system:*

$$\begin{aligned}\frac{dx}{dt} &= 2x - 0.001xy \\ \frac{dy}{dt} &= -10y + 0.002xy,\end{aligned} \quad (9.32)$$

where $x(t)$ denotes the hare population after t years, and $y(t)$ the lynx population. Suppose at some time there were 100 hares and 5000 lynx.

1. *Implement RK4 with $h = 0.01$ to approximate the solution and discuss the dynamics of both populations for the next 20 years.*

2. *What is the highest number of hare population and how often does the population reach this number?*

3. *What is the highest number of lynx population and what is the average period of its oscillation?*

Solution:

1. Since $N = (b-a)/h = (20-0)/0.01 = 2000$, the computations would be quite laborious and the use of computer becomes necessary in this case. We implement RK4 algorithm to obtain the numerical solutions for $x(t)$ and $y(t)$. The initial condition is given by $\mathbf{w}_0 = (100, 5000)^T$ with

$$\mathbf{f}(t, \mathbf{w}) = \begin{pmatrix} 2x - 0.001xy \\ -10y + 0.002xy \end{pmatrix}.$$

The time series graphs of $x(t)$ and $y(t)$ versus t are shown in Figure 9.4(a)-(b). From these graphs, we see that both hare and lynx populations follow a sinusoidal pattern, where their population size increases and decreases periodically. The direction field of the system (9.32) and a phase portrait given the initial condition of $(100, 5000)^T$ is shown in Figure 9.4(c). We note that the initial hare population is low compared to the lynx population. As a result, the lynx population would initially decrease due to lack of food. As lynx population decreases, the hare population would increases again, hence providing more food for the lynx. A high number of prey would cause the lynx population to rise again. The dynamics continue in this fashion periodically, as shown in the phase portrait.

(a) $x(t)$, the prey (hares) population

(b) $y(t)$, the predator (lynx) population

(c) The predator vs. prey population

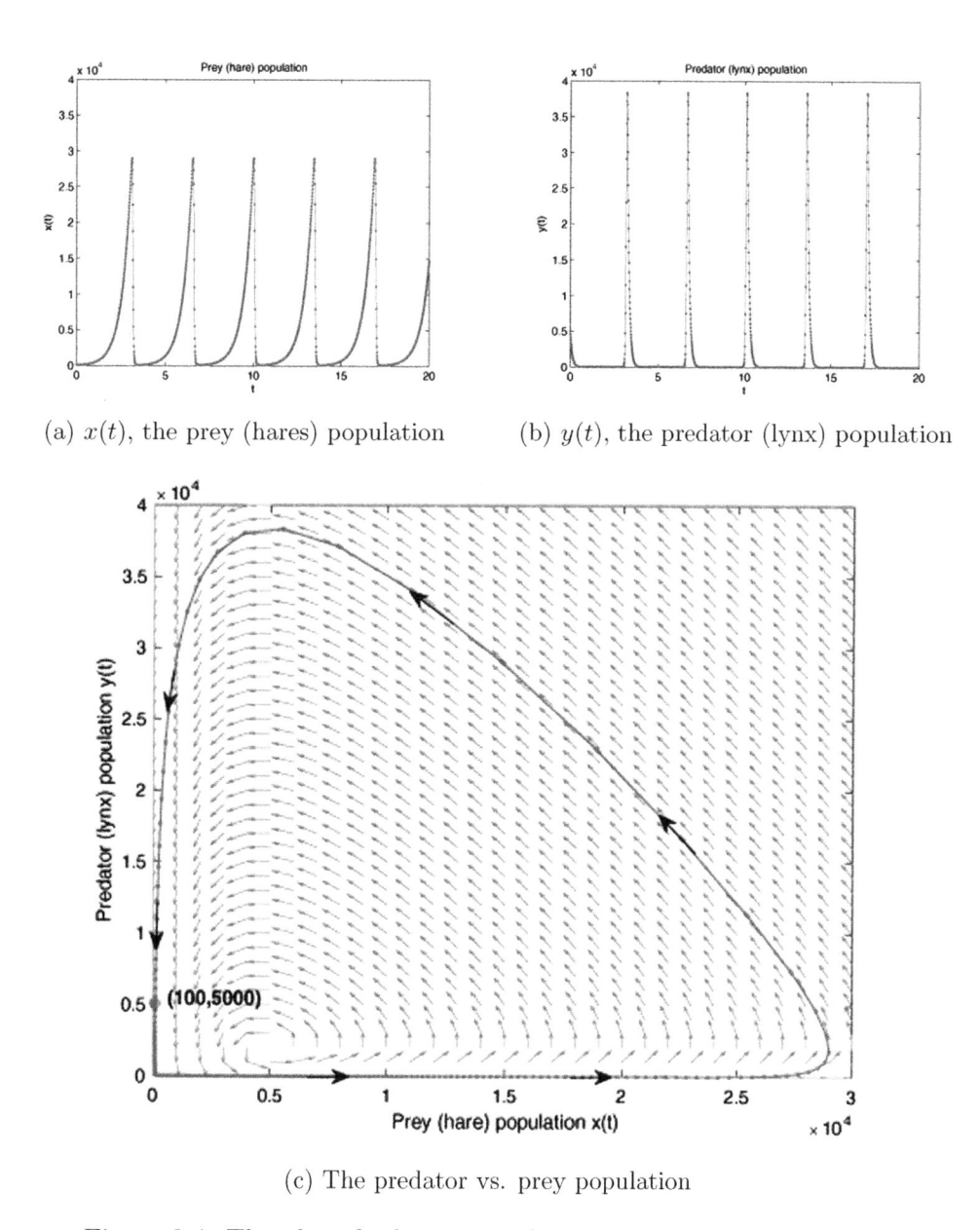

Figure 9.4: The plot of solutions to the predator-prey model (9.32)

2. From the time series graph in Figure 9.4(a), we can see that the peak of the hare population $x(t)$ is approximately 29,000. The curve $x(t)$ is periodic with period of the oscillation of approximately 3.45 years. This is how often the hare population will reach its highest.

3. Likewise, the highest number of lynx population is about 38,500 and its period is also 3.45 years as shown in Figure 9.4(b).

The Lotka-Volterra equations (9.31) can be easily modified to model the interaction of two competing populations that are not necessarily predator and prey. In ecology, this form of competition in which individuals of different species compete for the same resources, such as food and living spaces, is often called an *interspecific competition*. Interspecific competition models have also been used to study other types of competitive situations, such as businesses competing in the same market.

Consider two similar species, for instance, leopards and lions, that do not prey on each other but do compete for limited food supply. Let $x(t)$ and $y(t)$ be the populations of leopards and lions, respectively, at time t. When both species are present, each tends to diminish the available food supply for the other and consequently reduce the other's growth rate. This can be expressed in the simplest form by subtracting the interaction terms bxy and dxy from the right hand side of the system (9.31) giving us the following system:

$$\frac{dx}{dt} = ax - bxy$$
$$\frac{dy}{dt} = cy - dxy,$$

where a and c are the natural growth rate of leopards and lions, respectively, and b, d are the rates at which they interfere with each other.

We also note that since the competition occurs due limited resources, it is more common to describe the growth of each species by using the logistic growth rather than the exponential growth. As discussed in Section 2.5.4, the growth of leopard population in the absence of lions can be described by the following logistic equation:

$$\frac{dx}{dt} = x(a_1 - a_2 x) \qquad (9.33)$$

where a_1 is the growth rate of the leopards and the ratio a_1/a_2 is the maximum size of the leopard population that the environment can sustain. This maximum (saturation) level of the population is also known as the *carrying capacity* of the

Chapter 9. Numerical Methods   217

population. One can also think of the term $a_2 x^2$ in (9.33) as the competition among the leopards themselves. This competition within the same species is also known as the *intraspecific competition*. Similarly, the growth of the lions in the absence of leopards is given by
$$\frac{dy}{dt} = y(c_1 - c_2 y).$$

Incorporating the logistic growth into the competition model, we obtain the following system of first order equations:

$$\frac{dx}{dt} = x(a_1 - a_2 x - by)$$
$$\frac{dy}{dt} = y(c_1 - c_2 y - dx),$$

where $b, d, a_i, c_i, i = 1, 2$ are positive constants.

We will discuss the qualitative behavior of the solutions of the system through the following example.

Example 9.10. *Consider the competitive model describing the interaction between leopard and lion populations in an ecosystem given by the system*

$$\frac{dx}{dt} = x(1 - x - y)$$
$$\frac{dy}{dt} = y(0.5 - 0.25y - 0.75x), \quad (9.34)$$

where $x(t)$ and $y(t)$ represent the size of the leopard and lion populations (in thousands) over time. Solve the system numerically using RK4 for $t \in [0, 60]$ with $h = 0.2$. By sketching the phase portrait, determine the limiting size of each population, that is $x(t)$ and $y(t)$ as $t \to \infty$, for the following initial conditions:

(a) $x(0) = 0.1, y(0) = 0.1$

(b) $x(0) = 1, y(0) = 1$

(c) $x(0) = 0.5, y(0) = 0.5$

(d) $x(0) = 0.1, y(0) = 0.25$

(e) $x(0) = 1, y(0) = 0.6$.

Interpret the results in terms of the populations of the two species.

Solution:

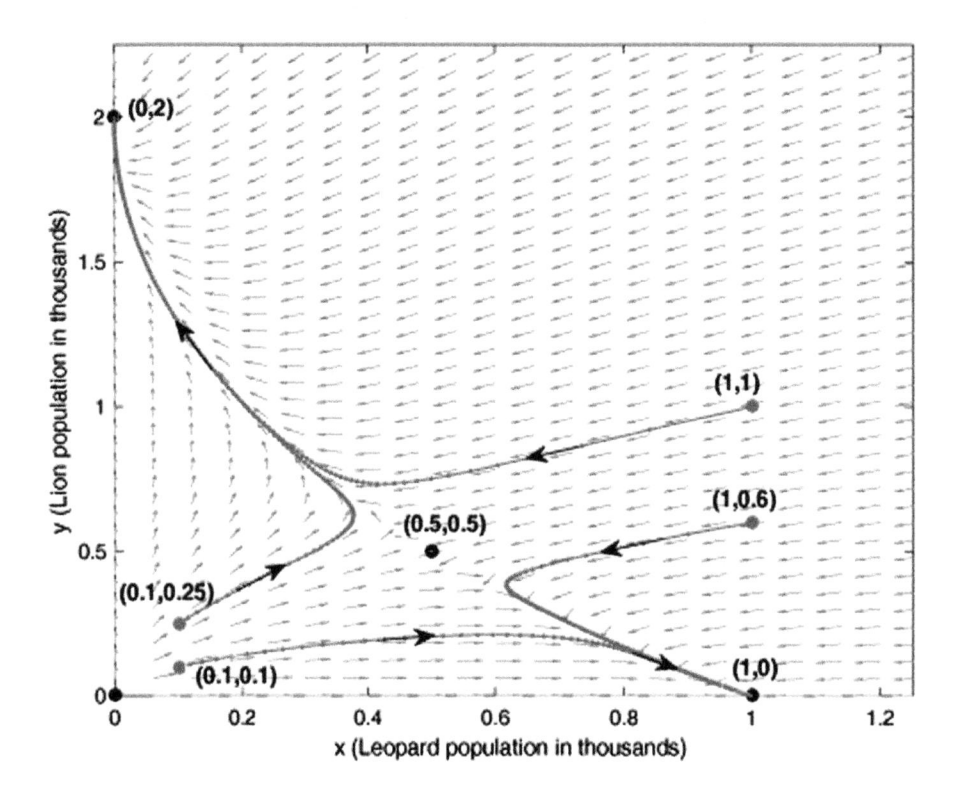

Figure 9.5: Direction field and phase portrait for the system (9.34)

The phase portrait for the system (9.34) is shown in Figure 9.5. We also sketch its direction field to see the flow and asymptotic behavior of the solution.

(a) With $(x(0), y(0)) = (0.1, 0.1)$, that is, initially there are 100 lions and 100 leopards, the solution curve approaches the point $(1, 0)$. This implies that the leopard population eventually saturates at 1000, while the lions extinct.

(b) With starting point $(1, 1)$, the solution curve shows convergence towards the point $(0, 2)$, which means that the leopard population will eventually extinct, while the lions reach 2000 individuals.

(c) When both populations start with 500 individuals, their population size remain constant for all time. This is the only starting point for which both species can coexist.

(d) With $(x(0), y(0)) = (0.1, 0.25)$, both populations initially increase. The leopard population then decreases leading to its extinction, while the lion population keeps increasing and reaches 2000.

(e) For the initial population of $(1, 0.6)$ the limiting population of leopard would be 1000 and the lion would eventually extinct.

9.6.3 Higher order equations

So far we have seen the use of numerical methods to solve first order equations. In fact, the use of numerical methods is not limited to this. Higher order equations can also be solved numerically by first writing the equation as a system of first order equations, and then solving the system numerically as discussed previously.

An n-th order differential equation of the form

$$y^{(n)} = g(t, y, y', \ldots, y^{(n-1)}) \tag{9.35}$$

can be rewritten as a first-order system by introducing a new variable for each derivative, with $y_1 = y$:

$$y_1' = y_2$$
$$y_2' = y_3$$
$$\vdots$$
$$y_{n-1}' = y_n$$
$$y_n' = g(t, y_1, y_2, , \ldots, y_n).$$

Hence, the equaton (9.35) is equivalent to the first order system

$$\mathbf{y}' = \mathbf{f}(t, \mathbf{y}), \tag{9.36}$$

where

$$\mathbf{y}' = \begin{pmatrix} y_1' \\ y_2' \\ \vdots \\ y_{n-1}' \\ y_n' \end{pmatrix} \text{ and } \mathbf{f}(t, y_1, y_2, \ldots, y_n) = \begin{pmatrix} y_2 \\ y_3 \\ \vdots \\ y_n \\ g(t, y_1, y_2, \ldots, y_n) \end{pmatrix}. \tag{9.37}$$

Example 9.11. *Given the second order equation*

$$y'' + 16y = e^{-3t} + \cos 4t, \tag{9.38}$$

with initial conditions $y(0) = 0, y'(0) = -1/25$. Write (9.38) as a system of first order equations, and for $t \in [0, \pi]$, solve the system numerically using Euler's and RK4 methods with $h = \pi/10$. Compare your approximations with the exact solution $y = -\frac{1}{25}\cos 4t + \frac{1}{50}\sin 4t + \frac{1}{25}e^{-3t} + \frac{1}{8}t\sin 4t$ (verify!).

Solution: We rewrite (9.38) as

$$y'' = -16y + e^{-3t} + \cos 4t.$$

Let $y_1 = y$. Then

$$\begin{aligned} y_1' &= y_2 \\ y_2' &= y_1'' = y'' \\ &= -16y + e^{-3t} + \cos 4t \\ &= -16y_1 + e^{-3t} + \cos 4t \end{aligned}$$

giving us the system

$$\begin{aligned} \mathbf{y}' &= \mathbf{f}(t, \mathbf{y}) \\ \text{with } \mathbf{y}' &= \begin{pmatrix} y_1' \\ y_2' \end{pmatrix} \text{ and } \mathbf{f}(t, \mathbf{y}) = \begin{pmatrix} y_2 \\ -16y_1 + e^{-3t} + \cos 4t \end{pmatrix}. \end{aligned} \tag{9.39}$$

The initial conditions are given by

$$\begin{aligned} y_1(0) &= y(0) = 0 \\ y_2(0) &= y_1'(0) = y'(0) = -1/25, \end{aligned}$$

hence,

$$\mathbf{y}(0) = \begin{pmatrix} 0 \\ -1/25 \end{pmatrix}.$$

Applying Euler's method (9.28) and RK4 method (9.29) with $h = \pi/10$, we obtain the approximations $\mathbf{w} = (w_1, w_2)$ at each $t_i = i(\pi/10)$. Note that w_1 is an approximation

Chapter 9. Numerical Methods

to $y_1 = y$ and w_2 is an approximation to $y_2 = y'$. Hence, when applied to second-order differential equations, numerical methods not only produce approximations to the exact solution y, but also approximations to its first derivative y'.

t	Exact $y(t)$	Euler $(w_1, w_2) \approx (y, y')$	Error $|y - w_1|$	RK4 $(w_1, w_2) \approx (y, y')$	Error $|y - w_1|$
0	0	(0,-0.04)	0	(0,-0.04)	0
$\pi/10$	0.0596	(-0.0126,0.5883)	0.0722	(0.0578,0.2870)	0.0018
$2\pi/10$	0.0964	(0.1726,0.8710)	0.0759	(0.0894,-0.1616)	0.0070
$3\pi/10$	-0.0463	(0.4459,-0.2013)	0.4922	(-0.0456,-0.5805)	0.0006
$4\pi/10$	-0.1799	(0.3826,-2.6782)	0.5625	(-0.1651,-0.0501)	0.0147
$5\pi/10$	-0.0396	(-0.4587,-4.4972)	0.4191	(-0.0331,0.7908)	0.0065
$6\pi/10$	0.2309	(-1.8716,-1.8743)	2.1025	(0.2095,0.5356)	0.0214
$7\pi/10$	0.2057	(-2.4604,7.6315)	2.6661	(0.1828,-0.6979)	0.0229
$8\pi/10$	-0.1640	(-0.0629,19.7451)	0.1011	(-0.1450,-1.1158)	0.0190
$9\pi/10$	-0.3675	(6.1402,19.8072)	6.5077	(-0.3221,0.1417)	0.0455
π	-0.0399	(12.3628,-10.9596)	12.4028	(-0.0387,1.4291)	0.0013

Table 9.6: Numerical and exact solutions of $y'' + 16y = e^{-3t} + \cos 4t$, $y(0) = 0, y'(0) = -1/25$. The numerical approximations are obtained by using Euler's and RK4 methods.

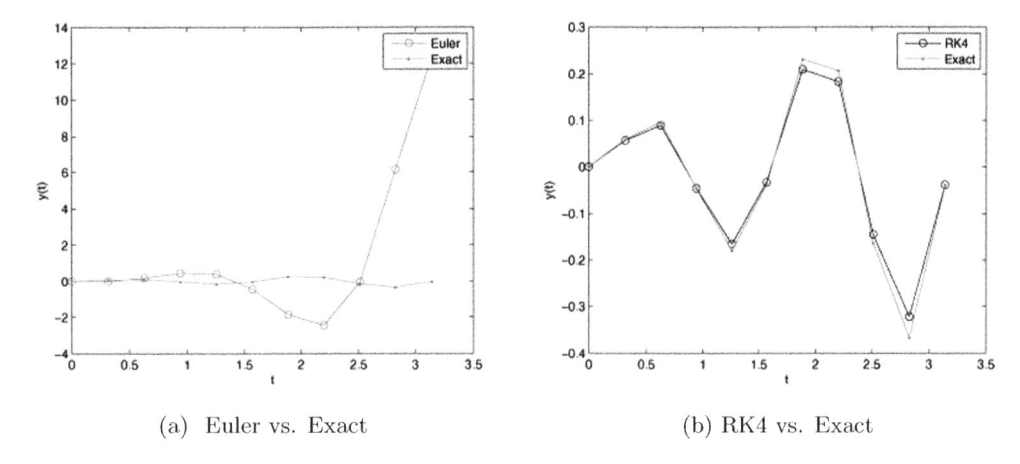

(a) Euler vs. Exact

(b) RK4 vs. Exact

Figure 9.6: Comparison between Euler's method, RK4, and the exact solutions for the second order equation (9.38).

Table 9.6 shows the approximations generated by Euler's and RK4 methods, as well as the exact solution $y(t)$. The approximation errors are computed at each iteration. Since w_1 approximates $y(t)$, the error is computed as the absolute value of the difference between the exact solution y and its approximation w_1. We can see in this table that the errors from RK4 are much smaller compare to the errors from Euler's method, indicating that RK4 gives much better accuracy to the actual solution. The plots of the exact solution and its approximations by Euler's and RK4 are also shown in the Figure 9.6.

9.7 Exercises

1. Use the Euler's method with the given step size to find the approximate values of the solution to the IVP at the points $t_i = t_0 + ih$, where $i = 1, 2, 3$ and t_0 is the point where the initial condition is imposed.

    (a) $y' = y(t - y)$, $y(0) = 1$; $h = 0.2$

    (b) $y' = 5t^3 e^{-2y}$, $y(1) = 0$; $h = 0.1$

    (c) $y' = ty/(t^2 + 1)$, $y(0) = 2$; $h = 0.25$

    (d) $(ty + y^2)dt - t^2 dy = 0$, $y(2) = 0.5$; $h = 0.5$

    (e) $y' = 2\sqrt{y+1}\cos t$, $y(0) = 1$; $h = \pi/4$

    (f) $dy/dt = 2t \sin^2 y$, $y(0) = \pi/4$; $h = 0.5$

2. Repeat Exercise 1 using the Modified Euler's method.

3. Given the IVP
$$y' = 1 - \cos y, \quad y(0) = \pi. \tag{9.40}$$

    (a) Use the Euler's method with $h = \pi/3$ to find an approximation to the solution at $t = \pi$.

    (b) Repeat part (a) using the Modified Euler's method.

4. Given the IVP
$$\frac{y'}{1+t^2} = \frac{t}{y}, \quad y(1) = 3. \tag{9.41}$$

    (a) Use the Euler's method with $h = 0.25$ to find the approximate solution to the above IVP on the interval $[1, 2]$.

    (b) Repeat part (a) using the Modified Euler's method.

    (c) The exact solution to the above IVP is
$$y = \sqrt{t^2 + 0.5t^4 + 7.5}. \tag{9.42}$$

Compute the exact solution at the points $t_i = ih$, where $h = 0.25$ and $i = 1, 2, 3, 4$. Compare the approximate values obtained in parts (a) and (b) with the exact solution, and compute their errors.

5. Use Taylor's method of order two to with the indicated step size to find approximate values of the solution to the IVP at the equally spaced points in the given interval.

   (a) $y' = 1 - y$, $y(0) = 0$; $h = 0.25$ on $[0, 0.5]$

   (b) $y' = t - 1 + y$, $y(0) = 1$; $h = 0.5$ on $[0, 1]$

   (c) $y' = \sin(t + y)$, $y(0) = \pi$; $h = 0.1$ on $[0, 0.3]$

   (d) $y' + y = e^t + 2\cos t$, $y(0) = 0.5$; $h = \pi/4$ on $[0, \pi/2]$

   (e) $y' = y(t - y)$, $y(0) = 1$; $h = 0.5$ on $[0, 1.5]$

   (f) $y' = e^y$, $y(1) = 0$; $h = 0.25$ on $[1, 1.5]$

6. Repeat Exercise 5 using Taylor's method of order four.

7. Repeat Exercise 5 using the fourth order Runge-Kutta method.

8. Solve the following system of differential equations using the Euler's method with the indicated step size for $t_i = t_0 + ih$, where $i = 1, 2, 3$ and t_0 is the point where the initial condition is imposed:

   (a) $x' = y$
   $y' = -x + 2y$
   $x(0) = 2$, $y(0) = 3$, $h = 0.2$

   (b) $x' + 2x - 3y = t$
   $y' - 3x + 2y = e^{2t}$
   $x(0) = 1$, $y(0) = 0$, $h = 0.1$

   (c) $3x - 3x' + 4y = 3t + 1$
   $3y' + 3y + 2x = e^t$
   $x(1) = 1$, $y(1) = 3$, $h = 0.25$

   (d) $x' = x(1 - y)$
   $y' = y(x - 1)$
   $x(0) = 2$, $y(0) = 5$, $h = 0.5$

   (e) $x' = -yz$
   $y' = xz$

$z' = xy/2$

$x(0) = 1,\ y(0) = 0,\ z(0) = 1,\ h = 0.1$

9. Repeat Exercise 7 using the fourth order Runge-Kutta method.

10. Rewrite the following higher order IVPs as a system of first order equations along with the associated initial values. Write your answer in matrix form $\mathbf{y}' = \mathbf{f}(t, \mathbf{y}),\ \mathbf{y}(0) = \mathbf{y}_0$:

    (a) $y'' - 3y' + 2y = e^t,\ y(0) = 1,\ y'(0) = 3$.

    (b) $y'' - 4y = e^{3t},\ y(0) = 0,\ y'(0) = 1$

    (c) $t^2 y'' - ty' + y = 0,\ y(1) = 3,\ y'(1) = 1$.

    (d) $(2t+1)y'' - 4(t+1)y' + 4y = 0,\ y(1) = 2, y'(1) = 0$.

    (e) $y'' = \sin(t - y) + y^2,\ y(0) = y'(0) = 1$.

    (f) $y^{(3)} - y'' + 5y = e^{2t},\ y(0) = 1,\ y'(0) = 2,\ y''(0) = 3$.

11. Convert the following higher order system of ODEs into a system of first order IVPs:

    (a) $x'' + x' - y = 0,\ x(2) = 4, x'(2) = 5$
    $y'' + y - x' = -1,\ y(2) = 0,\ y'(2) = 2$.
    (Hint: Set $y_1 = x, y_2 = x', y_3 = y, y_4 = y'$)

    (b) $x'' + x - 2y' = 5,\ x(1) = 1, x'(1) = 3$
    $y'' + 3y' - x = 0,\ y(1) = 0,\ y'(1) = 4$.

12. The dynamics of the interaction between fish and shark populations in an ocean can be described by the following Lotka-Volterra model:

$$\frac{dx}{dt} = x(10 - 5y)$$
$$\frac{dy}{dt} = y(-5 + 2x)$$

where $x(t)$ and $y(t)$ denote the fish and shark populations in thousands, respectively. Suppose there are 1000 fish and 2 0 sharks initially. Implement the RK4 with $h = 0.05$ to approximate the solution for the next 10 years. Plot your solutions $x(t)$ and $y(t)$ as a function of time. What can you say about the average of the fish and shark populations during this decade?

13. Suppose now we consider the intraspecies competition among the individuals in the fish population. The model in Problem 12 can be modified as follows:

$$\frac{dx}{dt} = x(10 - x - 5y)$$
$$\frac{dy}{dt} = y(-5 + 2x)$$

Note that the addition of the term $-x^2$ in the first equation represents the competition among the fish population, which would reduce the growth rate of the entire fish population. Using the same initial values as in Problem 12, implement the RK4 method and solve the system. How does the dynamic differ than the model in Problem 12? What will be the effect of this intraspecies competition to the average number of the fish and shark populations?

14. Two species of fish, bluegill and redear, compete with each other for food, but do not prey on each other. Suppose that both species occupy a pond and let $x(t)$ and $y(t)$ be the populations of bluegill and redear (in ten thousands), respectively, at time t. Their competition can be modeled by the following system:

$$\frac{dx}{dt} = x(1.5 - x - 0.5y)$$
$$\frac{dy}{dt} = y(2 - y - 0.75x).$$

(a) Draw a direction field and describe the behavior of the solutions.

(b) Using RK4 with $h = 0.5$ for $t \in [0, 60]$ solve the system numerically and sketch its phase portrait to determine the limiting behavior of x and y as $t \to \infty$ for the initial conditions $(0.1, 0.1), (1, 0), (1, 0.1), (0, 1), (0.1, 1)$, and $(1.4, 2)$. Interpret the results in terms of the populations of the two species.

(c) Determine the initial condition(s) that guarantee the coexistence of both species.

15. Repeat Exercise 14 for the following system:

$$\frac{dx}{dt} = x(1.5 - 0.5x - y)$$
$$\frac{dy}{dt} = y(2 - y - 1.125x)$$

with initial conditions $(0.1, 0.1), (1, 0), (0, 1), (1, 2.5), (0.8, 1.1),$ and $(2, 2)$.

Appendix A

Review of Basic Linear Algebra

A.1 Introduction

A vector space $\mathcal{V}$ over the real numbers $\mathbb{R}$ (often denoted by $\mathcal{V}/\mathbb{R}$) is a set of elements with two operations: "addition" $+$ and "multiplication" $\cdot$ such that

$$\mathbf{u}, \mathbf{v} \in \mathcal{V} \Rightarrow \mathbf{u} + \mathbf{v} \in \mathcal{V}$$

$$c \in \mathbb{R}, \mathbf{u} \in \mathcal{V} \Rightarrow c\,\mathbf{u} \in \mathcal{V}$$

$$\mathbf{u}, \mathbf{v}, \mathbf{w} \in \mathcal{V} \Rightarrow \mathbf{u} + (\mathbf{v} + \mathbf{w}) = (\mathbf{u} + \mathbf{v}) + \mathbf{w}$$

$$c \in \mathbb{R}, \mathbf{u}, \mathbf{v} \in \mathcal{V} \Rightarrow c\,(\mathbf{u} + \mathbf{v}) = (c\,\mathbf{u}) + (c\,\mathbf{v})$$

$$c, d \in \mathbb{R}, \mathbf{u} \in \mathcal{V} \Rightarrow c\,(d\,\mathbf{u}) = (cd)\,\mathbf{u}$$

$$1\,\mathbf{u} = \mathbf{u}$$

$$\exists\,\mathbf{0} \in \mathcal{V} \text{ such that } \forall\,\mathbf{u} \in \mathcal{V} \Rightarrow \mathbf{u} + \mathbf{0} = \mathbf{u}$$

Let us consider a couple of familiar examples.

The familiar 3-dimensional space $\mathbb{R}^3 = \{(x, y, z) : x, y, z \in \mathbb{R}\}$ is a vector space over $\mathbb{R}$. Here vector addition is defined by $(a, b, c) + (d, e, f) = (a + d, b + e, c + f)$ and vector multiplication by $c\,(x, y, z) = (cx, cy, cz)$ for any $c \in \mathbb{R}$. The "zero vector" is defined to be $\mathbf{0} = (0, 0, 0)$, i.e. the vector whose entries are all zero.

The space of 3×3 matrices with real entries,

$$M_{3\times 3} = \begin{pmatrix} a_{11} & a_{12} & a_{13} \\ a_{21} & a_{22} & a_{23} \\ a_{31} & a_{32} & a_{33} \end{pmatrix}$$

is a vector space. Vector addition here is the familiar matrix addition:

$$\begin{pmatrix} a_{11} & a_{12} & a_{13} \\ a_{21} & a_{22} & a_{23} \\ a_{31} & a_{32} & a_{33} \end{pmatrix} + \begin{pmatrix} b_{11} & b_{12} & b_{13} \\ b_{21} & b_{22} & b_{23} \\ b_{31} & b_{32} & b_{33} \end{pmatrix} = \begin{pmatrix} a_{11}+b_{11} & a_{12}+b_{12} & a_{13}+b_{13} \\ a_{21}+b_{21} & a_{22}+b_{22} & a_{23}+b_{23} \\ a_{31}+b_{31} & a_{32}+b_{32} & a_{33}+b_{33} \end{pmatrix}$$

For any scalar $c \in \mathbb{R}$,

$$c \begin{pmatrix} a_{11} & a_{12} & a_{13} \\ a_{21} & a_{22} & a_{23} \\ a_{31} & a_{32} & a_{33} \end{pmatrix} = \begin{pmatrix} ca_{11} & ca_{12} & ca_{13} \\ ca_{21} & ca_{22} & ca_{23} \\ ca_{31} & ca_{32} & ca_{33} \end{pmatrix}$$

and the "zero matrix" is simply the matrix all of whose entries are 0.

A.2 Linear independence

In a vector space $\mathcal{V}/\mathbb{R}$, the vectors $\mathbf{v}_1, \mathbf{v}_2, \cdots, \mathbf{v}_k$ are said to be **linearly dependent** if there are constants $c_1, c_2, \ldots, c_k$, not all zero, such that

$$c_1 \mathbf{v}_1 + c_2 \mathbf{v}_2 + \ldots + c_k \mathbf{v}_k = \mathbf{0}.$$

This simply means that one of the **v**'s can be written as a *non-trivial* linear combination of the others, that is, there is an i such that

$$\mathbf{v}_i = \sum_{\substack{j=1 \\ j \neq i}}^{k} d_j \mathbf{v}_j,$$

with at least one of the scalars d_js not equal to zero.

For instance, in $\mathbb{R}^2$, the vectors $\mathbf{v}_1 = (1,1), \mathbf{v}_2 = (0,3)$ and $\mathbf{v}_3 = (2,0)$ are linearly dependent since

$$c_1 \mathbf{v}_1 + c_2 \mathbf{v}_2 + c_3 \mathbf{v}_3 = c_1(1,1) + c_2(0,3) + c_3(2,0) = (c_1 + 2c_3, c_1 + 3c_2) = (0,0)$$

if we simply choose $c_3 = -c_1/2, c_2 = -c_1/3$. One obvious choice is $c_1 = 6, c_2 = -2, c_3 = -3$ and indeed $6(1,1) - 2(0,3) - 3(2,0) = (0,0)$.

The vectors $\mathbf{v}_1, \mathbf{v}_2, \cdots, \mathbf{v}_k$ are said to be **linearly independent** if they are **not** linearly dependent. Testing vectors for linear dependence is usually not easy! It often involves solving systems of equations. For example in $\mathbb{R}^3$, are the vectors

$(1,2,1), (-3,0,4)$ and $(6,-2,2)$ linearly independent? To check we try to find constants c_1, c_2, c_3 such that

$$c_1(1,2,1) + c_2(-3,0,4) + c_3(6,-2,2) = (0,0,0)$$

that is,

$$(c_1 - 3c_2 + 6c_3, 2c_1 - 2c_3, c_1 + 4c_2 + 2c_3) = (0,0,0),$$

which is equivalent to solving the system of equations

$$c_1 - 3c_2 + 6c_3 = 0$$
$$2c_1 \phantom{{} - 3c_2} - 2c_3 = 0$$
$$c_1 + 4c_2 + 2c_3 = 0$$

It is an exercise for you to show that the only solution for this system is $c_1 = c_2 = c_3 = 0$ and it follows that the vectors $(1,2,1), (-3,0,4)$ and $(6,-2,2)$ are indeed linearly independent.

A.3 Bases

Given a vector space $\mathcal{V}/\mathbb{R}$, a set of vectors $\{\mathbf{v}_1, \mathbf{v}_2, \cdots, \mathbf{v}_k\}$ is said to form a ***basis*** for $\mathcal{V}$ if for every vector $\mathbf{v} \in \mathcal{V}$, there exist *unique* constants $c_1, c_2, \cdots, c_k$ such that

$$\mathbf{v} = c_1\mathbf{v}_1 + c_2\mathbf{v}_2 + \cdots + c_k\mathbf{v}_k.$$

The integer k is called the ***dimension*** of $\mathcal{V}$. In this case $\mathcal{V}$ is said to be ***finite dimensional***. It is a deep theorem in Linear Algebra, that in a vector space $\mathcal{V}$ of dimension k, there can be many sets of basis vectors! *But any basis will contain exactly k vectors only.* In fact, any k linearly independent vectors form a basis!

In $\mathbb{R}^3$, of dimension 3, any basis will contain three linear independent vectors. The *standard* basis is the familiar set of vectors $(1,0,0), (0,1,0)$ and $(0,0,1)$ (often referred as **i, j, k**). But this is not the only basis. The set of vectors $\{(1,2,1),(2,0,1),(1,1,0)\}$ is also a basis. It is easy to verify that they are linearly independent. Note that there must still be three vectors in a basis.

In an n-dimensional vector space (e.g. $\mathbb{R}^n$), we require n constants $c_1, c_2, \cdots, c_n$ to determine a vector. For this reason we sometimes say we have n ***degrees of***

freedom. This point is worth noting for the rest of the course.

Appendix B

Operator Methods with Complex Coefficients

B.1 Introduction

In Chapter 4 we considered finding a particular solution for the equation

$$p(D)\,y = Q(x) \tag{B.1}$$

by using the method of undetermined coefficients and the operator method. However, while using the operator method we noticed it was easier to deal with some equations such as

$$y'' + a^2 y = \cos ax$$

by reverting to the UC method (Chapter 4 Remark 20). As you have seen, the UC method can become very tedious in some cases. If you wondered whether it was at all possible to avoid the method of undetermined coefficients and continue using the operator method while dealing with the trigonometric functions $\cos ax$, $\sin ax$, the answer is YES! This can be done elegantly by using complex numbers but one needs to be careful.

The operator method using complex coefficients is particularly useful when $Q(x)$ in (B.1) is of the form $x^k \cos ax$, $x^k \sin ax$ since the UC method may be very long and we cannot shift x^k. The method is also useful for those cases where $Q(x) = e^{kx} \cos bx$. Here one can simply shift e^{kx} and use the usual operator method. But the use of complex variables is equally well suited.

Recall Euler's formula,

$$e^{(a\pm ib)x} = e^{ax}(\cos bx \pm i\sin bx).$$

In particular $e^{iax} = \cos ax + i\sin ax$ and hence we can write

$$\cos ax = \Re(e^{iax}), \quad \sin ax = \Im(e^{iax}).$$

Here $\Re$ stands for the real part and $\Im$ for the imaginary part. It is useful to note that

$$1/i = -i \quad \text{and} \quad e^{iax}/i = \sin ax - i\cos ax.$$

These facts are used in problems involving complex numbers.

The following may seem a little heavy going at first. But if you study it carefully, it is no more difficult than the other methods. One just needs to keep track of real and imaginary parts at all times.

Consider Example 4.15 from Chapter 4 once again:

Example B.1. *Find y_p for the equation*

$$y'' + a^2 y = \cos ax$$

using the operator method.

Solution: We will find the particular solution η_p for the problem $y'' + a^2 y = e^{iax}$ and use the fact $y_p = \Re(\eta_p)$. We have

$$\begin{aligned}
\eta_p &= \frac{1}{D^2 + a^2} e^{iax} \\
&= e^{iax} \frac{1}{(D+ia)^2 + a^2} \cdot 1 \quad \text{(using exponential shift)} \\
&= e^{iax} \frac{1}{(D^2 + 2iaD)} \cdot 1 \\
&= e^{iax} \frac{1}{D} \frac{1}{(D+2ia)} \cdot e^{0x} \\
&= \frac{e^{iax}}{2ia} \frac{1}{D} \cdot 1 \quad \text{(from Remark 15)} \\
&= \frac{\sin ax - i\cos ax}{2a} \cdot x
\end{aligned}$$

Hence,

$$y_p = \Re(\eta_p) = \frac{x \sin ax}{2a},$$

as obtained by the method of undetermined coefficients.

Notice that as a bonus we have found y_p for the problem

$$y'' + a^2 y = \sin ax$$

since in this case

$$y_p = \Im(\eta_p) = \frac{-x \cos ax}{2a},$$

also as found by the method of undetermined coefficients.

This method is quite powerful! Consider the following example.

Example B.2. *Solve the equation*

$$(D^4 + 2a^2 D^2 + a^4) y = \cos ax.$$

Solution: First note that the left hand side can be factored as $(D^2 + a^2)^2 y$. Thus, the complementary solution is

$$y_c = (Ax + B) \cos ax + (Cx + D) \sin ax.$$

The method of undetermined coefficients is very involved. On the other hand, proceeding as in Example B.1,

$$\frac{1}{(D^2 + a^2)^2} e^{iax}$$
$$= e^{iax} \frac{1}{\left((D + ia)^2 + a^2\right)^2} \cdot 1$$
$$= e^{iax} \frac{1}{\left(D^2 + 2iaD\right)^2} \cdot 1$$
$$= e^{iax} \frac{1}{D^2} \frac{1}{(D + 2ia)^2} \cdot e^{0x}$$
$$= \frac{e^{iax}}{4i^2 a^2} \frac{1}{D^2} \cdot 1 \quad \text{(from Remark 15)}$$
$$= -\frac{e^{iax}}{4a^2} \frac{x^2}{2}$$
$$= -\frac{x^2}{8a^2} (\cos ax + i \sin ax).$$

It follows that

$$y_p = \Re\left\{\frac{1}{(D^2 + a^2)^2}\right\} e^{iax} = -\frac{x^2 \cos ax}{8a^2},$$

and the complete solution is

$$y = (Ax + B)\cos ax + (Cx + D)\sin ax - \frac{x^2 \cos ax}{8a^2}.$$

Now try doing that with the method of undetermined coefficients!

B.2 Exercises

Solve the following equations using the operator method.

1. $y'' + y = x^2 \cos x$.

2. $y'' + 4y = x \cos 2x$.

3. $(D - 2)^2 y = e^{2x} \sin x$.

Answers and Hints to Selected Exercises

Exercises 1.5

1. (a) First order.
   (c) Second order.
   (e) Second order.

2. (a) Trivial.
   (c) Differentiate the first equation to get $y' = (xy' + y)/\sqrt{1 - x^2y^2}$ and cross multiply.
   (e) Differentiate twice to get $y' = a\cos x - b\sin x$ and $y'' = -a\sin x - b\cos x = -y$ from which $y'' + y = 0$.

3. (a) $df = \cos(2x)dx$.
   (c) $df = 2/\sqrt{1 - 4x^2}dx$.
   (e) $df = e^{-t}(c_1(-\cos t - \sin t) + c_2(\cos t - \sin t))$.

4. (a) $(x^3 + y^2)dx - 2xdy = 0$.
   (b) $ydx - (x - \sqrt{1 - xy})dy = 0$.
   (c) $y\cot x\, dx + dy = 0$.
   (d) $e^{2x}dx - ydy = 0$.
   (e) $(x^2 + y)dx - x^3 dy = 0$.

5. (a) $y' = \dfrac{2xy^2 + y}{x}$
   (c) $y' = -y/x^2$.
   (e) $y' = 2x/(e^x - 1)$.

6. (a) The isoclines are the lines $2y = c$, where c is any constant. For any x_0, if $y(x_0) > 0$, then $y \to \infty$ as $x \to \infty$. If $y(x_0) < 0$, then $y \to -\infty$, and $y = 0$ if $y(x_0) = 0$.

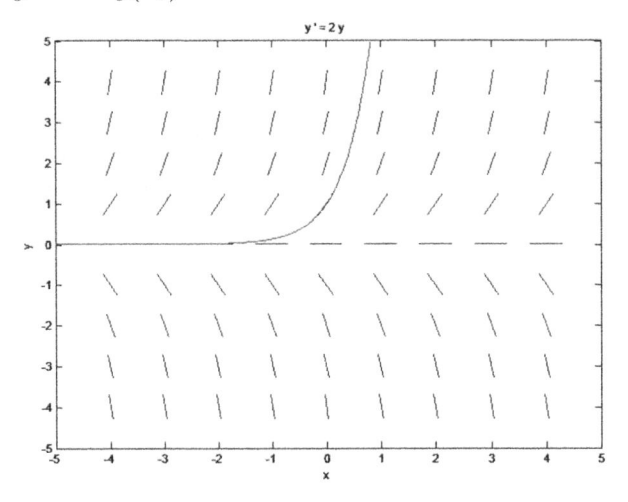

(c) The isoclines are the parabolas $y = x^2 - c$, where c is any constant.

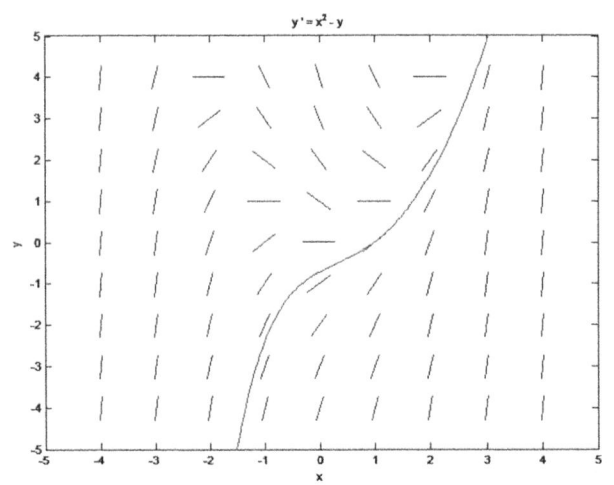

Exercises 2.6

1. (a) separable, exact
   (b) separable
   (c) linear
   (d) linear
   (e) exact

2. (a) $\frac{1}{3}y^3 + y = -e^x - \frac{1}{2}x^2 + c$.

ANSWERS AND HINTS

(b) $y = c\sqrt{1+x^2}$.

(c) $1/y^4 + 1/x^4 = c$.

(d) Rewrite as $dy/y = \tan x dx$. Solution is $y = c \sec x$.

(e) $y^2/2 + 2y = \arctan x + c$.

(f) Solution is $2y^2 = 2x^2 + x^4 + c$. From the initial conditions $c = 15$, the unique solution is $2y^2 = 2x^2 + x^4 + 15, y > 0$, or it can also be written as $y = \sqrt{x^2 + \frac{1}{2}x^4 + \frac{15}{2}}$.

(g) $-1/y = x^3/3 - 1/6$.

3. (a) $y = \frac{6}{7}x^3 + cx^{-4}$.

   (c) Dividing by x throughout, $\dfrac{dy}{dx} + \dfrac{2x+1}{x(x+1)}y = \dfrac{x-1}{x}$. This is linear with $P = (2x+1)/(x^2+x)$ so the integrating factor is (x^2+x). Hence the solution is $y(x^2+x) = x^3/3 - x + c$.

   (e) $xy = 1 + c\exp(-y^2/2)$.

   (g) $yx - x = cy$.

4. (a) Regroup as $(3x + x^2)dx + (y - \frac{1}{y^2})dy + 2(ydx + xdy) = 0$. Recall that $(ydx + xdy) = d(xy)$.

   (b) $x^2y^2 + 2xy = c$.

   (d) $y \ln x + 3x^2 - 2y = c$.

   (e) The given equation can be rewritten as $(6xydx + 3x^2dy) + (2y^2dx + 4xydy) = 0$ and the solution is $3x^2y + 2xy^2 = c$.

   (f) This is exact if written as $(bx + cy)dy + (ax + by)dx = 0$. Solution is $ax^2 + 2bxy + cy^2 = c$.

   (h) If you rewrite it as $(1/t)\{(3s^2 - 2)ds\} + (s^3 - 2s)\{\frac{-dt}{t^2}\}$ the solution is obvious!

   (k) Rewrite as $-\{dx/x^2 + dy/y^2\} + (-ydx + xdy)/x^2 = 0$ and remember the last term is $d(y/x)$.

   (l) $f(x,y) = 3x^2y + 2xy^2 - 5x - 6y + c$.

5. (c) $M_y = 2y, N_x = 0$, so $(M_y - N_x)/N = 1$ and integrating factor is e^x. Multiplying and solving $d(x^2e^x) + d(y^2e^x) = 0$, $x^2e^x + y^2e^x = c$.

(d) Here $M_y = 1, N_x = 2, (N_x - M_y)/M = 1/y$ so that the integrating factor is $e^{\int Pdy} = y$. Multiplying the equation by this factor, $y^2dx + 2xydy + ye^ydy = 0 \Rightarrow d(xy^2) + ye^ydy = 0$. Integrating $xy^2 + \int ye^ydy = c$, that is, $xy^2 + ye^y + e^y = c$.

6. (c) After you substitute $y = vx$, you should get $v + x(dv/dx) = v \ln v + v$ from which one gets $dv/(v \ln v) = dx/x$. This can be integrated as $\ln(\ln v) = \ln(cx)$ and the solution is $y = xe^{cx}$.

(d) $1/(Mx + Ny) = 1/x^4$ is the integrating factor. Multiplying and rewriting the given equation as

$$\frac{dx}{x} - \frac{1}{3}\left\{\frac{3x^3y^2dy - 3x^2y^3dx}{x^6}\right\} = 0$$

the solution is $\ln x - \frac{1}{3}(y^3/x^3) = c$ as before.

7. (a) $\tan x \tan y = c$

(b) $y = ce^{y/x}$

(c) $ye^{\sin x} = e^{\sin x}(\sin x - 1) + c$

(d) $y = x^2/(c - e^x)$.

(e) $(x^2 + y^2) = 2a^2 \tan^{-1}(y/x) + c$

(f) $x^3 - 2y^3 = cx$

(g) $\sqrt{1 + x^2} = -\sqrt{1 + y^2} + c$

(h) $\ln \frac{y^3}{x^2} + \frac{x}{y} = c$

(i) $2y(1 + x^3) = x - \sin x \cos x + c$

(j) $y = x + c_1e^{-x} + c_2$. (Hint: Set $z = y'$)

(k) $x(y - 1) = cy + 1$

(l) $y^3 \cos^3 x = -\frac{\cos^6 x}{2} + c$. (Hint: Bernoulli)

(m) $1 = y\left[-x + (1 - x^2)^{1/2}(\sin^{-1} x + c)\right]$

(n) $\ln(xy)^2 = y + c$

(o) $x + y + \frac{1}{2}(xy)^2 = c$

(p) $y = x/(1 - x + ce^{-x})$

8. (a) 256 ft.

ANSWERS AND HINTS

(b) 4 secs.

(c) 8 secs.

9. $\sqrt{gR}$.

10. (a) $\alpha = \sin^{-1}(2/3)$

(b) 64 feet

(c) 143 feet

12. $T_0 = 30$ degrees.

13. 32 times.

15. $250e^{-0.09}$ grams.

16. $100 - 90e^{-0.06t}$ pounds.

17. 0.044%.

18. 13.5 minutes.

19. 1.39 minutes.

20. $y^2 = 2xyy' + y^2(y')^2$.

21. (a) $y^2 = cx^3$.

(b) From the given equation we have $a = ye^{-2x}$. Taking the derivative we have $y' = 2ae^{2x} = 2(ye^{-2x})e^{2x} = 2y$. The slope of the tangents of the orthogonal trajectory is $y'_2 = -1/2y$, which leads to the differential equation $y' = -1/2y$. This is a separable equation which can be solved to get $y^2 = -x + c$.

(c) $y = ce^{-x}$.

(d) $y^3 - 3x^2y = c$.

24. $r^2 = c^2 \sin 2\theta$.

25. (a) $y^2 = 4(x+1)$.

(b) $xy = 0$.

(c) $4ay + x^2 = 0$.

(d) $c^2(x^2 + y^2) = x^2y^2$.

Exercises 3.4

1. (a) Linear, not homogeneous.

   (b) Not linear.

   (c) Linear, homogeneous.

   (d) Linear, homogeneous.

   (e) Linear, not homogeneous.

2. (a) Linearly independent.

   (c) Linearly dependent.

3. (d) $y = (c_1 \cos 2x + c_2 \sin 2x) + x(c_3 \cos 2x + c_4 \sin 2x)$.

4. (b) The auxiliary equation is $4m^2 - 7m + 3 = 0$ whose roots are $m = 1, 3/4$ and the general solution is $y = c_1 e^x + c_2 e^{3/4x}$.

   (e) The auxiliary equation is $(m+2)^2 = 0$ and has repeated roots -2, -2. The solution is $y = c_1 e^{-2x} + c_2 x e^{-2x}$.

   (f) The auxiliary equation can be factored as $(m^2 + 1)(m + 3) = 0$ whose roots are $m = \pm i, -3$. The solution is $y = c_1 \cos x + c_2 \sin x + c_3 e^{-3x}$.

   (g) One root of the auxiliary equation is -1.

   (h) $y = e^{-x}(c_1 \cos \frac{3}{4}x + c_2 \sin \frac{3}{4}x)$.

   (i) The auxiliary equation is $8m^3 + 12m^2 + 6m + 1 = 0$ which is really $(2m+1)^3 = 0$ with repeated roots $-1/2, -1/2, -1/2$.

   (j) Auxiliary equation is $m^3 - m = m(m-1)(m+1)$. General solution is $y = c_1 + c_2 e^x + c_3 e^{-x}$.

   (k) Auxiliary equation is $m^3 - 5m^2 + 9m - 5 = (m-1)(m^2 - 4m + 5)$. Roots are $m = 1, 2 \pm i$. General solution is $y = c_1 e^x + c_2 e^{2x} \cos x + c_3 e^{2x} \sin x$.

   (l) Auxiliary equation is $(m^2 - 4)^2 = 0$. Roots $m = \pm 2$ are double roots. General solution is $y = (c_1 + c_2 x)e^{2x} + (c_3 + c_4 x)e^{-2x}$.

5. (a) The general solution is $y = e^{3x}(c_1 \cos 4x + c_2 \sin 4x)$. Applying the initial conditions we get $c_1 = -3, c_2 = 2$ and the solution is $y = e^{3x}(-3\cos 4x + 2\sin 4x)$.

   (b) $y = 2e^{-x} - e^{-3x}$.

   (c) $y = xe^x$.

(d) $y \equiv 0$.

(e) Auxiliary equation is $16m^2 + 32m + 25 = 0$. Roots are $m = -1 \pm \frac{3}{4}i$. General solution is $y = e^{-x}(c_1 \cos \frac{3}{4}x + c_2 \sin \frac{3}{4}x)$. The condition $y(0) = 0$ implies $c_1 = 0$ and then the condition $y'(0) = 1$ implies $c_2 = \frac{4}{3}$. Final answer is $y = \frac{4}{3}e^{-x} \sin \frac{3}{4}x$.

(f) Auxiliary equation is $m^3 = 0$. Roots $m = 0$ is a triple root. General solution is $y = c_0 + c_1 x + c_2 x^2$. The condition $y(0) = 0$ implies $c_0 = 0$ and then the condition $y'(0) = 1$ implies $c_1 = 1$. The remaining constant c_2 is still arbitrary. Final answer is $y = x + c_2 x^2$.

6. $y = e^{2x}(c_1 \cos x + c_2 \sin x) + xe^{2x}(c_3 \cos x + c_4 \sin x)$.

7. The general solution is $y = c_1 e^{-x} + c_2 x e^{-x} + c_3 x^2 e^{-x} + c_4 x^3 e^{-x}$. The corresponding differential equation is $y^{(4)} + 4y''' + 6y'' + 4y' + y = 0$.

8. $y = c_1 e^{3x} + c_2 x e^{3x} + c_3 e^{2x} + c_4 e^{-x}$.

9. A parabola.

10. The equation of motion of the pendulum is $\theta(t) = c\cos(\omega t + \delta)$, where $\omega = \sqrt{g/\ell}$. The velocity is given by $v = -c\omega \sin(\omega t + \delta)$. At $t = 0, \theta = 1$ rad, $v = 0$. Hence, $\sin \delta = 0 \Rightarrow \delta = 0$. It follows that $c = 1$ and hence the equation of motion is $\theta(t) = \cos(\omega t)$. The amplitude is 1, period T is $2\pi/\omega = 2\pi/\sqrt{g}$, the frequency $f = \sqrt{g}/2\pi$. At the equilibrium position $\theta = 0 \Rightarrow \omega t = \pm \pi/2, v = \pm \omega = \pm \sqrt{g}$, which is the linear velocity. Then angular velocity is $v\ell = \pm \sqrt{g}$, same as v.

12. In equilibrium, the spring is stretched by six inches = 1/2 ft. The only forces on the object are the restorative force of the spring and its weight 4 lbs. If the mass of the object is m then $4 = mg, m = 4/32 = 1/8$. Assuming that the constant of proportionality of Hooke's law is k, $(1/2)k = 4$, from which $k = 8$. At any time time t, since the object stretches it by 1/2 ft, the total extension of the spring length is $y + \frac{1}{2}$. The restorative force of the spring acting upward is $k(y + 1/2) = 8y + 4$ acting upwards with its weight mg acting downwards. The net downward force then is $mg - (8y + 4) = -8y$. By Newton's law, $m\frac{d^2y}{dt^2} = -8y$, that is, $\frac{d^2y}{dt^2} + 64y = 0$ and this shows the motion is simple harmonic. The equation of motion is $y = c\cos(8t + \delta)$. Hence, $v = -8c\sin(8t + \delta)$. Since $y(0) = 1/2, v(0) = 0, \delta = 0$, and $c = 1/2$. Thus, the equation of motion is $y(t) = \frac{1}{2}\cos(8t)$. The period is $2\pi/8 = \pi/4$ sec, the frequency $f = 4/\pi$ cycles per second. The amplitude is 6 inches.

Exercises 4.4

1. (a) $y_p = Ax^2 + Bx + C$.
   (b) $y_p = Ae^x$.
   (c) $y_p = Ae^{3x}$.
   (d) $y_p = Ax\sin x + Bx\cos x$.
   (e) $y_p = (Ax^2 + Bx + C)e^x$.
   (f) $y_p = (Ax^2 + Bx) + (Cx^2 + Ex)\sin x + (Fx^2 + Gx)\cos x$.
   (g) $y_p = Ax^2 e^{2x}$.
   (h) The equation can be rewritten as $y'' + y = (1 + \cos 2x)/2$ so $y_p = A + (B\cos 2x + C\sin 2x)$.
   (i) $y_p = (Ax^2 + Bx)e^{-2x}$.
   (j) $y_p = (Ax^4 + Bx^3 + Cx^2)e^{-2x}$.

2. (a) $y = c_1 e^x + c_2 e^{2x} + e^{3x}$.
   (b) $y = c_1 e^{-x} + \cos x + \sin x$.

3. (a) $y_p = \dfrac{1}{D^4}e^{3x} = \dfrac{1}{3^4}e^{3x} = \dfrac{1}{81}e^{3x}$.
   (b) $y_p = \dfrac{1}{D-2}xe^{2x} = e^{2x}\dfrac{1}{(D+2)-2}x = e^{2x}\dfrac{1}{D}x = \dfrac{1}{2}x^2 e^{2x}$.
   (c) $y_p = \tfrac{1}{2}e^x + \cos x + \sin x$.
   (d) $y_p = -\tfrac{1}{12}x^4 e^{-2x}$.
   (e) $y_p = \tfrac{1}{17}e^{2x}(4\sin x - \cos x)$.
   (f) Note that
   $$\frac{1}{D^2 - 1} = -\frac{1}{1 - D^2} = -1 - D^2 - D^4 - D^6 - D^8 - \ldots$$
   so
   $$y_p = \frac{1}{D^2 - 1}x^4 = (-1 - D^2 - D^4 - D^6 - \ldots)x^4 = -x^4 - 12x^2 - 24.$$

4. (a) The auxiliary equation is $m^2 + 3m - 10 = 0$ with roots $m = -5, 2$. Hence $y_c = c_1 e^{-5x} + c_2 e^{2x}$. This is Case I. To find y_p, let $y_p = Ae^{4x}$. Therefore, $y_p' = 4Ae^{4x}, y_p'' = 16Ae^{4x}$. Substituting in the original equation we get $18Ae^{4x} = 6e^{4x}$ that is $A = \tfrac{1}{3}$ and the complete solution is $y = c_1 e^{-5x} + c_2 e^{2x} + \tfrac{1}{3}e^{4x}$.

(c) The auxiliary equation $m^2 - m - 6 = 0$ has roots $m = 3, -2$ and $y_c = c_1 e^{3x} + c_2 e^{-2x}$. This is Case II with $k = 0$ since e^{-2x} occurs on the right. We assume $y_p = Axe^{-2x}$ and get $y_p' = A(e^{-2x} - 2xe^{-2x})$, $y_p'' = A(-4e^{-2x} + 4xe^{-2x})$. Substitute in the original equation to get $-5Ae^{-2x} = 20e^{-2x}$ that is $A = -4$. The complete solution is: $y = c_1 e^{3x} + c_2 e^{-2x} - 4xe^{-2x}$. Again note cancelation of the term xe^{-2x} when we substitute in the original equation.

(e) From the auxiliary equation $m^2 - 2m + 1 = 0$ we get $m = 1, 1$, $y_c = (c_1 + c_2 x)e^x$. This is Case III. The roots $m = 1$ has multiplicity 2, that is $r = 2$. The right side is simply e^x so that $k = 0$. Hence we assume $y_p = Ax^2 e^x$ from which $y_p' = Ae^x(2x + x^2)$, $y_p'' = Ae^x(2 + 4x + x^2)$. Substitute to get $2Ae^x = 6e^x$, $A = 3$ and $y = c_1 e^x + c_2 x e^x + 3x^2 e^x$.

(g) The auxiliary equation being $m^2 + 4 = 0$, we have $m = \pm 2i$, $y_c = c_1 \cos 2x + c_2 \sin 2x$, $F = \{\cos 2x, \sin 2x\}$, $G = \{\cos 2x, \cos x, x^2, x\}$. The first term in G is case II, the others are case I. To find y_p we break the problem into three subproblems: (i) $y'' + 4y = 4\cos 2x$, (ii) $y'' + 4y = 6\cos x$, (iii) $y'' + 4y = 8x^2 - 4x$. We will write $y_{p_1}, y_{p_2}, y_{p_3}$ for the particular solutions of these subproblems.

  (i) Here $G = \{\cos 2x\}$, and this is case II. Hence, $y_{p_1} = x(A \sin 2x + B \cos 2x)$. This gives $y_{p_1}' = x(2A \cos 2x - 2B \sin 2x) + (A \sin 2x + B \cos 2x)$ and $y_{p_1}'' = x(-4A \sin 2x - 4B \cos 2x) + (4A \cos 2x - 4B \sin 2x)$. Substitute in (a) to get $y_{p_1}'' + 4y_{p_1} = 4A \cos 2x - 4B \sin 2x = 4\cos 2x$. Thus, $A = 1, B = 0$ and $y_{p_1} = x \sin 2x$.

  (ii) Here $G = \{\cos x\}$ so this is case I and $y_{p_2} = A\cos x + B \sin x$ so that $y_{p_2}' = -A \sin x + B \cos x$, $y_{p_2}'' = -A \cos x - B \sin x$. Therefore, $y_{p_2}'' + 4y_{p_2} = 3A \cos x + 3B \sin x = 6 \cos x$, that is, $A = 2, B = 0, y_{p_2} = 2\cos x$.

  (iii) It is trivial to see this is also case I so $y_{p_3} = Ax^2 + Bx + C$ to get $y_{p_3}' = 2Ax + B$, $y_{p_3}'' = 2A$, $y_{p_3}'' + 4y_{p_3} = 4Ax^2 + 4Bx + (2A + 4C) = 8x^2 - 4x$. Hence, $A = 2, B = -1, C = -1$ so $y_{p_3} = 2x^2 - x - 1$.

From (i), (ii) and (iii), the particular solution of the original problem is $y_p = y_{p_1} + y_{p_2} + y_{p_3} = x \sin 2x + 2 \cos x + 2x^2 - x - 1$. The general solution is $y = y_c + y_p = c_1 \cos 2x + c_2 \sin 2x + x \sin 2x + 2 \cos x + 2x^2 - x - 1$.

(i) Here $y_p = \frac{10}{(D+2)(D+2)} x^3 e^{-2x} = \frac{10 e^{-2x}}{D^2} x^3 = 10 e^{-2x} x^5 / 20 = \frac{1}{2} x^5 e^{-2x}$. Thus, $y = c_1 e^{-2x} + c_2 x e^{-2x} + \frac{1}{2} x^5 e^{-2x}$.

(k) Here $y_p = \frac{1}{D^2-D+1}(x^3-3x^2+1) = \frac{1}{1+D^2-D}(x^3-3x^2+1) = \{1-(D^2-D)+(D^2-D)^2-(D^2-D)^3+...\}(x^3-3x^2+1) = \{1-(D^2-D)+(D^4-2D^3+D^2)-(D^6-3D^5+3D^4-D^3)\}(x^3-3x^2+1) = \{1+D-D^3\}(x^3-3x^2+1) = \{(x^3-3x^2+1)+(3x^2-6x)-6)\} = x^3-6x-5$, where we have dropped powers of D higher than 3. Hence, $y = e^{1/2x}(c_1 \cos \frac{\sqrt{3}}{2}x + c_2 \sin \frac{\sqrt{3}}{2}x) + x^3 - 6x - 5$.

(m) $y_p = \frac{1}{D^3-8}16x^2 = -\frac{16}{8}\frac{1}{1-D^3/8}x^2 = -2(1+D^3/8+D^6/64+..)x^2 = -2x^2$. The general solution is $y = c_1e^{2x} + e^{-x}(c_1 \cos\sqrt{3}x + c_2 \sin\sqrt{3}x) - 2x^2$.

(o) $(D-2)^2 = e^{2x}\sin x$. The auxiliary equation is $(m-2)^2 = 0$ with roots $m = 2, 2$. Hence, $y_c = c_1e^{2x} + c_2xe^{2x}$ and $y_p = \frac{1}{(D-2)^2}e^{2x}\sin x = e^{2x} \cdot \frac{1}{D^2}\sin x = -e^{2x}\sin x$ and $y = c_1e^{2x} + c_2xe^{2x} - e^{2x}\sin x$.

5. (a) $y = e^{4x}(c_1e^{\sqrt{7}x} + c_2e^{-\sqrt{7}x}) + \frac{5}{29}\cos 5x - \frac{2}{29}\sin 5x$.

(b) $y = c_1e^x + c_2e^{3x} + \frac{10}{884}\cos 5x - \frac{11}{884}\sin 5x + \frac{1}{20}\sin x + \frac{1}{10}\cos x$.

(c) $y = c_1e^{-x} + (c_2 + c_3x)e^x + x^2 + 2x + 5$.

(d) $y = -\frac{1}{25}\cos 4x + \frac{1}{50}\sin 4x + \frac{1}{25}e^{-3x} + \frac{x}{8}\sin 4x$.

(e) $y = c_1e^{4x} + c_2e^{-2x} - \frac{3}{10}\cos 2x - \frac{1}{10}\sin 2x$.

6. (a) $y'' - 2y' + 2y = xe^x$; $\quad y = e^x(c_1 \cos x + c_2 \sin x) + xe^x$.

(b) $y'' + 4y = e^x \cos x$; $\quad y = c_1 \cos 2x + c_2 \sin 2x + \frac{e^x}{10}(\sin x + 2\cos x)$.

(c) $y'' + 16y = e^{-3x} + \cos 4x$; $\quad y = c_1 \cos 4x + c_2 \sin 4x + \frac{x}{8}\sin 4x + \frac{1}{25}e^{-3x}$.

Exercises 5.5

1. (a) $y'' - 6y' + 9y = 0$, $p(x) = -6$, $e^{-\int p dx} = e^{6x}$.

$$v = \int \frac{e^{-\int p dx}}{y_1^2}dx = \int dx = x.$$

General solution: $y = c_1e^{3x} + c_2xe^{3x}$.

(b) $p(x) = 2/x$, $e^{-\int p dx} = x^{-2}$.

$$v = \int \frac{e^{-\int p dx}}{y_1^2}dx = \int x^{-2}dx = -x^{-1}.$$

General solution: $y = c_1 + c_2x^{-1}$.

(c) $y = c_1 x + c_2 x \ln x$.

(d) $y = c_1 x^{-2} + c_2 x$.

(e) $y = cx + dx^4$, where c, d are constants.

(g) $y = c_1 \sqrt{x} + c_2 x^{-1}$.

(h) $y = ce^{2x} + d(x+1)$, where c, d are constants.

(j) $y = c_1 x^{-1/2} \sin x + c_2 x^{-1/2} \cos x$.

(k) If $y = e^x$ is a solution then substituting for y in $y'' + py' + qy = 0$ gives $e^x + pe^x + qe^x = 0$ which is possible only if $1 + p + q = 0$. Clearly the converse is also true. This condition applies in this problem since $(x-1) - x + 1 = 0$. Thus, as can easily be verified $y = e^x$ is a solution. To find another solution, in this problem $p = -x/(x-1)$, $\int (-p dx) = x + \ln(x-1)$, $\exp(\int (-p) dx = (x-1)e^x$. Hence, $v = \int (x-1)e^x/(e^{2x}) dx = \int (x-1)e^{-x} dx = -xe^{-x}$. Hence $y_2 = -x$ as can be verified. The complete solution is $y = c_1 x + c_2 e^x$.

2. (a) $y_1 = e^{2x}$, $y_2 = e^{-2x}$, $W = y_1 y_2' - y_2 y_1' = -4$.

$$v_1 = \int \frac{-y_2 Q(x)}{W} dx = \int \frac{1}{4} e^x dx = \frac{1}{4} e^x,$$
$$v_2 = \int \frac{y_1 Q(x)}{W} dx = \int -\frac{1}{4} e^{5x} dx = -\frac{1}{20} e^{5x}.$$

Thus, $y_p = v_1 y_1 + v_2 y_2 = \frac{1}{5} e^{3x}$.

(b) $y = c_1 e^{2x} + c_2 e^x - x e^x$.

(d) $y = c_1 \cos x + c_2 \sin x + \cos x \ln(\cos x) + x \sin x$.

(f) $y_c = c_1 \cdot 1 + c_2 = e^{2x}$ and $y = y_c + 2x^2 e^{2x} - 2x e^{2x}$.

(h) $y_c = c_1 e^{-x} + c_2 x e^{-x}$, $y_p = x^2 e^{-x} \left(\frac{1}{2} \ln x - \frac{3}{4} \right)$ and $y = y_c + y_p$.

(k) $y = \frac{x^4}{6} - \frac{x^2}{2}$.

3. (a) $y = c_1 x + c_2 x \ln x$.

(c) The auxiliary equation is $\theta^2 - 4\theta + 6 = 0$ with roots $2 \pm i\sqrt{2}$. So the solution is $e^{2t}(c_1 \cos \sqrt{2} t + c_2 \sin \sqrt{2} t) = x^2(c_1 \cos(\sqrt{2} \ln x) + c_2 \sin(\sqrt{2} \ln x))$.

(e) The auxiliary equation is $(\theta - 2)(\theta - 1)\theta + 2(\theta - 1)\theta - 10\theta - 8 = 0$. By inspection, $\theta = -1$ is a root so $(\theta + 1)$ is a factor. Dividing by $(\theta + 1)$ we get $(\theta + 1)(\theta^2 - 2\theta - 8) = (\theta + 1)(\theta - 4)(\theta + 2) = 0 \Rightarrow y = c_1 e^{-t} + c_2 e^{-2t} + c_3 e^{4t} = c_1 x^{-1} + c_2 x^{-2} + c_3 x^4$.

(g) $y_c = x^2(c_1 \cos(\ln x) + c_2 \sin(\ln x))$, $y_p = 5x^2$, $y = y_c + y_p$.

4. (a) $y = c_1/x + c_2(x + 1/x)$.

(b) $y = c_1 x + c_2 \cos x$.

(c) $y = \dfrac{1}{4x} - \dfrac{1}{9x^2} + \dfrac{1}{6}x \ln x - \dfrac{5}{36}x$.

(d) $y = x^2 - 2x \ln x$.

Exercises 6.6

1. $\sum_{k=0}^{\infty}(k+2)(k+1)c_{k+2}\,x^k$.

2. $\sum_{n=0}^{\infty}(n+3)(n+2)(n+1)x^n$.

3. Same.

4. (a) $y = ce^{-x}$.

(b) Here $a_1 = 1 = a_0$ and a_1/a_0 is analytic.

(c) $y' = c_1 + 2c_2 x + 3c_3 x^2 + \ldots = \sum_{n=1}^{\infty} nc_n x^{n-1}$.

(d) $\sum_{n=0}^{\infty} c_n x^n + \sum_{n=1}^{\infty} nc_n x^{n-1} = 0$.

(e) $\sum_{n=0}^{\infty}\{c_n + (n+1)c_{n+1}\}x^n = 0$, $(c_0 + c_1) + (c_1 + 2c_2)x + (c_2 + 3c_3)x^2 + (c_3 + 4c_4)x^3 + \ldots = 0$.

(f) $c_0 + c_1 = 0, c_1 + 2c_2 = 0, c_2 + 3c_3 = 0, \ldots c_n + (n+1)c_{n+1} = 0$. Hence $c_1 = (-1)c_0, c_2 = -c_1/2 = (-1)^2 c_0/2, c_3 = -c_2/3 = (-1)^3 c_0/3!, \ldots c_n = (-1)^n c_0/n!, \ldots$.

(g) $y = c_0 - c_0 x + c_0 x^2/2! - c_0 x^3/3! + \ldots = c_0\{\sum_{n=0}^{\infty}(-1)^n x^n/n!\}$. The answers are the same since the power series within the braces is the series for e^{-x}.

5. (b) a_0 and a_1 are arbitrary, $a_2 = a_0$ and $a_{n+2} = -\dfrac{(n-2)a_n + 3a_{n-1}}{(n+2)(n+1)}$, $n \geq 1$.

(d) $a_2 = -\dfrac{1}{4}a_0$, $a_{n+2} = -\dfrac{1}{2(n+2)}a_n$, $n \geq 1$. One quickly computes that

$$a_2 = -(1/2^2)a_0, \quad a_4 = (1/(2^4 2!))a_0, \quad a_6 = -(1/2^6 3!)a_0, \ldots,$$
$$a_{2n} = [(-1)^n/(2^{2n} n!)]a_0 \ldots$$

and likewise we have $a_3 = -(1/2 \cdot 3)a_1$, $a_5 = (-1)^2(1/(2^2 \cdot 3 \cdot 5)), \ldots, a_{2n+1} = (-1)^n/[2^n(1 \cdot 3 \cdot 5 \ldots (2n+1)]a_1$, both formulas valid for $n \geq 1$.

7. Using Leibniz's theorem we get

$$\left\{(1+x)^2 y_{n+2} + \binom{n}{1} 2x\, y_{n+1} + \binom{n}{2} 2\, y_n\right\} - \left\{x y_{n+1} + \binom{n}{1} y_n\right\} + \left\{x y_n + \binom{n}{1} y_{n-1}\right\} = 0,$$

which simplified becomes $(1+x^2)y_{n+2} + (2n-1)\,xy_{n+1} + (n^2 - 2n + x)y_n + ny_{n-1} = 0$.

8. (a) $y_{n+1} + y_n = 0$.

   (b) $c_{n+1}(n+1)! = -c_n \cdot n!$

   (c) $c_{n+1} = -c_n/(n+1)$, the answers are the same.

9. (a) Hint: Show that $(1-x^2)(y')^2 = 1$ and differentiate once.

   (b) $(1-x^2)y_{n+2} - (2n+1)xy_{n+1} = n^2 y_n$.

   (c) $a_0 = a_2 = a_4 = \ldots a_{2n} = 0$. $a_{2n+1} = \dfrac{(2n-1)^2}{2n(2n+1)} a_{2n-1}^2$, $n > 0$.

   (d) $a_1 = 1, a_3 = 1/6, a_5 = 1/480$.

10. (b) $a_{n+2} = -\dfrac{1}{(n+1)(n+2)}\{(n-1)a_n + 2a_{n-2}\}$, $n \geq 2$, where a_0, a_1 are arbitrary, $a_2 = \frac{1}{2}a_0$, and $a_3 = 0$.

    (d) $a_{n+2} = \dfrac{(n+1)a_{n+1} - 2a_{n-1}}{(n+1)(n+2)}$, $n \geq 1$, $a_2 = (1/2)a_1$ and a_0, a_1 are arbitrary.

    (f) $a_{n+2} = -\frac{1}{2}\dfrac{1}{(n+2)}a_n$, $n \geq 0$, a_0, a_1 arbitrary.

    (g) By Leibniz's theorem, $y_{n+2} - xy_n - ny_n = 0$ and at $x = 0$ this becomes $y_{n+2} = ny_n$. After substituting $(n+2)!a_{n+2}$ for y_{n+2} and $(n_1)!a_{n-1}$ for y_{n_1} we get the recurrence relation $a_{n+2} = \dfrac{1}{(n+2)(n+1)} a_{n-1}$, $n \geq 1$. Since a_{n+2} is given in terms of a_{n-1}, the subscripts for a_n jump by three. From the given equation, $y_2 = 0 = a_2$. Hence $a_2 = a_5 = a_8 = a_{11} = \ldots = 0$. In general, $a_{3n+2} = 0$, $n \geq 0$. From the recurrence formula it is easy to compute that

$$a_3 = \frac{a_0}{3 \cdot 2}, \quad a_6 = \frac{a_3}{6 \cdot 5} = \frac{a_0}{6 \cdot 5 \cdot 3 \cdot 2}, a_9 = \frac{a_0}{9 \cdot 8 \cdot 6 \cdot 5 \cdot 3 \cdot 2} \cdots,$$

and likewise

$$a_4 = \frac{a_1}{4 \cdot 3}, \quad a_7 = \frac{a_4}{7 \cdot 6} = \frac{a_1}{7 \cdot 6 \cdot 4 \cdot 3}, \quad a_{10} = \frac{a_7}{10 \cdot 9} = \frac{a_1}{10 \cdot 9 \cdot 7 \cdot 6 \cdot 4 \cdot 3}, \ldots$$

These results seem to show that

$$a_{3n} = \frac{a_0}{2 \cdot 3 \cdot 5 \ldots (3n-1)(3n)}, \quad a_{3n+1} = \frac{a_1}{3 \cdot 4 \cdot 6 \cdot 7 \ldots (3n)(3n+1)}, \quad n \geq 1.$$

Thus the general solution is

$$y = a_0 \left\{ 1+\sum_{n=1}^{\infty} \frac{x^{3n}}{2\cdot 3\cdot 5 \cdots (3n-1)(3n)} \right\} + a_1 \left\{ x+\sum_{n=1}^{\infty} \frac{x^{3n+1}}{3\cdot 4\cdot 6\cdot 7 \cdots (3n)(3n+1)} \right\}.$$

11. $(n+2)(n+1)a_{n+2} = a_n + a_{n-1}$, a_0, a_1 are arbitrary, $a_2 = a_0/2$, $a_3 = (a_0+a_1)/6$.

12. $a_{n+2} = -\dfrac{1}{n+2} a_n$.

Exercises 7.5

1. $2Dx - 3x + Dy + 4y = 1$
   $Dx - Dy = t + 1$.

2. $(2D+3)x - 2Dy = e^t$
   $(2D-3)x + (2D+8)y = e^t$.

3. The order of the system is the order of

$$\begin{vmatrix} D-1 & 2D-3 \\ D+1 & -D \end{vmatrix},$$

that is the order of $(D-1)(-D) - (2D-3)(D+1) = D - D^2 - 2D^2 + D + 3 = -3D^2 + 2D + 3$ which is 2.

4. Rewrite the system using D in the standard form:

$$(D-1)x + (D-1)y = t$$
$$(2D+2)x + (2D-1)y = 0.$$

The number of arbitrary constants equals the order of

$$\begin{vmatrix} D-1 & D-1 \\ 2D+2 & 2D-1 \end{vmatrix},$$

that is the order of $2D^2 - 3D + 1 - (2D^2 - 2) = -3D + 3$ which is 1.

5. (a) Using D notation we have $Dx - y = 0$, $x + (D-2)y = 0$. Eliminating y

and using the determinant notation we get

$$\begin{vmatrix} D & -1 \\ 1 & D-2 \end{vmatrix} x = - \begin{vmatrix} -1 & 0 \\ D-2 & 0 \end{vmatrix}$$

which reduces to $(D^2 - 2D + 1)x = 0$. Hence, $x = (c_1 + c_2 t)e^t$. We use the first equation to find y, that is $y = Dx = (c_1 + c_2)e^t + c_2 t e^t$.

(b) $x = c_1 e^{-2t} + \frac{1}{2} e^{4t}$, $y = -\frac{2}{3} c_1 e^{-2t} - \frac{1}{3} e^{4t}$.

(d) $x = c_1 e^{-2t} + \frac{1}{6} e^t + \frac{1}{10} e^{3t}$, $y = -\frac{1}{2} c_1 e^{-2t} - \frac{1}{3} e^t + \frac{1}{5} e^{3t}$.

(f) $x = c_1 e^{-3t} + c_2 e^t - \frac{1}{3} t + \frac{1}{9}$, $y = \frac{5}{3} t - 5 c_1 e^{-3t} - c_2 e^t - \frac{5}{9}$.

(h) $x = c_1 \cos t + c_2 \sin t - t - 2$, $y = -(c_1 + c_2) \cos t + (c_1 - c_2) \sin t - 2$.

(j) In determinant form this is

$$\begin{vmatrix} 2D-1 & D-1 \\ D+1 & D-1 \end{vmatrix} x = - \begin{vmatrix} D-1 & 2e^t \\ D-1 & e^t \end{vmatrix}.$$

In this example, $p_2(D) = p_4(D)$, that is the coefficients of y in both equations are the same and any attempt to eliminate y' will also eliminate y (this is the degenerate case). We cannot use the determinant method here since this will introduce an additional factor $(D-1)$ and hence the additional term $c_1 e^t$ in x_c. We eliminate y (and y') simply by subtraction to get $x' - 2x = e^t$ from which $x = c_1 e^{2t} - e^t$. From the second equation, $y' - y = e^t - x' - x$ from which $y = c_2 e^t - 3 c_1 e^{2t} + 3 t e^t$.

(l) $x = c_1 e^{4t} + c_2 e^{-2t}$, $y = c_1 e^{4t} - c_2 e^{-2t}$.

(m) In determinant form, this problem becomes

$$\begin{vmatrix} D^2 - 1 & D+1 \\ D-1 & D^2+1 \end{vmatrix} x = - \begin{vmatrix} D+1 & \sin t \\ D^2+1 & \cos t \end{vmatrix} = \sin t - \cos t$$

or $(D^4 - D^2)x = \sin t - \cos t$ and whose solution is

$$x_c = c_1 + c_2 t + c_3 e^t + c_4 e^{-t},$$
$$x_p = \frac{1}{D^2(D^2-1)}(\sin t - \cos t) = \frac{1}{D^2-1}(\cos t - \sin t)$$
$$= (\sin t - \cos t)/2.$$

To find y_p, we subtract the second equation from the first to get

$$x_p'' - y_p'' - (x_p' - y_p') = \sin t - \cos t,$$

that is

$$(D^2 - D)(x-y)_p = (\sin t - \cos t), \quad (x-y)_p = \frac{1}{D^2 - D}(\sin t - \cos t)$$

from which

$$x_p - y_p = (x-y)_p = -\frac{1-D}{1-D^2}(\sin t - \cos t) = \cos t.$$

It follows that

$$y_p = \tfrac{1}{2}\left(\sin t - 3\cos t\right).$$

Finally to find y_c we have from the second equation,

$$(D^2 + 1)y_c + (D-1)x_c = 0 \quad \text{from which} \quad (D^2+1)y_c = x_c - x_c'.$$

Hence,

$$\begin{aligned}(D^2+1)y_c &= \{c_1 + c_2 t + c_3 e^t + c_4 e^{-t}\} \\ &\quad - \{c_2 + c_3 e^t - c_4 e^{-t}\} \\ &= (c_1 - c_2) + c_2 t + 2c_4 e^{-t},\end{aligned}$$

from which $y_c = (c_1 - c_2) + c_2 t + c_4 e^{-t}$. It follows that

$$\begin{aligned} x &= c_1 + c_2 t + c_3 e^t + c_4 e^{-t} + \tfrac{1}{2}(\sin t - \cos t) \\ y &= (c_1 - c_2) + c_2 t + c_4 e^{-t} + \tfrac{1}{2}(\sin t - 3\cos t).\end{aligned}$$

(n) $x = c_1 e^t + c_2 e^{-5t} - \dfrac{13}{25} - \dfrac{2t}{5} + \dfrac{3e^{2t}}{7}, \quad y = c_1 e^t - c_2 e^{5t} - \dfrac{12}{25} - \dfrac{2t}{5} + \dfrac{4e^{2t}}{7}.$

(o) $x = (c_1 + c_2 t)e^t + (c_3 + c_4 t)e^{-t}, \quad y = e^t(-c_1 + c_2 - c_2 t)/2 - e^{-t}(c_3 + c_4 t + c_4)/2.$

(p) $x = c_1 e^{t/3} + c_2 e^{-t/3} + e^t/2 + 3t + 10, \quad 2y = 11 - 3t - c_1 e^{t/3} - 2c_2 e^{-t/3}.$

(q) $x = c_1 e^{2t} + c_2 e^{-3t}, \quad y = c_2 e^{-3t} - 2c_1 e^{2t}.$

Exercises 8.5

1. (a) Diverges.

(c) Converges.

2. (a) $6/s^3$.

   (c) $1/(s+1)^2$.

   (e) The integral becomes $\int_4^\infty 2e^{-st}dt$, which after taking the limit becomes $(2/s)e^{-4s}$.

3. (a) $1/s - 12/s^4$.

   (c) $2/s^3 + 2/(s^2+4)$.

   (e) $\frac{3}{(s-1)^2+9} - \frac{6}{s^4} + \frac{2}{s}$.

4. (a) $\frac{1}{2}t^2$.

   (c) $\cosh\sqrt{2}t$.

   (e) $4e^{-2t} - 2e^t$.

5. (a) $y = \frac{-1}{2}e^{-t} + \frac{3}{2}e^t$.

   (c) $y = -te^{2t}$.

   (e) Write $g(t) = 1 - u_3(t)$, where u_3 is a unit step function with jump discontinuity at $t = 3$. Taking Laplace transform on both sides and simplifying gives $\mathcal{L}\{y\} = \dfrac{2s^2+s+1-e^{-3s}}{s(s+1)(s-1)}$. Using partial fractions, $\dfrac{2s^2+s+1}{s(s+1)(s-1)} = \dfrac{-1}{s} + \dfrac{1}{s+1} + \dfrac{2}{s-1}$ and $\dfrac{e^{-3s}}{s(s+1)(s-1)} = \dfrac{-e^{-3s}}{s} + \dfrac{1/2e^{-3s}}{s+1} + \dfrac{1/2e^{-3s}}{s-1}$. Taking the inverse transform we have $y = e^{-t} + 2e^t - 1 + (1 - \frac{1}{2}e^{-t+3} - \frac{1}{2}e^{t-3})u_3(t)$.

   (f) Write the input rate $g(t)$ as $g(t) = 3.6 - 1.8u_{10}(t)$.

Exercises 9.7

1. (a) $y(0.2) \approx 0.8$, $y(0.4) \approx 0.7040$, $y(0.6) \approx 0.6612$.

   (b) $y(1.1) \approx 0.5$, $y(1.2) \approx 0.7448$, $y(1.3) \approx 0.9396$.

   (c) $y(0.25) \approx 2$, $y(0.5) \approx 2.1176$, $y(0.75) \approx 2.3294$.

   (d) We rewrite the equation as $dy/dt = (ty + y^2)/t^2$. Hence $f(t,y) = (ty + y^2)/t^2$. The approximations are $y(2.5) \approx 0.6563$, $y(3) \approx 0.8220$, $y(3.5) \approx 0.9965$.

   (e) $y(\pi/4) \approx 3.2214$, $y(\pi/2) \approx 5.5035$, $y(3\pi/4) \approx 5.5035$.

   (f) $y(0.5) \approx 0.7854$, $y(1) \approx 1.0354$, $y(1.5) \approx 1.7751$.

2. (a) $y(0.2) \approx 0.8520$, $y(0.4) \approx 0.7712$, $y(0.6) \approx 0.7344$.

   (b) $y(1.1) \approx 0.3724$, $y(1.2) \approx 0.6394$, $y(1.3) \approx 0.8542$.

   (c) $y(0.25) \approx 2.0588$, $y(0.5) \approx 2.2284$, $y(0.75) \approx 2.4869$.

   (d) $y(2.5) \approx 0.6610$, $y(3) \approx 0.8326$, $y(3.5) \approx 1.0142$.

   (e) $y(\pi/4) \approx 3.2518$, $y(\pi/2) \approx 4.3969$, $y(3\pi/4) \approx 3.1067$.

   (f) $y(0.5) \approx 0.9104$, $y(1) \approx 1.5080$, $y(1.5) \approx 2.2717$.

3. Since $h = \pi/3$ we need to apply the methods iteratively three times to obtain the approximate solutions at the points $t = \pi/3, 2\pi/3$, and $\pi/3$.

   (a) Euler's method: $y(\pi) \approx 5.8999$.

   (b) Modified Euler's method: $y(\pi) \approx 5.5376$.

4. We first rewrite the equation as $y' = (1 + t^2)(t/y)$, giving us $f(t, y) = (1 + t^2)(t/y)$. The approximate values obtained by the Euler's and Modified Euler methods are shown below:

t	Exact	Euler	Error	Modified Euler	Error
1	3	3	0	3	0
1.25	3.2067	3.1667	0.0401	3.2098	0.0030
1.5	3.5045	3.4195	0.0849	3.5107	0.0062
1.75	3.9054	3.7760	0.1294	3.9146	0.0092
2	4.4159	4.2467	0.1692	4.4278	0.0119

5. (a) $y(0.25) \approx 0.2188$, $y(0.5) \approx 0.3896$.

   (b) $y(0.5) \approx 1.1250$, $y(1) \approx 1.6406$.

   (c) $y(0.1) \approx 3.1366$, $y(0.2) \approx 3.1226$, $y(0.3) \approx 3.1006$.

   (d) $y(\pi/4) \approx 2.0009$, $y(\pi/2) \approx 3.0075$.

   (e) $y(0.5) \approx 0.8750$, $y(1) \approx 0.8716$, $y(1.5) \approx 1.0261$.

   (f) $y(1.25) \approx 0.2813$, $y(1.5) \approx 0.6673$.

6. (a) $y(0.25) \approx 0.2212$, $y(0.5) \approx 0.3935$.

   (b) $y(0.5) \approx 1.1484$, $y(1) \approx 1.7173$.

   (c) $y(0.1) \approx 3.1368$, $y(0.2) \approx 3.1229$, $y(0.3) \approx 3.1010$.

   (d) $y(\pi/4) \approx 2.0492$, $y(\pi/2) \approx 3.1910$.

   (e) $y(0.5) \approx 0.7891$, $y(1) \approx 0.7860$, $y(1.5) \approx 0.9576$.

(f) $y(1.25) \approx 0.2874$, $y(1.5) \approx 0.6916$.

7. (a) $y(0.25) \approx 0.2212$, $y(0.5) \approx 0.3935$.

    (b) $y(0.5) \approx 1.1484$, $y(1) \approx 1.7173$.

    (c) $y(0.1) \approx 3.1368$, $y(0.2) \approx 3.1229$, $y(0.3) \approx 3.1010$.

    (d) $y(\pi/4) \approx 2.0520$, $y(\pi/2) \approx 3.1978$.

    (e) $y(0.5) \approx 0.7432$, $y(1) \approx 0.7498$, $y(1.5) \approx 0.9274$.

    (f) $y(1.25) \approx 0.2877$, $y(1.5) \approx 0.6932$.

8. (a) $\mathbf{y}(0.2) \approx (2.6000, 3.8000)$, $\mathbf{y}(0.4) \approx (3.3600, 4.8000)$, $\mathbf{y}(0.6) \approx (4.3200, 6.0480)$.

    (b) We first rewrite the equations as

    $$x' = t - 2x + 3y$$
    $$y' = e^{2t} + 3x - 2y.$$

    Hence,

    $$\mathbf{f}(t, \mathbf{y}) = \begin{pmatrix} t - 2x + 3y \\ e^{2t} + 3x - 2y \end{pmatrix}.$$

    The approximations obtained by Euler's method are:
    $\mathbf{y}(0.1) \approx (0.8000, 0.4000)$, $\mathbf{y}(0.2) \approx (0.7700, 0.6821)$, $\mathbf{y}(0.3) \approx (0.8406, 0.9259)$.

    (c) We rewrite the system as follows:

    $$x' = (1/3)(3x + 4y - 3t - 1)$$
    $$y' = (1/3)(-2x - 3y + e^t)$$

    so that

    $$\mathbf{f}(t, \mathbf{y}) = \begin{pmatrix} (1/3)(3x + 4y - 3t - 1) \\ (1/3)(-2x - 3y + e^t) \end{pmatrix}.$$

    The Euler's method gives the following approximations:
    $\mathbf{y}(1.25) \approx (1.9167, 2.3099)$, $\mathbf{y}(1.5) \approx (2.7699, 1.7038)$, $\mathbf{y}(1.75) \approx (3.5720, 1.1897)$.

    (d) $\mathbf{y}(0.5) \approx (-2, 7.5)$, $\mathbf{y}(1) \approx (4.5, -3.75)$, $\mathbf{y}(1.5) \approx (15.1875, -10.3125)$.

    (e) $\mathbf{y}(0.1) \approx (1, 0.1, 1)$, $\mathbf{y}(0.2) \approx (0.99, 0.2, 1.005)$, $\mathbf{y}(0.3) \approx (0.9699, 0.2995, 1.0149)$.

9. (a) $\mathbf{y}(0.2) \approx (2.6871, 3.9085)$, $\mathbf{y}(0.4) \approx (3.5803, 5.0721)$,
$\mathbf{y}(0.6) \approx (4.7374, 6.5595)$.

(b) $\mathbf{y}(0.1) \approx (0.8749, 0.3517)$, $\mathbf{y}(0.2) \approx (0.8678, 0.6454)$,
$\mathbf{y}(0.3) \approx (0.9479, 0.9240)$.

(c) $\mathbf{y}(1.25) \approx (1.8868, 2.3490)$, $\mathbf{y}(1.5) \approx (2.7226, 1.7804)$,
$\mathbf{y}(1.75) \approx (3.5254, 1.3005)$.

(d) $\mathbf{y}(0.5) \approx (0.7293, 4.1431)$, $\mathbf{y}(1) \approx (0.2219, 3.0051)$,
$\mathbf{y}(1.5) \approx (0.1067, 1.9636)$.

(e) $\mathbf{y}(0.1) \approx (0.9950, 0.0999, 1.0025)$, $\mathbf{y}(0.2) \approx (0.9799, 0.1993, 1.0099)$,
$\mathbf{y}(0.3) \approx (0.9547, 0.2976, 1.0219)$.

10. (a) Set $y_1 = y$ and $y_2 = y'$. Then $y_1' = y' = y_2$ and $y_2' = y'' = 3y' - 2y + e^t = 3y_2 - 2y_1 + e^t$. The initial conditions $y_1(0) = y(0) = 1$ and $y_2(0) = y'(0) = 3$. In matrix form, we write

$$\begin{pmatrix} y_1' \\ y_2' \end{pmatrix} = \begin{pmatrix} y_2 \\ 3y_2 - 2y_1 + e^t \end{pmatrix}, \quad \mathbf{y}(0) = \begin{pmatrix} 1 \\ 3 \end{pmatrix}.$$

(b) Let $y_1 = y$ and $y_2 = y'$. Hence, $y_1' = y' = y_2$ and $y_2' = y'' = 4y + e^{3t}$. In matrix form, this becomes

$$\begin{pmatrix} y_1' \\ y_2' \end{pmatrix} = \begin{pmatrix} y_2 \\ 4y_1 + e^{3t} \end{pmatrix}, \quad \mathbf{y}(0) = \begin{pmatrix} 0 \\ 1 \end{pmatrix}.$$

(c) Setting $y_1 = y$ and $y_2 = y'$, we obtain $y_1' = y' = y_2$ and $y_2' = y'' = (ty' - y)/t^2$. In matrix form, this can be written as

$$\begin{pmatrix} y_1' \\ y_2' \end{pmatrix} = \begin{pmatrix} y_2 \\ (1/t)y_2 - (1/t^2)y_1 \end{pmatrix}, \quad \mathbf{y}(1) = \begin{pmatrix} 3 \\ 1 \end{pmatrix}.$$

(d) Set $y_1 = y$, $y_2 = y'$. Then $y_1' = y' = y_2$ and $y_2' = y'' = [4(t+1)y' - 4y]/(2t+1) = [4(t+1)y_2 - 4y_1]/(2t+1)$. Writing it in matrix form,

$$\begin{pmatrix} y_1' \\ y_2' \end{pmatrix} = \begin{pmatrix} y_2 \\ \frac{4(t+1)}{2t+1}y_2 - \frac{4}{(2t+1)}y_1 \end{pmatrix}, \quad \mathbf{y}(1) = \begin{pmatrix} 2 \\ 0 \end{pmatrix}.$$

ANSWERS AND HINTS 255

(e)
$$\begin{pmatrix} y_1' \\ y_2' \end{pmatrix} = \begin{pmatrix} y_2 \\ \sin(t - y_1) + y_1^2 \end{pmatrix}, \quad \mathbf{y}(0) = \begin{pmatrix} 1 \\ 1 \end{pmatrix}.$$

(f) Since the ODE is a third-order ODE, we introduce three new variables: $y_1 = y, y_2 = y', y_3 = y''$. It follows that

$$y_1' = y' = y_2$$
$$y_2' = y'' = y_3$$
$$y_3' = y''' = y'' - 5y + e^{2t} = y_3 - 5y_1 + e^{2t}.$$

The initial condition is given by $y_1(0) = y(0) = 1, y_2(0) = y'(0) = 2, y_3(0) = y''(0) = 3$. The system in matrix form is

$$\begin{pmatrix} y_1' \\ y_2' \\ y_3' \end{pmatrix} = \begin{pmatrix} y_2 \\ y_3 \\ y_3 - 5y_1 + e^{2t} \end{pmatrix}, \quad \mathbf{y}(0) = \begin{pmatrix} 1 \\ 2 \\ 3 \end{pmatrix}.$$

11. (a) We let $y_1 = x, y_2 = x', y_3 = y, y_4 = y'$. Then the derivatives are given by

$$y_1' = x' = y_2$$
$$y_2' = x'' = -x' + y = -y_2 + y_3$$
$$y_3' = y' = y_4$$
$$y_4' = y'' = x' - y - 1 = y_2 - y_3 - 1$$

The initial values are $y_1(2) = x(2) = 4, y_2(2) = x'(2) = 5, y_3(2) = y(2) = 0, y_4(2) = y'(2) = 2$. In matrix form, we can write this system as

$$\begin{pmatrix} y_1' \\ y_2' \\ y_3' \\ y_4' \end{pmatrix} = \begin{pmatrix} y_2 \\ -y_2 + y_3 \\ y_4 \\ y_2 - y_3 - 1 \end{pmatrix}, \quad \mathbf{y}(2) = \begin{pmatrix} 4 \\ 5 \\ 0 \\ 2 \end{pmatrix}.$$

(b)
$$\begin{pmatrix} y_1' \\ y_2' \\ y_3' \\ y_4' \end{pmatrix} = \begin{pmatrix} y_2 \\ -y_1 + 2y_4 + 5 \\ y_4 \\ y_1 - 3y_4 \end{pmatrix}, \quad \mathbf{y}(1) = \begin{pmatrix} 1 \\ 3 \\ 0 \\ 4 \end{pmatrix}.$$

12. The oscillations of the two populations can be seen clearly here even though their amplitudes are slowly decreasing.

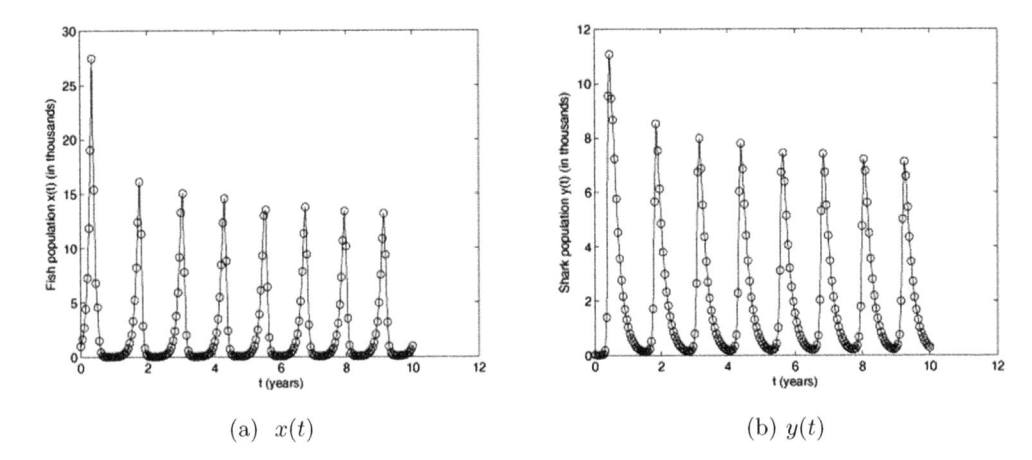

Figure B.1: Fish $x(t)$ and shark $y(t)$ populations for Chapter 9 Exercises problem 12.

13. The oscillations are quickly damped out. Starting at year 4, the fish population reaches the average (steady-state) population of 2500, while the shark population reaches an average of 1500.

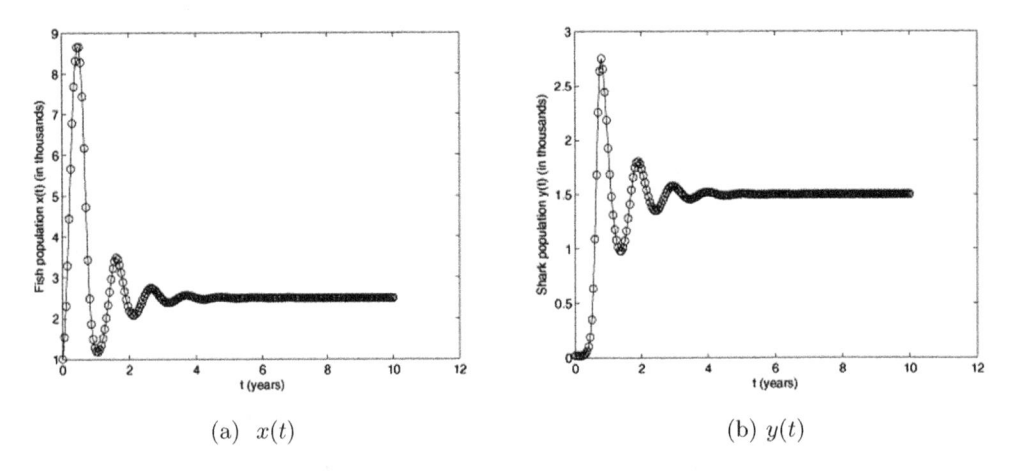

Figure B.2: Fish $x(t)$ and shark $y(t)$ populations for Chapter 9 Exercises problem 13.

14. For the initial conditions $(0.1, 0.1), (1, 0.1), (0.1, 1)$ and $(1.4, 2)$ the solution curves converge to the point $(0.8, 1.4)$, indicating the coexistence of both species with bluegill and redear population stabilize at 0.8×10^4 and 1.4×10^4, respectively. The initial condition of $(1, 0)$ represents the condition where there is no redear population initially and the bluegill population eventually saturates at 1.5×10^4. Likewise, when there is no bluegill initially, that is, $(0, 1)$ being the initial condition, the redear population reaches 2×10^4. We conclude that as $t \to \infty$,

$$(x, y) \to \begin{cases} (0.8, 1.4), & \text{for } x_0 \neq 0, y_0 \neq 0 \\ (1.5, 0), & \text{for } x_0 \neq 0, y_0 = 0 \\ (0, 2), & \text{for } x_0 = 0, y_0 \neq 0 \\ (0, 0) & \text{for } x_0 = y_0 = 0. \end{cases}$$

The coexistence occurs whenever both species are nonzero initially.

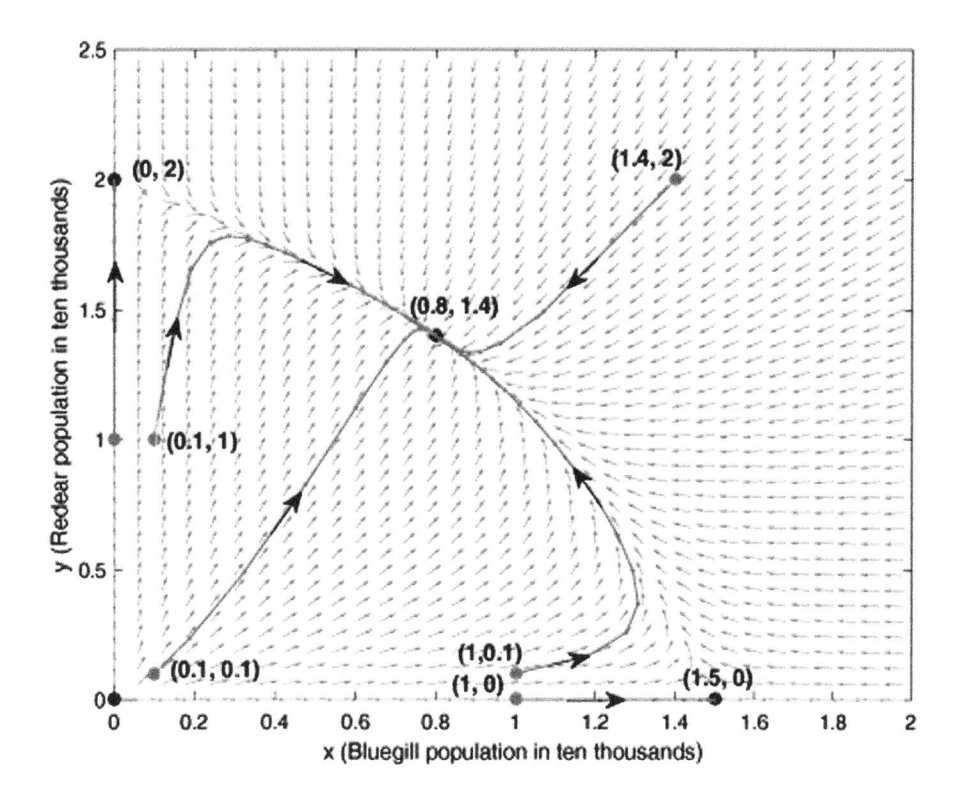

15. From the direction field and phase portrait, the only initial condition that yields to coexistence of both species is $(0.8, 1.1)$.

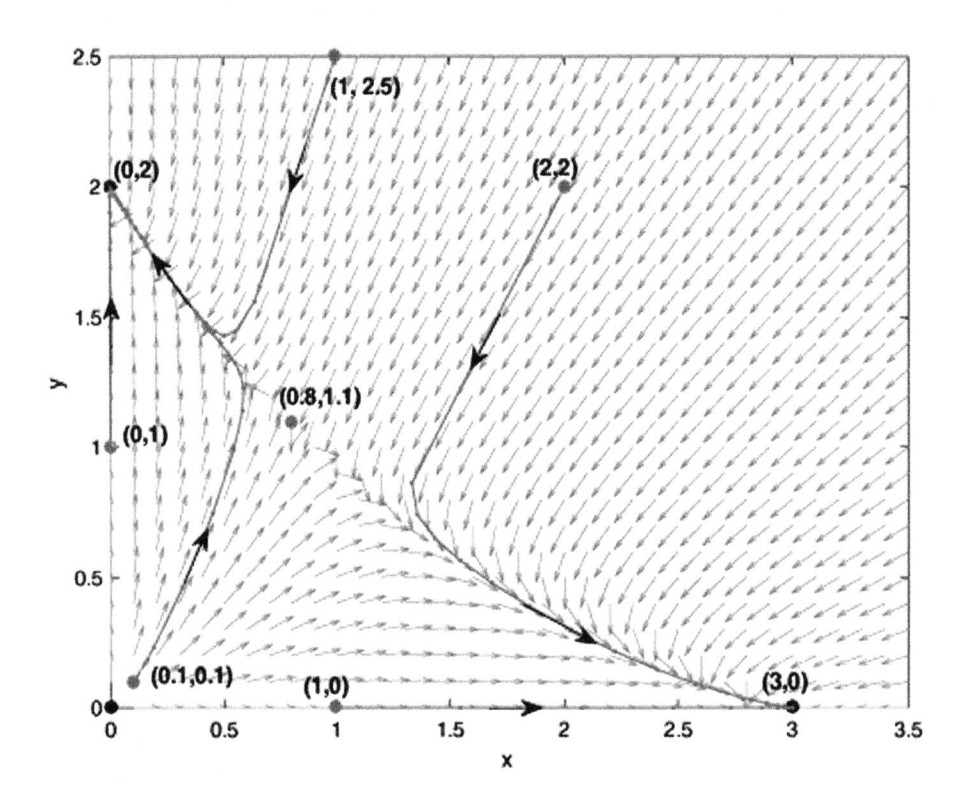

Exercises B.2

1. $(D^2 + 1)y = x^2 \cos x$. You should not dream of shifting x. Instead we will use complex numbers. Let $z = \{1/(D^2 + 1)\}x^2 e^{ix}$. Then $y_p = \Re(z)$ and we have $z = \frac{1}{(D^2+1)}x^2 e^{ix} = e^{ix}\frac{1}{(D+i)^2+1}x^2 = e^{ix}\frac{1}{(D^2+2iD)}x^2 = e^{ix}\frac{1}{D(D+2i)}x^2 = \frac{e^{ix}}{2i}\left\{\frac{1}{D}\frac{1}{(1+D/2i)}\right\}x^2 = \frac{e^{ix}}{2i}\left\{\frac{1}{D}\left(1 - \frac{D}{2i} + \frac{D^2}{4i^2}\right)\right\}x^2 = \frac{e^{ix}}{2i}\left\{\frac{1}{D}\left(x^2 - \frac{2x}{2i} + \frac{2}{4i^2}\right)\right\} = \frac{-ie^{ix}}{2}\left\{\frac{1}{D}\left(x^2 + ix - \frac{1}{2}\right)\right\} = \frac{-ie^{ix}}{2}\left(\frac{x^3}{3} + \frac{ix^2}{2} - \frac{x}{2}\right) = \frac{(\sin x - i\cos x)}{2}\left(\frac{x^3}{3} + \frac{ix^2}{2} - \frac{x}{2}\right)$, where we have used $1/i = -i$. Since $y_p = \Re(z)$, it follows that $y_p = (\sin x)/2\{x^3/3 - x/2\} + (x^2 \cos x)/4$.

3. The auxiliary equation is $(m-2)^2 = 0$ with roots $m = 2, 2$. Hence, $y_c = c_1 e^{2x} + c_2 e^{2x}$ and $y_p = \frac{1}{(D-2)^2}e^{2x}\sin x = e^{2x} \cdot \frac{1}{D^2}\sin x = -e^{2x}\sin x$ and $y = c_1 e^{2x} + c_2 e^{2x} - e^{2x}\sin x$.

Made in the USA
Las Vegas, NV
21 September 2021